Better Bicycling
—— Book ——

Harry Barber began cycling again as part of his education at ANU Canberra and University of Melbourne. Since then he has worked in teaching, conservation and as a writer. He has written for, or edited, bicycle magazines, such as *Freewheeling*, *Bicycle* (UK), and *Pedal Power*. He was author or editor of cycling books such as VicBike's *The Cyclist's Handbook*, the second edition of the *Melbourne Bike Paths Book* and the State Bicycle Committee's *BMX Guidelines*.

Harry Barber has a long involvement in transport planning and improving the safety and convenience of cycling, including bicycle plans for a number of local government authorities in Victoria.

He has ridden to work in cities as various as Canberra, Salonica, Edinburgh and New York. He has toured on cycling holidays over much of Australia, some of New Zealand and a good part of Europe.

Harry Barber lives in Melbourne with his partner, Jeanette, and baby daughter, Cecilia.

**SILVER
GUM PRESS**

The **Better Bicycling** *Book*

SILVER
GUM PRESS

First published in 1994 by Silver Gum Press,
an imprint of Jackie Yowell Productions P/L
PO Box 713
Camberwell South
Victoria 3124
Australia

Copyright text © Harry Barber 1994
Designer and illustrator: Andrew Bond
Typeset in 10/12 pt Palatino by Aird Books
Production: Morgan Blackthorne Productions
Printed on Australian-made chlorine-free paper
by Australian Print Group, Maryborough

National Library of Australia
Cataloguing-in-publication data

Barber, Harry
The Better Bicycling Book

Bibliography.
Includes index.
ISBN 1 875843 04 3

1. Cycling. 2. Cycling – Safety measures. I. Title. II. Title:
Better bicycling book.

796.6

CONTENTS

Chapter 1

BICYCLING IS A THRILL

A bicycle ride can make a good day better. A bright winter sun sparkled on the water as I rode to work one day along the seafront promenade of Salonica in northern Greece. It had snowed the night before and, as I pedalled towards the crisp outline of the centre of town, my wheel-tracks were the first marks crunched into the snow.

A bicycle ride can give you a good time when all around people are grumbling. Just recently someone riding past my place was surprised by sudden rain. It was coming down like snooker cues; the bike had no mud-guards, the rider had no raincoat and was just short of being drenched. As she freewheeled down the street, she was laughing.

A bicycle ride is a good way to be with friends. You can talk as you ride along, telling stories, debating questions of the universe, or sharing silent companion-ship. Talking and riding allows for pauses that develop the conversation in a special

bicycle way.

Another pleasure is sharing a ride with youngsters. Taking kids on a bike ride to the zoo and back, with a stop at the ice-cream shop, makes a day to remember. If you don't have any children of your own, go and borrow a couple of kids and see if I am right.

A bicycle gets you into a large and friendly club. You will meet other cyclists on the road, waiting at traffic lights, at campsites on organised cycling expeditions. And it is not just other cyclists who will be friendly: bicycling brings out a warm side in other people. I've been on holidays where I've had drinks shouted, meals paid for, invitations to stay – all offered just because I was a cyclist.

Children know cycling is a thrill. Watch them. They will just ride round and round for hours, on their own or with friends. But adults are serious people who are often too busy or too grown up just to have fun. Imagine an adult saying, 'I think I'll just spend

Sunday morning mucking about on my bike'. So for the grown-ups, let's look at some serious, practical reasons for cycling.

PRACTICAL REASONS TO RIDE

• **Bike riding makes you fitter.** We all need to exercise and there is no gentler way of getting it than on a bike. You'll be surprised how far you can ride, even on your first outing; and, at the other end of the spectrum, some of the fittest athletes in the world are bike riders.

• **Bikes can double up transport and exercise.** Many people drive home first and then drive to the gym or swimming pool for exercise. As a bike rider you will be getting bonus exercise while you pick up the milk, go to work or chat with a friend. If you ride to work five days a week – say a twenty-minute trip each way – that's ten good exercise sessions. You get fit for free. This exercise also pays off in alertness when you arrive at work and in easing the stresses and strains of the day on the way home.

• **Bikes are a quick way to get about**, especially in cities and towns. The more congested the traffic, the better you'll do on a bike. Most people know that a bike is faster than a bus or tram and there are no timetable restrictions. Regular riders can often get from A to B faster than by car. The denser and slower the traffic, the more the cyclist has the advantage. I find it quick and convenient to nip down to the supermarket on my bike: the supermarket delivers the shopping to my front door for the price of a packet of chips.

• **Bikes are convenient.** Like a car owner, bike riders can go where they want, when they want. This gives you a great feeling of independence. But, unlike a car, a bike will take you *right* to where you are going, not to the carpark two blocks away. Next time you go out to do a few things and have to park a couple of times, think about the extra convenience of a bike. A bike will also improve the convenience of public transport, allowing you to get to the bus more quickly or to reach a more direct service. If it is too far to walk from home to the local milk bar, your bike will bring the shop closer. If your kids are old enough for bicycle independence, that can free you from ferrying them to school or sport or ballet.

• **Bikes are cheap.** If you are a long way from public transport or are stuck at home without a car, a bike will get you mobile for less than the price of a year's rego on a car.

• **Bikes can save you money.** Using your car less, or even replacing a car with a bike, saves money. The operating costs (1993) of a two-litre car is about 14¢ a kilometre or $130 a week. For that weekly cost you could buy a basic bike; for the annual running cost of $6500, you could buy a pretty flashy bike *and* a cycling holiday in France.

• **A bike is a simple, efficient machine** with not much to go wrong; and if it does, it's much easier and cheaper to put right than a car.

• **Bikes are great for growing up.** Bike riding gives children more exercise than twiddling a video game and helps develop important physical skills like balance and coordination. Young riders also appreciate the way a bike brings them a taste of adult independence.

• **Bikes put less stress on the planet.** The smog cocktail that blows from a car exhaust is gaining a bad reputation: old cars put lead in the air, lowering the IQ of children; badly tuned new cars emit gases that cause leukaemia and particles that provoke asthma; even the latest and most efficient cars contribute significantly to global warming. Compared with a car, a bike takes less energy to make, a lot less to run and leaves little pollution.

• **Bike riding is good for your neighbourhood.** Bikes are a good way to leave a party, there are no doors to slam and no loud exhausts. No one minds the noise of bicycle commuters whizzing past their house. Bike riders don't need hectares of asphalt outside the shops for parking nor do they need freeways channelled through the neighbourhood park. If you love where you live, one of the nicest things you can do, in return, is to use a bike.

LEAVE YOUR WORRIES AT THE DOORSTEP

Some people miss out on the thrill of bicycling because they worry that they are too this or too that. Don't worry about the worries:

• **Don't worry about your age**: people still ride bikes in their eighties. You can get back to riding however old you are.

• **Don't worry if you aren't big and strong**: you don't need to be to ride a bike. Bike riding requires less effort than walking, running or swimming.

• **Don't worry if you aren't a boy.** In the past nearly all cyclists were boys but that is no longer true. If you like getting out and about, if you like to run things yourself and make your own decisions, then you will like riding a bike. Why should boys have all the fun?

• **Don't worry about turning into a muscle-bound weight lifter.** Unless you go into competition, cycling isn't going to give you big leg muscles. The muscle that is likely to grow significantly stronger is your heart.

• **Don't worry if you don't know, or remember, how to ride.** Plenty of people learn to ride, or return to riding, when they are older, and go on to enjoy decades of cycling. I know great violinists start before they are seven but you don't want to be a great cyclist, you just want to have fun on your bike.

• **Don't worry if you don't have the flashiest bike.** It's nice to have a new bike but you can have a good time on the oddest or the simplest of bikes. Dervla Murphy rode from Ireland to India on her one-gear, round-town bike 'Roz'.

• **Don't worry about the fashion freaks.** You know whom I mean: they have matching bikes and shoes and fancy tops and their sunglasses cost more than your bike. You can have fun on a bike whatever clothes you are wearing.

• **Don't worry about bike jargon.** All bikes are variations of the same simple, efficient machine, although you can be sure the marketing people will always be promoting a new, more fashionable model.

• **Don't worry about the speed and distance travelled by other cyclists.** Some people will sound off about how they generally ride at around 84 kph or how they only just made it up both mountains before lunch. Don't compare yourself with these people. What matters is if you felt the thrill of cycling. If you haven't ridden for years, then a ride around the block is a hundred per cent improvement.

• **Don't worry if the hill is too steep**: get off and walk. My cycling friend says: 'They haven't made a hill yet that we can't walk up'. The more you ride, the further or faster you will be able to go, but most people have a good time on bikes without getting exhausted.

- **Don't worry if you have nowhere nice to ride.** Not everyone lives in a scenic spot where the birds twitter in the morning sun. There are often unexpected joys wherever you ride. Once, my work-place moved for a short time to one of the more dismal parts of town. On the ride there I discovered some wonderful old houses as well as a cliff-top view just before a walloping downhill.

- **Don't worry about the mechanical aspect of your bicycle.** By and large it will survive with little attention, and repairs are cheap. I have ridden for thousands of kilometres between punctures.

- **Don't worry about the weather.** It is true that rain, hail and wind or excessive heat can make bike riding less pleasant. But when you think that Holland is one of the rainiest and yet one of the most bicycle-ridden places in the world, you can see that weather doesn't stop people enjoying bikes.

- **Don't worry about danger.** Cycling can be dangerous but we should keep it in perspective: five times more people die each year in Australia from swimming. If you are out on the roads, you have the same rights and responsibilities as other road users. Take the same care that you would with driving: learn how to handle your bike, how to ride in traffic, and make sure that all the family know and follow the road rules. Don't let fear keep you from the joy of cycling.

- **Don't worry about reading this whole book at once.** Pick what you need as you need it.

- **And don't hesitate** to send me your comments and suggestions on the book, through the contact given at the very end of the book.

Now, grab the handlebars and put the thrill of bicycle riding in your life. Gloria Steinem said that it is never too late to have a happy childhood. As far as bicycles are concerned she is right. Bicycles are a part of a happy childhood that is ready and waiting for you to enjoy at any age.

See you in the saddle.

Chapter 2

A MAP OF YOUR BIKE

You might think that all bicycles look pretty much the same – and you'd be right. Although it's also true that an expert could point out many little ways that one bike differs from another. This short chapter presents a map of the five main features of a typical bike and, for your reference while reading other chapters, a kind of pictorial glossary of terms.

Don't try to learn all the names of all the parts now. If, later in the book, you are unsure of a term, or to which part I am referring, check back to these diagrams for help. Bicycle parts have collected names from a number of languages and even in English the parts have different names in different places. Where possible I have tried to use the more common term for a part and included common alternatives in square brackets.

HOW THE MAIN PARTS WORK TOGETHER

There are five main structures to a bicycle. The frame holds everything together and you up on your seat. The wheels roll it all along. The drive train describes all the parts that make the thing go, from the turning pedals and sprockets through the chain and gears to the rear wheel. The handlebars and saddle support you. The brakes stop you. That's it.

• The **frame** is made up of a number of tubes: *top tube, seat tube, down tube, chain stays*, and *seat stays*. This frame is called a *diamond* frame because it has two triangles: the *rear triangle* and the *front triangle*. Some frames are made without a top tube, some have a lowered top tube, and on a *mixte* the top tube runs from the top of the head tube to the back of the rear triangle.

• The tubes are sometimes joined by *sleeves* called *lugs*. The tubes can be assembled with different *head angles* and *seat angles*.

• The forks are made up of a threaded *steerer tube* (which you might never see as it hides inside the head

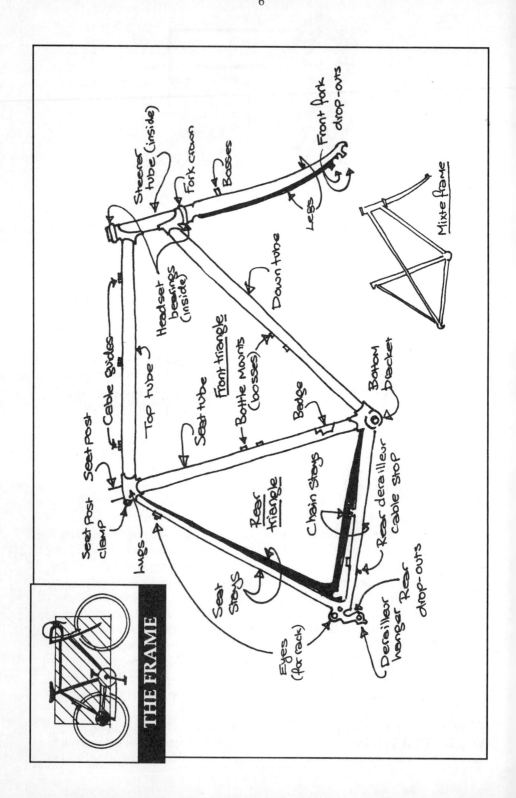

THE FRAME

Seat Post clamp

Seat Post

Cable guides

Lugs

Top tube

Steerer tube (inside)

Headset bearings (inside)

Fork crown

Bosses

Legs

Front fork drop-outs

Down tube

Mixte frame

Seat tube

Front triangle

Bottle Mounts (bosses)

Badge

Bottom Bracket

Rear triangle

Chain Stays

Rear derailleur Cable Stop

Seat Stays

Eyes (for rack)

Derailleur hanger

Rear drop-outs

tube) and the *crown* and the *legs*. The amount that the forks bend from the straight is called the *rake*.

- On a bike frame you will also see:
- two pairs of *drop-outs*, one for each wheel axle. The front drop-outs are always vertical; the rear drop-outs are sometimes horizontal. The distance from the front to the rear drop-out is called the *wheelbase*.
- *eyes*, for the mudguards and racks;
- *cable guides*, through which the *gear cable* and *brake cable outers* run;
- *cable stops*, which hold the end of the brake and gear cable outers;
- *bosses*, for the brake calipers and water-bottle [*bidon*] *cage*;

- a *hanger*, with a threaded hole for the derailleur arm;
- a *seat clamp*, to grip the *seat post*;
- a threaded tube, or *bottom bracket*, to hold the *crank-axle bearing*;
- *bearings*.

Anything on a bike that spins, such as wheels or pedals, runs on a *bearing*. A typical bike has a dozen sets of bearings, made up of a number of *balls* or *ball bearings* of hardened steel which are held between two curved channels or *races* tightened together and held in place by a *lock nut* which is sometimes hidden behind a *dust cap*.

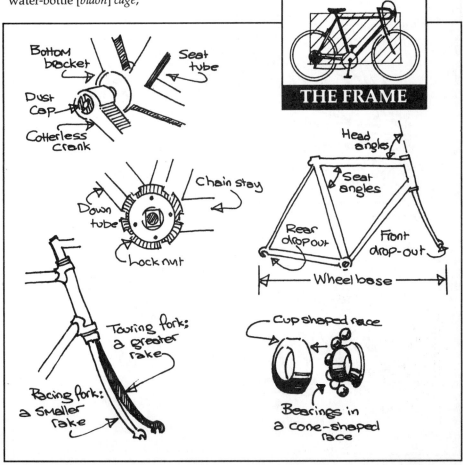

THE FRAME

• The **drive train** describes all the parts that make the bicycle go forward. Start at your feet with the *pedals*. Pedals (possibly with toe clips) can be made for ordinary shoes, or to hold special cycling shoes fitted with cleats. The pedals spin on *pedal bearings* and are screwed onto *cranks*.

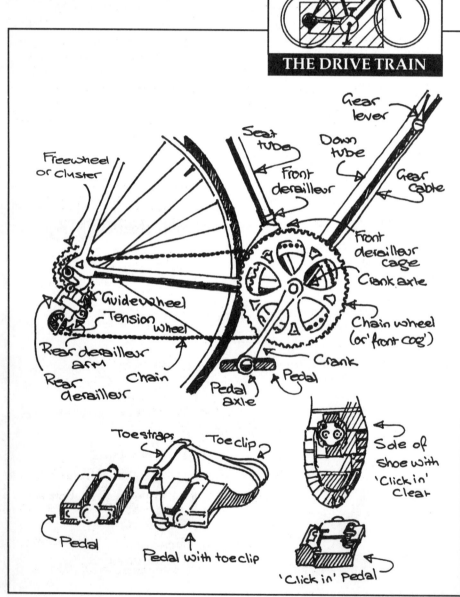

THE DRIVE TRAIN

Gear lever

Seat tube

Down tube

Freewheel or cluster

Front derailleur

Gear cable

Front derailleur cage

Crank axle

Guidewheel

Tension wheel

Chain wheel (or 'front cog')

Rear derailleur arm

Rear derailleur

Chain

Pedal axle

Pedal

Crank

Toe straps

Toe clip

Sole of shoe with 'Click in' Cleat

Pedal

Pedal with toe clip

'Click in' Pedal

- **Cranks** can be made of steel or alloy, can come in different lengths, and are fixed by either a 'push fit' [or 'cotterless'] system, or a wedge called a *cotter pin*, to the *crank axle*, which turns on the crank-axle bearings. (Some bikes have *one-piece* [or *Ashtabula*] cranks where the cranks and crank axle are made out of one piece of metal.)

The right-hand crank is attached to a *sprocket* called the *chainwheel* [or *front cog*], which pulls the links of the *chain* when the pedals are turned.

- **Gears.** A *hub-gear*, or *single-speed*, bike has only two sprockets and might carry a *chain guard* to protect the rider from the greasy chain. A *derailleur*, or *ten-speed*, bike can have two or three front sprockets [*double* or *triple*

chainwheel], and the chain pulls a group of five to seven sprockets which are collectively known as the *cluster* or *freewheel*.

– The *gears* are usually worked by *levers*, which can be on the down tube, handlebars or bar ends. The levers pull a *gear cable* which, on a derailleur bike, moves a front or rear *derailleur* [or *derailleur arm*].

– The front derailleur *cage* works by pivoting and lifting to push or pull the chain between the two front sprockets.

– The rear derailleur arm carries two pulleys. The *top pulley*, or *jockey wheel*, moves back and forth guiding the chain between the sprockets. The *lower pulley*, or *tension wheel*, pushed to the rear by a spring, keeps the bottom half of the chain in tension.

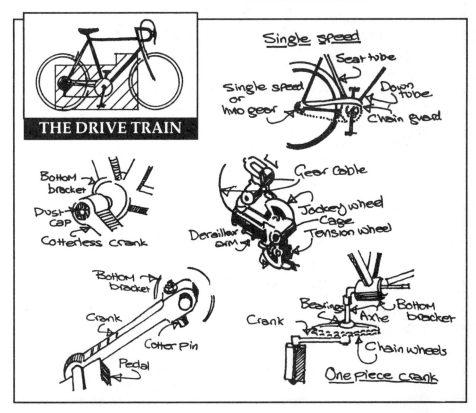

THE DRIVE TRAIN

• **Wheels**. *Tyres*: the *diameter, width* and *pressure capacity* of the tyre is written on the wall of the tyre. The tyre holds the *inner tube* which sits on *rim tape*. You pump up the inner tube through a *valve*, which is protected by a *valve cap*. Tyres sit on *rims* of *steel* or *alloy*. The rim is supported by *spokes*, which connect to the *hubs*, which can have a *high* or *low flange*.

• Inside the hub is the *hub bearing* and the *wheel axle* which turns on the *wheel bearings*. The ends of the axle sit in the drop-outs and are held on by *nuts* or by a *quick-release lever*.

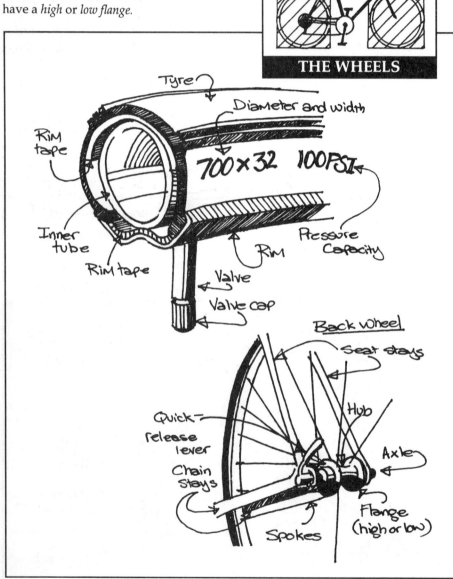

THE WHEELS

• When you sit on the bike your bum will be on the **seat** (*saddle*). The saddle sits on *rails*, which are clamped to the *seat post*, which can be moved up and down in the seat tube and is clamped by the *seat clamp*.

• Your hands will be on the **handlebars**, which can be bent back towards you, straight (*flat*), or curved down towards the ground (*drop* or *racing* bars). Some bikes are fitted with *bar extensions*. The bars will have *grips* or *handlebar tape* for comfort. Taped bars are fitted with *bar-end plugs*. The centre of the bars will be held in the *stem*. The other end of the stem can be moved up and down in the head tube where it is wedged into place by the *stem bolt*.

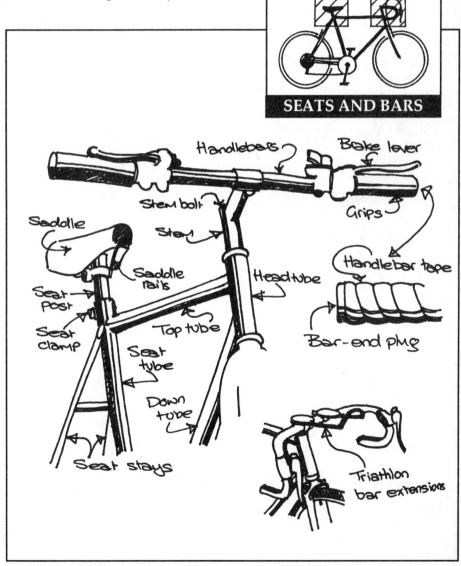

SEATS AND BARS

• When you put on the **brakes** you pull a *brake lever*, which pulls the *brake cable*, through a cable *outer*, pivoting the *brake calipers* towards the wheel rim. These calipers come in a number of types, including *centrepull*, *sidepull* and *cantilever*. At the end of the calipers are brake *pads* (*blocks*), which press on the rim and slow the turning wheel.

We look at each of these main structures in more detail in Chapters 8 and 14.

BRAKES

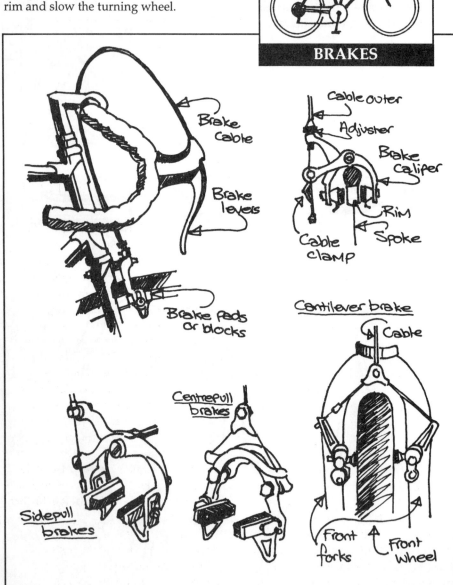

Chapter 3

SHORT RIDES:
AN HOUR OR TWO

A BREATH OF FRESH AIR

Let's look at going out for a ride just for an hour or two. This is one of the great ways to experience the thrill of cycling. It combines the fresh air and exercise of a walk in the park with the watch-the-world-go-by relaxation of a Sunday drive. It is a pleasant way to pass some time with a friend and, if you have a family, it's a great chance for the kids to burn off excess energy.

A couple of hours' riding is a good way to explore a new place you are visiting for a holiday, and it can be an excuse to get out of the way for a while if you are staying with friends. Or you could use your bike to rediscover your own neighbourhood, or put a fresh slant on a visit to a familiar destination such as a zoo, historic home, gallery, park or playground. Regular walkers will find that a bike gets them much further in the same time. Dog owners who cycle find they can give Woofer a more strenuous workout than on a walk.

Most people associate these sorts of short rides with bike paths. There are a couple of bike paths nearby that we use. One has been built alongside the creek. As the path meanders downstream it changes from concrete to boardwalk and back to concrete. When it gets to a road bridge it connects to another path that takes you right near the local cinema. We usually walk up the hill to the road bridge because it is a bit steep. If you keep going on this path you'll arrive at an old boathouse which serves ice cream for humans and stale bread for ducks. We sometimes ride the path upriver to visit friends. It is further and takes longer than getting to their place by road, but you get to ride through the newly planted trees and over a charming wooden pedestrian bridge. There is another favourite ride which is further away. We put the bikes on the back of the car and drive to the start. The path runs alongside another creek through some bushland and ends at a park with barbecues. You can retrace the path back to the car or return more directly on the roads.

Not that you need a bike path to have a pleasant couple of hours on a bike. Country people have little trouble finding a quiet road, but even city people can usually find some quiet streets to pedal around.

FINDING SOMEWHERE TO RIDE

Finding somewhere to ride for the first time is a bit hit and miss. If you are looking for bike paths, you might be lucky enough to find an up-to-date guide book or pamphlet describing bike paths. (See Appendix 4.) Failing that, some street directories show bike paths. Your state bicycling authority, the local government, the water authorities or the state road authorities should give you some clues because they are usually the ones responsible for building and maintaining bike paths. Tourism or town promotion groups might know of bike paths in the area. You could ask cyclists you meet or bike-shop owners if they know of paths nearby. If you go sniffing around yourself, you might find bike paths alongside creeks or freeways, in large areas of parkland, through sports grounds and through some new housing estates.

Two of my favourite guide-books have nothing to do with cycling. One book describes a series of walking tours of interesting suburbs; the other is the National Trust series of guides to historic sites: these sorts of walking

routes work really well for cyclists.

If you are not near any bike paths then don't be afraid to take to the roads on a quiet day. Working out which roads are quiet takes a bit of local knowledge, a bit of reconnaissance and maybe a bit of trial and error. You might come across busy intersections even on a quiet day, but you can always get off and walk for a bit. Riding on the roads gives you a much wider choice of destinations and activities.

GETTING THERE

Obviously the most convenient short ride begins at your front door. Even if you are heading to a bike path, by picking a quiet day, riding backroads and with the judicious and considerate use of footpaths, you can often manage to ride all the way to the bikepath. Once you are confident your children can brake and corner safely and will follow your instructions, it is safe to take them with you on quiet roads. This sort of riding is hard work for the adult as you will have anticipate traffic situations for them and you will do a lot of talking: reminding them to stop at the red Stop sign, for example. Such an expedition can be a very grown-up and therefore exciting thing for the young rider. It will also lay the foundation for safe cycling when they are able, at around nine years old, to go out on their own. This sort of trip is also a good way for adult novices to begin to learn how to ride on the roads. (Chapter 6 and 7 look at basic riding skills, while Chapter 5 discusses riding in traffic.)

If you live near a railway station you can use a train to get to a path a long way from home, though it might not be possible to get your bike on the train during peak periods. If you plan to use your car to get the bikes to the path, you'll need to invest in a bike rack. You could even share one with a neighbour or friend. (See Chapter 4 for more on racks.)

Another possibility is to get to the path and rent a bike. Popular paths and tourist towns often have a bike-hire company that operates on or near the path. Cycle shops near popular paths sometimes rent bikes out. Some tourist towns let you hire unusual pedalled machines like tandems and sociables (where you sit side by side) which are entertaining for a hour or so.

PLANNING THE RIDE

You don't have to make massive preparations when you are riding only for an hour or two, but a little bit of planning can make the outing more enjoyable. Above all, think about how much time you will spend in the saddle. This is most important if you are taking children with you. If there is a lot of pedalling to do after they have lost interest or the energy has run out, the ride is not much fun for anyone.

First, decide how long you want to be pedalling. Be conservative with children or adult novices, especially if they don't ride their bikes a lot or aren't keen on exercise. Don't be too ambitious on hire bikes: they are rarely at the pinnacle of mechanical efficiency. Multiply your time estimate by your average speed, which will probably be somewhere between 5 and 15 kph, depending on your party, how long you want to pedal for and how often you stop. That will give you an idea of how far you can go and let you check a map to work out some landmarks. Use the map to guestimate where the hills might be and whether it will be easier

riding there or riding back. For example, you will need to turn for home sooner if it is uphill on the way back. Don't forget to allow for what the weather's doing, how windy it is and when it will be dark.

Whatever you decide before you start, don't hesitate to change your plans. It is better to get back a bit early, and leave 'em wanting more, than to turn a pleasant outing into a Burke-and-Wills expedition which, as you remember, Tried To Do Too Much.

WHAT TO TAKE
• **Food and drink**: Whatever time of day you are out for a ride, make sure you carry water and something to snack on like fruit or sandwiches. Don't rely on finding a shop. It is unpleasant cycling on a thirsty day with no relief. You don't need special cycling waterbottles: fill up a plastic lemonade bottle or take a thermos. The classic rule is to have a rest, a drink or something to eat before you feel tired, thirsty or hungry. (Chapter 12 has more on healthy drinking and eating.)

– If you plan to include lunch, you could ride to a cafe or kiosk you know is open. Some people like to take a packed lunch and have it at a scenic spot. Or you could organise with someone to meet you with the tucker bag at the halfway point, or return to the car and eat there.

• **A raincoat** is a sensible precaution. The usual rule is that if it looks like rain and you take a raincoat, it won't rain, and vice versa.

• **Lock.** Take your U-locks in case you want to leave the bikes. (See Chapter 11 for more on locks.)

• **Tool kit.** Candidates for the tool kit include: pump, puncture kit or replacement tube, tyre levers and an adjustable spanner. (See Chapters 4 and 14 for more on tools.)

• **First aid** might include dressing strips for blisters, antiseptic for a scratch or graze, and maybe some aspirin for a headache. (Hypochondriacs can find more suggestions in Chapter 4.)

WHAT TO WEAR

• **Helmet.** *Always* wear a helmet. Your head is just as delicate, whether on a path or a road.

• **Sunscreen and sunglasses** in summer. Protect yourself from sunburn and glare, especially between 11 am and 3 pm in summer when the ultraviolet light is at its strongest. The glasses will also keep bugs and wind-blown grit out of your eyes.

• **Clothing.** Wear bright clothing so other path-users will spot you. In summer, wear a light, comfortable shirt and loose-fitting trousers or shorts. In winter, wear gloves, clothes that will keep you warm, especially your legs, and take an extra jumper.

• **Shoes.** Wear comfortable lace-up shoes. Try to find some shoes with hard soles. Thongs are not a good idea.

• (There is more about helmets and cycle clothing in Chapter 11.)

PREPARING YOUR BIKE

Give your bike a bit of a check-over before setting off.

• Pump the tyres until they are hard so that the bike will be easier to pedal.

• Check that the brakes work so you don't run into people or spin off the track.

• Lubricate the chain to help pedalling and changing gears.

• Check over the nuts you can see, tightening them up with a spanner.

• Check that luggage is held on tight to the rack or is safely in a pannier so it won't fall off, wobble or get in the spokes.

• (Chapter 12 details more about these things.)

SHARING THE PATH

Bring your road skills with you on your ride, even if you are on a bike path:

• **Keep on the left and stay alert.** It is especially important to set a good example if you are out with young riders. Impress on the children that they have to ride responsibly.

• **Don't hog the road.** In some places cyclists can ride two abreast on the road. This is more sociable and in some cases makes more safety sense. But there are few bike paths that are wide enough for cyclists to ride two abreast all the time. If you are out in a group, work out *beforehand* what you are going to do if there is someone else on the path. Two cyclists might agree that one will brake and the other will move ahead into single file. This sort of prior agreement is even more important if there are more than two of you. Confusion about what you are going to do could result in a crash.

• **Don't race.** Bike paths are for recreation, not competition. If you want to ride like the wind and not watch too closely where you are going, please find a velodrome.

• **Don't endanger other path users.** One reason cyclists take to bike paths is because they are concerned about safety on the roads. Unfortunately once they feel safe, some cyclists terrorise other users. Some feel that the paths belong only to cyclists and everyone else should give way. But there are very few bike paths that are for cyclists alone. The dog walkers, roller skaters, joggers and kids on tricycles have as much right to be there. Remember that children under nine years old do not have fully developed judgement of the speed and distance of other path users (see Chapter 6).

• **Be courteous.** Bikes are silent and, compared with a pedestrian, move quickly. It is easy to frighten walkers, especially if you approach from behind, and a startled walker could jump in your way. Let them know you are coming: ring your bell, flick your brake levers a few times, pedal backwards to make the freewheel click, even sing out, 'Hello, I'm coming past on your right.'

If you need a selfish reason for being considerate, it might be that we will get more bike paths if cyclists behave in a considerate manner. A council near where I live bans cyclists from its paths because they don't think cyclists mix well with everyone else.

PROBLEMS WITH PATHS

Riding a bike path can be surprisingly hard work, requiring concentration, skill and a good sense of direction.

Bike paths are rarely built as well as roads. They are often too narrow or cambered the wrong way on corners; sometimes the hills are too steep and the corners too sharp. Frequently there are bollards in the middle of the track as well as fences, posts and signs dangerously overhanging the path. The surface is rarely maintained and can be covered with loose gravel, pitted with holes or littered with glass. Often poorly designed drains pour water across the path, making it slippery. I remember one time rounding a corner and finding myself bouncing down a set of steps that was part of a bike path!

Not much planning has gone into the bigger picture either. Few paths run continuously for five kilometres, enough for about half an hour's gentle cycling. Sometimes, without warning, a path can dump you in the middle of a busy road intersection. Paths are sometimes in inappropriate places, such as next to a golf course, where the cyclist has to dodge whistling golf balls. You will rarely find direction or distance signs, even when the path goes on the road for a while, making navigation difficult. Often a path suddenly stops in the middle of nowhere, marking the spot where the land-owner wouldn't give permission, or where the route needs some construction more complicated than just slapping the path down or, simply, where the money ran out.

The short-term solution is to go carefully. The long-term solution is to join the crusade for better bike paths. Write to your local council, praise them for what they have done well and ask them to improve the path where it is below standard.

SUPPORT YOUR LOCAL BIKE PATH

Building and improving bike paths is one of the great contributions we can make to a city. Bike paths can be our opportunity to turn an creek full of old car bodies into a fabulous new park. We can then have the pleasure of passing it on to future generations, like the parks we've inherited from the city founders. As your part in the crusade you might consider adopting your local bike path. Keep an eye open for community clean-up days and volunteer tree-planting sessions. It really adds to a ride when you go past one of 'your' trees and see it flourishing. Financial help is always welcome as well: there are few councils who would knock back the offer of a seat or barbecue donated by a local business, for which it would be good public relations.

OUT ON THE ROAD

Charity rides and organised fun rides are a good way to enjoy a few hours in the saddle, not to mention the benefits of raising money for a worthy cause. Usually these events take place on a path or on roads that are closed off to cars. This makes them well suited to bike-path riders looking for a new experience without worrying about traffic. The Great Melbourne Bike ride attracts over 10 000 riders, which makes it hard to get lost or feel intimidated by the traffic.

The organisers of these rides go to some trouble to make it easy for participants. They usually have lots of back-up: first-aid crews, police or service clubs watching the intersections, radio contact to base and a 'sag wagon' to pick up anyone who can't go on. This means anxious parents need have no worries about letting younger riders go with a friend or in a group.

Some rides can be as short as 6 km, which should take an hour or so. Then there are longer rides: for example, Community Aid Abroad in Melbourne runs an annual 30-km or 40-km ride. The Great Melbourne Ride is usually around 45 km which, with a long lunch, takes most of the day to complete. There will probably be a map of the course, giving the distance. Have a go at working out how long it will take you or your group to ride the course. Start early and give yourselves plenty of time. There is no rule that says you have to ride it all in one go and it is common for riders to stop for breaks on the circuit.

Chapter 4

LONGER RIDES: A DAY OR MORE

After a few successful short outings on your bike, you will probably start to consider longer rides. By putting together two of your bike-path jaunts, one either side of lunch, you could easily spend most of the day away on your bike: five hours in the saddle perhaps. If you put two of those rides together and stay somewhere overnight, you will have completed a weekend bike ride. Then it is only a small step to spending a couple of nights away on a cycling holiday.

THE PLEASURES OF A LONGER RIDE

If you have never been out for a day or more on a bike, you have a great treat in store. You will find all the pleasures of a short ride, but you will also, like Alice slipping through the looking glass, find that you pass into Cycling World.

In Cycling World you discover new facets of familiar places. I had been to the Barossa Valley a couple of times but to return by bike was to find roads, views, people and places we had missed in the car. It is not unusual for cyclists to discover things unknown even to car-bound locals.

In Cycling World you see more vividly. Bicycling will marinate you in the sights and smells and sounds of an area: the hill that leads into town, the view just past the turn-off and the locally made pastries at the cafe. The road over Arthur's Pass in New Zealand is a popular tourist route, but motor travellers will not absorb it as deeply as a cyclist. You pedal over the cleared, windy plains near Christchurch, feel them give way to the climb, as if up giant steps into the mountains, see the vegetation change as you approach the summit, and then zing down the other side, past waterfalls and probably through rain, to the gold town of Hokitika and the land of the Westcoasters.

In Cycling World you can travel back in time. I remember stumbling on the home-town of C J Dennis, author of *The Sentimental Bloke*. Arrive there by car and you would think of the poet as a suburbanite, living just a few minutes drive out of the city. But we had ridden up the winding road to the top of the hill and so knew what it had been like for him to live out in the bush. We knew it would have taken a day to ride his horse to the local town and back. Another instance was the two towns in Italy, which, though only a few minutes' bus ride from each other, were enemies for hundreds of years. If you ride down the hill from one and across the plain for most of an hour and then up the hill to the other, you feel as people in the Middle Ages did – that they are two completely different places.

But the best part of travelling in Cycling World is that you come to enjoy the journey as much as the destination. Like walkers who set off for 'a walk on the beach', cyclists out on a longer ride are not necessarily going anywhere. Going somewhere is not the point. There is a bicycle ride near my place that is quite popular. It goes from one unremarkable town to another, but it is along a joyful, windy, riverside road, and, if you go in the right direction, it is largely downhill. As Robert Louis Stevenson said of his twelve-day donkey tour in southern France, 'I travel not to go anywhere but to go. I travel for travel's sake.'

You might set out on your longer ride to enjoy the road, to enjoy the company, to take in the surroundings, to enjoy the local produce or to experience life at a different pace. Whatever the reason, once you have visited Cycling World, you will want to go back there.

SOMEONE ELSE TO ORGANISE IT

The easiest way to get into longer cycling trips is to get someone else to organise it. There are all sorts of organised rides you can join. Some go for a day around town, others for a fortnight across the state, and there is everything in between. Some tours are organised for twenty people, others gather a travelling army of five thousand riders.

There are a lot of advantages in going on an organised ride:

• There will be no need to pedal a heavily laden bicycle, as all necessary gear will go in a truck or van.

• The organisers will have ridden the route and its alternatives and will know that it is achievable and interesting.

• The route survey means there will be no surprises such as big hills, closed milk bars or busy roads.

• Accommodation and food will be sorted out for you. Organised rides may get you a bed in pubs or motels but most will put you up in a tent.

• The organised tour will provide medical, mechanical and emotional back-up.

• Parents will be able to wave off the kids knowing there will be some supervision.

• There are usually many other thoughtful extras, such as evening entertainment, rest-day trips on a boat or in a balloon, and a support van for vineyard purchases.

As well as these advantages, many

people find that travelling in a group is a good thing in itself: you can make friends, have a bicycle romance or just enjoy sharing cycling with other like-minded people.

PREPARING FOR AN ORGANISED RIDE

In the last chapter we looked at the preparation you might do for a short ride. If you tackle a longer ride on an organised tour, that basic preparation might be enough. Some organised rides even supply the bike.

But however well-supplied the tour is, and whether you are out for one day or ten, your contribution is the pedalling. I would recommend a look at:
– Chapter 7, which talks about the best way to pedal;
– Chapter 12, which looks at how your body works best and about bicycle fitness.

If you are taking your own bike but are uncertain if it is right for the job, you might want to look at Chapter 8.

Other relevant chapters for long rides are:
– Chapter 5, which discusses skills for riding on the road;
– Chapter 14, which gives you a start at fixing mechanical problems;
– and of course this chapter, which will help you to check the tour company's planning and get an idea of how demanding the ride is.

ORGANISING A LONGER RIDE YOURSELF

Careful people often use organised rides as a way to gain the experience and confidence to go off and do a ride on their own. I heard of a couple of school kids who had been on three long organised rides while they were at

school. To celebrate the end of their school career they worked out their own ride around Tasmania and completed it successfully. Another way to do-it-yourself is to copy an organised ride by getting family or friends to drive the support vehicle for the day, or to manage the wagon train between stops on a longer trip.

But you might want to dive in the deep end like Hard-ways Harry and learn from your mistakes. On my first long ride, which lasted from breakfast to a late lunch, I packed an unnecessary tent and sleeping bag but took no water. On my first bike camping trip, a friend and I set off with very little experience. Nine days later we arrived at our destination having made every mistake possible but having had a great time. On subsequent rides we never made quite that many mistakes again, but those rides didn't produce as many good stories. For careful deep-enders, this chapter, and those chapters I just mentioned above, will brief you on the things that would have helped us back then.

Plan for longer trips in two parts: the basic plan and the details.

THE BASIC PLAN
First you should fill in the big picture. How many days are you going for? What type of ride are you going to do? Where are you going to go?

How many days?
There are three ways to travel by bike: unloaded, lightly loaded and fully loaded. The way you choose will depend on the length of time you are away, and how want to handle meals and accommodation.
• **Out for a day: unloaded.** The unloaded day trip is a good way to

enjoy a longer ride. You don't have to carry anything more than you would on a short ride and you don't have to organise accommodation. This is the sort of riding that the French call *ciclotourisme*. In France, especially on summer Sundays, you will see men and women, teenagers and pensioners, in spotless cycling clothes, riding their gleaming bikes out on a day trip. This sort of trip has a limited range.

- **Out overnight: lightly loaded.** If you want to go out for the weekend, or you need more than a day to ride a particular road, then you are looking at an overnighter. The British have a long tradition of this sort of riding, usually done in a group and symbolised by the saddlebag, a sort of sports bag slung behind the saddle. In the saddlebag goes your youth-hostel sleeping sheet, soap and towel, cut lunch, raincoat and other essentials. Your bike is still light and easy to pedal but you need to organise accommodation.

In Europe you can just pop over the hill to the next village if there is no room at the inn, but in Australia you need to book ahead. As you have no doubt gathered, the French and British methods are not unlike an organised tour.

The French do go on overnighters, but they still refuse to carry luggage and so have to stay in hotels. When I win the lottery I am going to go riding this way, just with a credit card in my pocket. I'll stay each night at the Hilton and if I get a puncture I'll buy a new bike.

- **Out for longer: bicycle camping.** This is like a holiday in a camper van except that you load the bikes with everything that would go in the van. At night you camp by the side of the road or in caravan parks, lobbing in a hotel

every so often for a bit of luxury. This method allows you to be independent of towns and to stop and go when you want. Once you have bought the camping gear, it is a cheap way to travel, which means you can probably stay on the road longer. On the other hand, the self-sufficient bicycle is quite heavy, you will need low gears (see Chapter 8) and you won't go very fast.

All round the world you will see this type of touring cyclist, sometimes travelling alone, sometimes in a small group. Some will be laden to the gunwales with gear; others will cut down their luggage by tearing out the pages of books as they read them and each night washing their one pair of socks.

A circuit or A-to-B
There are two types of longer bike ride: a circuit ride and an A-to-B ride. As a general rule, cyclists don't like riding there-and-back on the same road. Like the short ride on a bike path, your longer trip might begin and end at home. Or you could get a lift to the start by train or car, do a circuit and return to your starting point. Or you could head off to another car or train rendezvous and complete an A-to-B ride. If you are basing your riding around a holiday you could do an A-to-B ride to the holiday spot and join others there. Or you take your bike with you on holiday and then go out on a number of circuits, first in one direction and then in the other. Then of course you could turn the whole holiday into a ride.

Where to go
Three common ideas to build a longer ride around are: places, town-to-town and themes.

- **Places.** The best places for longer rides have interesting natural features with spectacular views and pleasant towns. Some of Australia's best riding includes the east coast of Tasmania, the Ocean Road in Victoria, the Hunter Valley in NSW, the Barossa and Clare Valleys in SA, the south-west of WA and the Atherton Tablelands near Cairns. New Zealand offers the loop from Christchurch through Arthur's Pass and the Haast Pass in the South Island and the wine areas of the North Island. In fact, wine areas in every State attract cyclists, and not just the bibulous. For example, the Barossa and Clare Valleys in South Australia give you rolling hills, vineyards, old stone buildings, vine-clad villages, and of course the wine. Goldfields are another winner. The old goldfields in Victoria and NSW have plenty of atmospheric old towns with museums, old pubs and scenic roads. If you lack inspiration, tourism brochures are full of ideas. Appendix 5 advises on books that suggest cycling trips in Australia.
- **Town-to-town.** Some riders like to build their longer ride around a ride from town-to-town. Travelling is the point rather than arriving, so the route is often circuitous and the destination town usually marks the end rather than the purpose of the ride. Usually the towns are chosen because they have transport to get you to the start or home again. There is, for example some great riding to be had between Brisbane and Sydney or Sydney and Melbourne.
- **Themes.** A theme can inspire a longer ride. History buffs, for example, could ride around the area where a bushranger such as Ned Kelly or Ben Hall roamed. On such a trip you could go to the birthplace, hide behind the rock at the site of the first hold-up, imagine the capture and so on. You could trace the steps of white explorers, follow the roads the Chinese took to the goldfields, a shearers' round, a First World War recruiting march or an Aboriginal trading route. Geographers could follow a river down through its catchment, balance along the Divide, ride over the highest road in the State or go as far as possible to one point of the compass. Sporting enthusiasts could ride the route of past cycle races. You could even use your cycling holiday for work purposes. In the years before the First World War, British intelligence officers took a lot of paid cycling holidays in northern France and Belgium. I don't know if it did much good militarily, but I'm sure they had a good time.

The theme of your ride could also be one of your other interests, such as birdwatching, plant spotting, fishing or photography. You could do a reconnaisance of potteries, nurseries or country art galleries. Some riders grumble that pushing-a-bicycle-uphill is a hobby that goes well with longer rides.

PLANNING DETAILS

Once you have the basic plan organised, then you can work out the details: estimating how long it will take you, studying the route in detail and breaking down the day into riding time and breaks.

How far and how fast?

The first job is to get a rough idea of the time the trip will take and the distance you'd like to travel. I recommend you decide first how long you want to spend in the saddle.

- **Time**: Obviously, the longer you spend in the saddle, the further you will go, but the less time you will have for sightseeing, resting, or talking to the locals. It makes sense to set yourself an easily achievable goal for your first longer rides. A ride made up of two 'bike path rides', one either side of lunch – or about five hours in the saddle for the day – is plenty to start with. But if you are accustomed to riding and are fit, perhaps from regular riding to work, then you could plan for a longer day in the saddle. (Chapter 12 has more on fitness and how to prepare for a longer ride.)

If you are out for a couple of days, make sure you build rest days into your plans. Robert Louis Stevenson took twelve days to do his walking trip with a donkey, and made sure he had three rest days. He would have adapted well to bicycle touring.

A holiday cyclist, riding about five hours a day at about 10-15 kph would cover 50-70 km. Your average speed will be closer to 15 kph if you are a fit and experienced, if you are lightly loaded and if the roads are mostly downhill. Your average will be closer to 10 kph if you are carrying all the gear for cycle camping. You could, at this daily rate, spend a pleasant two weeks holiday in Tasmania. Nine 75-km days would take you down the east coast of Tasmania from Launceston via Port Arthur to Hobart. Your holiday, like RLS' donkey trip, would include three rest days but you would travel more than three times as far as him, and not be faced with the problem of trying to sell a donkey in Hobart. If you find you travel at 10 kph, you could add another four days to the ride and still only pedal for five hours each day. Equally

you could shorten the ride or increase the number of hours in the saddle.

A fit cyclist – say someone who commutes half an hour each way five times a week – might treat the riding like a job and enrol themselves in the mythical holiday cyclists' union. Over a week's holiday they could ride for 38 hours at the regulation 7.6 hours a day. They would travel between 80 and 110 km each day and, assuming a five-day cycling week, would travel 400 to 570 km in a week. They might only take six riding days to complete the Tasmanian trip.

- **Distance.** Sometimes riders will set a distance and stay in the saddle until they arrive. But riding a set distance only makes sense if you are trying to get between two towns or between two water stops in the outback, or are trying to break a personal record or reach an athletic goal. One popular goal that some people get excited about is to ride the old 'century' of a hundred miles, now 160 km, in daylight.

For most people, though, the number of kilometres covered in a day is not the point. At 160 km each day you'd polish off the east coast of Tassie in four days but you'd have to pass the apple museum without going in.

In the end, your longer ride will probably be based on a calculation that includes average speed, time in the saddle, distance each day, rest days and the length of your holiday. The answer in days and kilometres will give you an idea whether you will be out for the weekend or if you can have a go at crossing the Nullabor.

Speaking of deserts, Lawrence of Arabia reported that an 80-km day was easy for the camel-mounted guerillas with whom he worked, 130 km was a good day, and 230 km was possible in twenty-four hours. When necessary the guerillas could ride 2400 km in 30 days, which again is about 80 km a day. If you can match Lawrence's camels, you are doing all right.

Studying the maps and guides
Once you have decided the basic plan and how many hours you are going to spend in the saddle, it is time to study some maps and guides to get a more accurate idea of how the day might turn out.

In the best of all possible worlds you will find detailed maps where one centimetre represents two kilometres (1 : 200 000) and you will have a guide-book with suggested routes and comprehensive commentaries written by cyclists. German speakers riding in Europe can reach this nirvana.

In Australia it is possible to find some books and pamphlets with suggested itineraries and commentaries but probably only at bicycle organisations or at specialist touring bike shops. It is also possible to find some detailed maps prepared by cyclists for cyclists. These are usually to a good scale, and do all sorts of nice bicycle things like indicate hills and distinguish between a town that once had a shop and a town that has a shop today.

If you can't find specialist maps and guides for where you want to go, the road maps put out by the major petrol companies are adequate. It is a good idea to carry a couple of road maps as this allows you to get a better picture by comparing and combining information. The Commonwealth government sells large-scale maps in which one centimetre represents one kilometre for the whole country. These maps have great accuracy and detail but are expensive as you'd need a few of them to cover one ride. Tourist information maps are good for inspiration but not reliable for planning or navigation.

Use your maps and guides to do three things:

• **Look for busy roads and quiet roads.** Your maps should help you suss out which road a car-driver would pick between A and B. This allows you to avoid Toad of Toad Hall in his shiny new motor car. The less-improved roads are more likely to carry less traffic, allowing you to hear the cars from a long way off and the motorists to move well over as they pass you. The quiet roads often have more roadside trees and better gradients for cyclists. An old road, built for a horse-drawn vehicle, twists and bends up hills and is much easier to ride.

• **Check how big the towns are**, the distance between them and whether the road is sealed or dirt. This will let you work out how long it will take to get from A to B. The size and location of towns will help you decide where to stop and have lunch or whether to carry food.

• **Check out ups and downs.** Ideally your guide and commentary will have a gradient cross-section of the recommended road. These gradient graphs, which show height against distance, have been used for years by racers. The height and distance on the gradient chart should be same scale, otherwise the hills will be exaggerated. A gradient map will not get you up the hill quicker but it will stop you anticipating an early finish when there is a small piece of the Himalaya between you and your destination.

Contours are a help but maps with contours tend to be expensive and large scale. Standard maps will usually carry some clues to the topography. Look for rivers and creeks, shaded or painted representations of mountains and very winding roads. Sometimes the height of a summit will be marked or a name like 'Christmas Hills' will give you a direct clue.

If you know how hilly your chosen road is, then you will be able to estimate time in the saddle more accurately. People who hate the idea of hills can of course look for an alternative route. But hills need not be a problem if your bike has low gears, if you have some pedalling technique and a bit of fitness. You can always walk. Hills can even be an advantage. With hills come twisty roads which can be a relief from ruler-straight roads that stretch to the horizon. Hills give a view of the surrounding country-side rather than just the fence next to the road. And best of all, in the hills you will find that most pleasant of all road signs, 'Steep Descent', which warns you of a speedy, eye-watering blast down the other side. Even if you don't become an afficionado of the Steep Descent like me, it is worth learning to love hills; they turn up wherever you ride.

The day's ride

After studying the maps you will be able to work out the day's ride and break it down further into meal-breaks and rests. When you are on the road, use a clock to monitor your progress rather than a kilometre-counter. The kilometre-counter tells you how the bike is going, not how *you* are going. A wristwatch will tell you how long you have been pedalling and therefore

whether you need a break. A rule of thumb for beginners might be a ten-minute break after every 20-30 minutes of riding. This allows you to stretch your legs and upper body and to drink water (see Chapter 12). Experienced cyclists, who are more used to riding and who can drink and stretch while in the saddle, will probably only want to take a break every hour. Planning breaks and rests is something you will get better at the more you do it and the more you know about your cycling ability.

No matter how much careful preparation you have made, you must be prepared to change your plan as the day unfolds with its unexpected downhills and unanticipated setbacks.

The weather is one factor that might affect your day plan. The temperature will set your dehydration rate or the chill factor. Humidity, cloud cover and ultraviolet radiation will all influence how long you want to ride and how fast you go. Wind speed and direction will also be a big influence.

Tourist interest is another. You might decide to stop early at one town or spend longer in the saddle to arrive at another. Fixating only on a certain number of kilometres, no matter what, can spoil the fun.

WHAT YOU NEED FOR BICYCLE CAMPING

In some ways bicycle camping is a contradictory activity. For the bicycling bit you want to carry as little as possible; for the camping and comfort bit you want to have everything you need. The following suggestions should help you to remember things to pack but you won't be able to move if you take them all!

- **Clothing for riding:** cycling gloves, cycling shorts, cycling shoes, shirt, socks, underwear. (See Chapter 11 for details about cycling clothing.)
- **Sun-protection:** collar and cuffs on your shirt, lip screen, sunglasses, sunscreen. (A long-sleeved cotton shirt with collar and cuffs will save you having to baste your arms in sunscreen. Sweat will wash away the sunscreen you put on and you will need to re-coat frequently.)
- **Clothing for cold weather:** balaclava and/or windproof helmet cover, woollen cycling jumper, sleeved sweater and/or sleeveless sweater/s, and/or synthetic 'thermal' T-shirt, insulated cycling gloves, overshoes, cycling leg warmers or cycling long tights or thermal long johns.

The usual way to stay warm in the saddle is to have a number of thin layers that you can take off and put on as you warm and cool while riding and resting. Your feet and hands will get coldest. Gloves will protect your hands but feet are more difficult. Extra socks, overshoes and even plastic bags will do for emergencies.

- **Clothing for staying dry:** raincoat, waterproof over-mittens, waterproof over-pants.

It is hard to stay dry on a bike, but you can stay warm. These things can also be your last line of warmth. Stick them on if all the cold-weather gear isn't effective. (Chapter 11 talks about rainwear in more detail.)

- **Be-seen clothing:** bright colours during the day, helmet, reflective gear at night. (Chapter 11 talks about be-seen clothing in more detail.)
- **Après-saddle clothing:** Comb or brush, jumper, nice clothes, swimmers, walking shoes. When you pull up for a meal or a rest you will probably need a jumper or jacket you can throw on to stay warm. You might need another pair of shoes if you can't walk in your cycling shoes. Many people carry a light and not-too-bulky change of clothes so that when they have a pub tea at the Commercial Hotel or spend a night at the casino they don't stick out in their cycle shorts and multi-coloured cycling jumper.
- **Water:** water bottle(s) on the bike and back-up water bottle. Water is very important if you are in the saddle for any length of time. The further it is between water sources, the more you will have to carry.
- **Personal hygiene:** soap, sponge or face washer, toothbrush and paste, towel, toilet paper, shaving tackle, deodorant, moisturiser, tampons.
- **Recreation gear:** camera, book, journal, playing cards, hobby gear such as paints.
- **Extra things for your bike:** Carrying gear such as panniers, handlebar bag and so on, bike computer, lights, U-lock. You might wonder if it is worth taking lights, but if you do have to ride at night – back to your campsite after a meal in town, for example – you would be putting yourself at risk without lights.

It is hard to lock up a touring bike with all its bags and you will probably stay near your bike most of the time. For these reasons many people leave their U-lock behind. But there are bound to be some occasions when you want to leave it, and so it is worth having a lock. Some people carry a light but less secure cable lock as a deterrent. (See Chapter 11 for more on locks and lights.)

- **Other important items:** day pack

for walks, identification, emergency contact numbers and addresses, maps, money, credit cards, phonecard, plastic bags or stuff sacks (it is a rare pannier that is waterproof), sewing kit, useful string and rope, wristwatch.

The following suggestions are for cyclists camping and cooking for themselves in caravan parks or in the bush.

• **Cooking:** cooker, fuel, pots, matches; meal ingredients, hot drink ingredients, back-up dehydrated meal.

• **Eating:** knife, fork, spoon, cup, plate, sharp knife; scourer, soap, Swiss-army knife (has lots of useful things such as sharp knife, scissors, bottle/can opener, corkscrew, etc.), water bag or old wine-cask bladder; cold drink ingredients, e.g., cordial, fruit, snacks. (Chapter 12 talks about cycling food in more detail.)

• **Sleeping:** tent or bivvy bag, sleeping bag, sleeping mat, candle, torch, spare batteries and bulb.

If you are camping in the bush, please follow the basic rules: don't burn wood but use a stove; take away your rubbish; don't put soap into streams; and bury your shit.

Body repair

If you are away for a while and could be a long way from assistance it is a good idea to do some first-aid training, such as for resuscitation and burns. It is also good to have a comprehensive first-aid kit on hand if you need one. Such a kit could be designed to tackle:

– Wounds: soap, or something to clean cuts and grazes (another reason to have plenty of water on board), cotton buds, antiseptic powder or cream, gauze bandage (say 2 m by 2.5 cm), non-stick gauze pads, several sizes of bandage strips, adhesive tape, scissors.

– Sprains and twists: elastic bandage, crepe bandage.

– Burns: cream.

– Blisters: adhesive tape.

– Splinters: needle, tweezers.

– Pain and itch: pain relievers, insect repellent, insect-bite cream.

– **Also:** personal medicines (e.g. asthma); first-aid manual.

Bike repair

Mechanical problems are not part of the thrill of bicycle holidays so the first thing to do is to service your bike or have someone service it for you *before* you go off on a longer ride. If you take a well-serviced bike, the chances are that nothing will go wrong.

You should also take with you some basic mechanical knowledge and experience. It would be unwise to set off on a longer ride when no-one in the party knows how to change a tube or fix a puncture. Chapter 14 describes basic repair skills and begins with a quick test that can alert you to problems.

You also need to take some tools – generally the fewer the better, as they're are heavy and not much use for anything other than fixing a bike. Chapter 14 looks in more detail at bike repairs and the tools you need.

HOW TO GET YOUR BIKE THERE AND BACK

The ride is planned, your bags are packed. Now all you have to do is get yourself there. To get yourself to or from a ride you could use: car, train, bus or plane.

Cars

The most common ways to transport bikes is to stick them in a car boot, on a

Roof racks are suitable for racing bikes but towbar racks are good for bikes of different size, and shape.

rack or on the roof. A stationwagon or trailer will also accommodate several bikes, but the bikes need to be well packed and strapped, so as not to damage each other.

- **Boot.** A large car boot can accommodate a bike, with the front wheel removed. (See Chapter 14 for removing the front wheel.) If the car has a small boot and the bike sticks out, use lots of padding above and below the frame to protect the bike from the edge and boot lid. Tie the bike down, with a rope through the bumper bar or tow bar.

- **Rack.** If you are going to carry bikes regularly, it is worth getting a rack. One common type fits on the towbar in place of the towball and comes up in an L-shaped angle, or beak. Others strap onto the boot of the car. Most L-racks clamp three bikes, facing in alternate directions, by their top bars. Kid's bikes or bikes without a top tube might have to be clamped by the seat tube. You can buy a false top bar that clamps on the seat tube and head tube, allowing you to attach the bike horizontally to the L-rack.

Whatever way you clamp them, make sure the nuts that clamp the bikes and the nut that holds the L-rack to the towbar are all done up tight with lock washers. Tighten these nuts when you break your journey. If a nut vibrates loose, you could spill the bikes onto the road. This is dangerous to other road users and will damage the bikes. Tie the bikes so they can't move and pad the places where they might rub on each other or on a rope.

If you can take the wheels off and carry them inside the car, you will burn less petrol. It is illegal and dangerous to drive around with a bike rack mounted and no bikes on it. Nor should your number plate be obscured by the rack. In some states you can buy an extra plate to fit to the rack.

- **Roof rack.** Racers generally use specially designed bicycle roof-racks where each bike is clamped into its own cradle. But these roof-racks are hard to use if you are not tall, and they don't generally allow you to install lots of different sizes and shapes of bike. Bikes can also be strapped, securely, horizontally onto a standard roof-rack.

Trains
Trains are a vital part of many longer rides. You can usually take your bike on a city train if you don't travel in rush

hour. On country trains, bikes usually travel in the luggage van. Sometimes you have to book the bike on, but on some services you only need to turn up half-an-hour before the train leaves. It is best to ring and check.

It is heartbreaking to see some of the damage caused to bicycles that have travelled by rail. But there are a few things you can do:

• Often rail staff will let you put your bike in the luggage van yourself if you ask politely. You can then make sure it is not threatened by any other luggage.

• Pad it well to protect it from rubbing against other things. Leaving panniers on the bike provides a bit of padding.

• Improvise a handbrake to stop the bike rolling. Squeeze the brake levers and jam something, such as a block of wood, into the gap near the lever to hold the brake on.

• Lash the bike to something so it won't be thrown about during the trip. But don't tie your bike up too comprehensively as you might have only a few minutes to get it out at your destination. If possible, go down to the luggage van and untie the bike before the train gets into the station.

Long-distance buses

Buses won't always carry bikes, so make sure you ask when you book your ticket. Sometimes the bus company will leave the decision to the driver. In that case you will have to decide whether to risk it or go with another bus line. The bike usually goes on its side into the luggage compartment under the bus. Give your bike the best chance of avoiding damage by doing four things:

• Take off the pedals (see Chapter 14).

This allows the bike to lie flat and do less damage to other people's luggage.

• Wrap a cloth around the chain and gears to protect other people's luggage. You won't necessarily be doing this out of altruism but to ensure that the driver lets you put the bike on the bus.

• If you have to take the front wheel off, try to protect the forks from being squashed together by securing something like an old axle or piece of wood between them.

• If you can, try to make sure your bike is on top of the suitcases rather than vice versa.

Aeroplanes

Getting a bike on a plane requires a bit of bicycle knowledge. Weight is not usually a problem for the airlines because if your luggage weighs too much, you just pay more; but airlines are paranoid about space. So you need to origami your bike down to the size of a suitcase. It is a lot of work but it is probably the least damaging method of transport for a bike. Once you have made your bike suitcase size, most airlines will take it without a murmur. (The adjustment section of Chapter 14 will help with this process.)

• Take off the wheels and tie them securely alongside the frame.

• Lower the seat post into the frame if necessary.

• Loosen the handlebar stem in the frame and swing it to one side.

• If necessary, loosen the handlebars in the stem and swing them so that they are parallel to the frame. You might have to take the stem out of the frame and strap it to the frame if the bars stick out too far in front.

• Wrap the chain and gears in a cloth.

• Let down the tyres a little so they

don't burst in the unpressurised cargo hold.

• Take off the pedals, (it might be easier to take off the cranks: see 'Servicing the drive train' in Chapter 14), pump, water bottle and any other removables and put them in your other luggage.

• You might want to protect your darling further with cardboard, bubble packing sheets or hot-water-pipe insulation.

Reassembling takes a while; try to get a lift to to your accommodation at the other end so that you can put the bike back to rights at your leisure. Racers fit their bikes into special carrybags or stiff-sided bicycle cases, not unlike a cello case. These bags are great for transportation but can be a problem to store while on your ride.

OVERSEAS CYCLING HOLIDAYS
There is no better way to see another country than from the saddle of a bike; it is an experience not to be missed. Australia is good for cycling but you won't find here the understanding and support for cycling that exists in some other places. People in Australia don't clap when you ride into town. Europe and North America especially are worth a visit as they are criss-crossed with excellent formal and informal bicycle trails that, as yet, we cannot match.

The main decision you will have to make when cycling overseas is whether you hire a bike, take your own, or buy one there.

• **Hiring a bike** is expensive if you are out for more than a few days.

• **Taking your bike.** It is possible to take your bike on a plane. But it might be hard to get spare parts over there. Some metric countries don't sell tyres in our old imperial size. Unless you have somewhere cheap and safe to leave it, a bicycle becomes very inconvenient if you are going to be travelling around but not riding.

• **Buying and selling abroad.** This ensures you will be able to get spares during your ride. But you might not be able to get the sort of bike you want or you might not be able to wait while they order one in your size. It is not easy to sell the bike for a fair price quickly just before you leave. Some shops do offer buy-back agreements, where they guarantee to take your machine when you return which is good if you are returning to that place.

• **Buying and bringing back.** Make sure before you bring the foreign bike home that it has standard parts. You might have trouble trying to find replacement parts for a Yugoslavian derailleur.

Unfortunately there is no perfect answer to the overseas bike problem and not many of the friends you are leaving behind will sympathise with your holiday dilemma. Don't worry, it will be worth it.

Chapter 5

RIDING AROUND TOWN

You don't have to wait for weekends and holidays to ride your bike, you can enjoy bicycling every day if you ride around town.

I've had some great rides to work. For a while I used to ride past the zoo, which has its own unique smells and early-morning sounds. On misty, cool mornings it was easy to imagine that I was riding in Africa with the exotic birds calling above the chattering of the chimps. Another trip to work had me going through a city park where I often saw the woman with the two dachshunds. She spears bread on the end of her stick and holds it up to the hollows in the trees for the possums to grab. I suppose you don't mind being woken up if it's room service. That park is full of deciduous trees so in winter you get to see the sky, but it's almost total shade in summer. Autumn is best, as you ride through the leaves pasted on the ground as if the path were a asphalt scrap-book. It's hard to have a bad day when you start work like that.

Coming home is all right as well. I've found you can pedal off a few frustrations, and you get to watch the evening starting to happen around you. On one ride, there'd be a jazz sax busker towards the end of the week who used to entertain me when I stopped at the lights. What did people do before saxophones? My last job had me coming home past a florist which, though it was on a busy road, over-powered the fumes with a strong scent of flowers and freshly cut stalks, reminding me of Jeanette's warning 'Don't ever not buy me flowers'.

Not that all your round-town riding has to be to work and back. Cycling has a lot going for it on any round-town trip:

- You'll get fitter with regular riding.
- You'll get there quickly.
- You'll save time with regular riding.
- Bikes are cheap.
- Bikes can save you money.
- Bikes are convenient.
- Bikes are kind to where you live.

You can see that, even though we don't do it as much as we could, there is a lot to be gained from riding around town.

Is town riding safe?

The one question at the front of your mind about riding around town is probably 'Is it safe?' The answer is that you are at risk of death or injury riding your bike just as you are in a car or on foot. The next question is, 'How risky is it?' The answer is that there are many things that are more risky. Swimming, for example: five times as many people die each year in Australia from swimming than from cycling. The risk of a fatal disease provoked by smoking is around 400 times greater than death from cycling. In fact you could argue from a health point of view that it is riskier not to cycle: deaths from cardiovascular disease are 24 times as common as deaths from traffic crashes.

The British Medical Association considered the safety issue at some length in their 1992 book, *Cycling: towards health and safety*. They said that although there was some risk, (statistically a cyclist in Britain could ride 330 000 km before being seriously injured and 17 million km before being killed), the 'benefits gained from regular cycling are likely to outweigh the loss of life through cycling accidents'. They concluded that cycling should be promoted vigorously.

That still leaves us with the perception that cycling is dangerous. Perception is a funny thing: people fear air travel and think cars are safe, yet the facts show the opposite is true. The facts show that cycling is much safer than it was: the number of cycle fatalities has fallen significantly in the

last couple of years. For example, in Victoria in 1983 there were 30 cyclists killed, whereas in 1992 the number was 13 (Vic Roads, 1993).

I think that's because the crackdown on speeding and drunken motorists has made the roads a lot safer, and that if cyclists do crash, they are more likely to be wearing a helmet. We don't have much data on the number of bicycle crashes or injuries but there is some reassurance in the research which suggests that 80 per cent of bicycle crashes have nothing at all to do with a motor vehicle (Federal Office of Road Safety, 1985).

Despite all the studies and statistics, I can think of two good reasons to be careful when cycling around town.

First of all cars dominate our roads. Much has been done over the last 40 years to make the roads more suitable for cars and less suitable for other road-users, including cyclists. For example, traffic lanes are commonly made too narrow for a car and a cyclist to share. But changes are already taking place that make the roads more suitable for all users. Cyclist groups are, for example, pressuring government to reorganise lane marking so that the kerbside lane is wide enough for a car and a cyclist to share. I think there are many potential cyclists who are waiting for such changes before they join us on the roads.

The second reason for caution is the attitude of car drivers. Constant emphasis on car priority has bred an attitude in the minds of some drivers that the roads are solely for them. Some become quite aggressive in defence of their imagined right to rule the road. 'You don't pay registration – get off the road,' a driver yelled at me the other day. He was wrong – like most bike riders, I own a car – and I didn't get off the road. This sort of thing does not happen in bicycle-friendly countries and you just have to develop a thick skin.

But arrogant and aggressive drivers are probably not as much of a problem as careless drivers. Careless drivers pay little attention to the road, often concentrating on changing the CD or talking on the phone. They do not expect to meet anything other than cars and will drive through a Stop sign, turn in front of you or shoot past you with centimetres to spare. If you are riding in traffic, you have to watch out for careless drivers at all times.

In the end the decision whether to ride in traffic is up to you alone. I hope you do decide to vote with your pedals. What follows will help you improve your riding-in-traffic skills if you are already on the road. And if you have just moved to a busy town, or have just got into bike riding, or are thinking about riding to work, warm up to it slowly. Start on quieter roads and build up your confidence. Riding in traffic is one of those things that look difficult from the outside but is quite com-fortable once you are in the swing of it.

PREPARING FOR REGULAR TOWN RIDING

First, we will look at how you might prepare for a regular ride around town, using the ride to work as an example.

TIME AND DISTANCE

Most people set their ride-to-work limit somewhere around 30 to 40 minutes. This is about where the advantage of the bicycle ends and it becomes quicker and easier to go by public transport or by car. There are some people who are happy to ride for over an hour each

way but this is a big commitment, especially if you are doing it each weekday.

If it is just too far to ride to your destination, there are a number of ways to shorten the ride:

- Take your bike on the car to a spot where it is easy to park and then ride the rest of the way.
- A more common solution is to ride until you reach a public transport connection. If you are leaving your bike all day, you will need either a good lock or an undesirable bike.
- If the public transport doesn't leave you near your destination, you could pay to take your bike with you or use a folding bike that can travel without a ticket. Another solution is to use two bikes to do a three-part trip. Ride the first bike to the transport stop near home and lock it up. Leave the other bike locked up at the stop where you get off, ready for the ride to your destination.

WHAT TO WEAR

For a short trip of 10 minutes, it doesn't matter what you wear. But the longer you are in the saddle and the harder you pedal, the more you will want to wear cycling gear for your trip and the less you will want to wear your work clothes or shoes. Chapter 11 discusses clothes that make it easier to ride. Riding in cycling gear probably means that you will need somewhere to change, and maybe have a shower, at the other end. If you are lucky, there will be a shower at work or possibly at a nearby local swimming pool, gym or fitness centre.

If you wear cycling clothes on your bike, you will need work clothes to change into. Some regular riders carry their good clothes with them but bike bags can crease an ironed dress or shirt. Other riders keep good clothes at work and either carry them home at the end of the week or get them cleaned locally. Another strategy is to leave the bike at home once a week and carry in a week's worth of clothes. Some people do ride in their good clothes but wear cycling shoes, keeping a pair of ordinary shoes at work. If you are going to change into work clothes after your ride, establish a routine or write a list to make sure you have everything you need. The day I forgot my shirt I had to go out and buy one.

HOW OFTEN?

There is nothing that says that you have to ride to work every day to get the benefits of cycling. Some people ride twice or three times a week. Nor do you have to ride there-and-back on the same day; you can shuffle your trips around. Someone I worked with would ride in the morning, leave the bike that evening and go home on public transport. The next day she might come in on public transport and then ride home that evening. This allowed her to dodge rain, stay in town late or just take it easy. If you found it easy to ride in on mornings but inconvenient to ride back at night you could use a couple of bikes for the morning trips and then take them back one night on a car rack. Some people keep a bike at work so they can get their exercise at lunchtime, or can do quick work trips from the office. Don't stint on getting a taxi every so often: a cab ride once a fortnight will not cost anything like regular car or public-transport use. You can combine cycling with regular car-pooling, or just ask a colleague for a lift when you can't be bothered riding.

WORKING OUT YOUR ROUTE

Take some time to work out a low-stress route. If possible, get an experienced cyclist to help you at each of the following stages.

Study a street map that shows your home and your destination, and weigh up alternative routes. Use a pencil to mark in one or two possibilities. Try to build your route out of the easier and safer left turns, rather than right turns across traffic. This might mean using a different route morning and evening. Keep an eye open for parks, bike paths, open areas or carparks that might allow you to take a short-cut or get away from the traffic.

A direct route along the roads will probably be the quickest way, but some people prefer a more circuitous route, perhaps along quiet residential streets. One cyclist I know enjoys an hour-long ride on a bikepath through the bush and under the kookaburras. He could get to work in half an hour on the road.

• **Test the route** on a quiet weekend when there's not too much traffic. This will tell you how long the ride takes. You will also be able to familiarise yourself with the intersections (see below). The test will reveal things you can't see on a map, such as whether the roads have a smooth surface or wide traffic lanes, and if there are any potential problems, like multi-lane roundabouts or multiple turning-lanes.

Your test ride might reveal an unavoidable problem, such as a narrow bridge. If there is no detour or alternative, you can always walk your bike through the problem area. Some people in these situations ride on the footpath which can be illegal. (See 'Riding on footpaths' in Chapter 6.)

Your test ride will also reveal ups

and downs. Don't give up if you find a difficult hill: you will get fitter. Often the impossible hill you avoided at first becomes quite manageable after a few months of riding.

• **Look at the map again** for better alternatives after your test ride.

• **Leave early the first time** you do the real thing. Allow yourself lots of time, so you can go nice and carefully. If you can ride in with a cycling colleague and benefit from their experience, so much the better.

• **Evaluate the route again**. What was a nice quiet suburban street during your test run can, in peak hour, turn into a racetrack with drivers zipping along a short-cut and jumping Stop signs. Traffic conditions change throughout the day and you might use one road that is good in the morning and come home on another in the evening. If you like the route but not the drivers, you might be able to change the time you get to work, arriving earlier or later to avoid the worst of peak hour.

BE PREPARED FOR TOWN RIDING
Regular riders will also consider the following things:

• **A roadworthy bike** is essential. Chapter 14 has a list of quick diagnostic tests.

• **Be visible**: wear reflective and be-seen clothing, as discussed in Chapter 11.

• **Rain gear** is a good idea. Make sure the coat itself is bright and reflective. Or else wear be-seen gear over the top of the raincoat. See Chapter 11 for more on riding in the rain.

• **Luggage.** You will need some way of carrying things, such as work needs,

swimming togs, lunch or library books. Chapter 11 looks at luggage carriers.

• **Reliable lights** are obviously important if you are riding at night. Chapter 11 describes the options.

• **A U-lock** is vital if you want to be able to ride home as well. Chapter 11 discusses locks. Sometimes you can organise a locker or can put your bike in a shed or cupboard at work. Some people leave a big chain and lock at work so they don't have to carry it back and forth. Some railway stations will rent you a secure bike locker.

• **Carry some water** if you are riding for half an hour or more. Chapter 12 explains why cyclists need so much water.

• **Medical kit,** for prevention – face or hand cream, lip salve, sunscreen – or to treat minor accidents. (A comprehensive kit is described in Chapter 4.)

• **A breakdown kit** to make minor repairs. The simplest bike breakdown kit is your U-lock and a twenty-dollar note, so that you can secure the bike, jump in a cab and solve the problem later. Solving the problem later could be done by taking the bike to a shop, by taking the bike home to your tools or by taking your tools back to the bike. Chapter 14 lists tools to choose from for your on-the-road repair kit.

• **Roadcraft.** Always concentrate and practise to improve your skills.

ROADCRAFT: HOW TO TRAVEL SAFELY IN TRAFFIC

FOLLOW THE ROAD RULES
Road rules are not very fashionable among some cyclists. This is wrong. The rules – or, more importantly, the ideas behind the rules – should shape

our attitude to riding around town. If you have the right attitude then you will have laid the foundation for your roadcraft and road safety.

- **The road rules are an agreement on how to share the road.** If you follow them, other people are going to be more willing to share the road with you.

Some cyclists ignore the road rules because they say the road system is biased to the car and, for as long as car drivers continue to ignore or endanger cyclists, cyclists can ignore the rules. It is true that the road rules are not a guarantee of cycling safety. Despite the rules, people can endanger you by driving through Stop signs or traffic lights. But if you do not stop at red lights yourself, how can you expect others to? Also, when cyclists break the rules, they make drivers resentful, which doesn't increase cyclists' safety.

A more dangerous excuse among cyclists is that it is okay to break the rules because bicycles are all about freedom and independence and that sort of thing. But that can make government inclined to bring in stricter rules and harsher enforcement against cyclists.

- The road rules are based on two important safety principles:
  - One is that you must always ride in a way that will allows you to avoid a collision. For example, a green light is not a guarantee of safe passage but an indication that you may proceed if it is safe.
  - The other is 'giving way'. No road-user ever has absolute right of way over another: the rules describe in particular instances who should give way. For example, the rules say a vehicle coming up to the Stop sign should stop and give way; they do not

say that a vehicle on the priority road has absolute right-of-way. That means cyclists have to go carefully.

For cyclists these two principles are perhaps more important than the detail of the rules. Car drivers who have had a collision can indulge themselves in legal argument about the rules but cyclists can get hurt even if they are technically in the right.

I strongly recommend that every so often you refresh your knowledge of the road rules that apply in your area. Get a learn-to-drive book from the newsagent and test yourself as if you were going for your licence.

Special bicycle regulations
Part of the blame for cyclists disrespecting the law must be laid at the door of the regulators who have not addressed some basic problems with bicycle regulations:

- **Standards are not enforced:** e.g., few reflectors on new bikes meet the Australian Standard.
- **Regulations are not enforced:** e.g., few cyclists are booked for not using lights at night.
- **Unnecessary regulations are on the books:** such as requirements for hand signals which can contribute to loss of control.
- **Necessary regulations are missing:** such as a requirement that bicycles are assembled by a trained mechanic.
- **There are anomalies between States:** e.g., the hook turn, which is recommended below at intersections, is legal in Victoria and South Australia for cyclists but not in Tasmania or New South Wales.

Road authorities around Australia are inching towards a uniform set of road rules for each State which will sort out some of these anomalies. In the meantime it is worth checking with your State road authority on the special bicycle rules that apply where you live.

TAKE YOUR PLACE ON THE ROAD

Bicycles have a right to be on the road and they have a correct place on the road. Some cyclists don't believe this and skulk around like a shy person at a party, trying to be invisible. Other cyclists believe they are outside the law and act as if they can do anything they like on the road. Neither of these approaches is safe or sensible. Most motorists look before they turn, open a door or pull in; if the cyclist is trying to be invisible, she or he is at greater risk. The lawless are obviously in danger when they go through red lights and Stop signs. The best thing you can do is to take your rightful place among the other road-users. These seven rules will help achieve it:

1. *Learn competent bike-handling*

Part of the job of any car or motorcycle test is to ensure that you have adequate handling skills: that you can concentrate on the road situation while operating the machine. Handling skills are equally important for cyclists. When you can handle your bike competently without much conscious thought, you can give most of your attention to the traffic. If you wobble all over the road while getting on and off, changing gears, riding slowly and looking behind you, then you need to improve your bike handling before riding in traffic. You should also be able to ride in a straight line, brake properly and corner safely. (Chapter 6 looks at getting on and off, while Chapter 7 discusses these other basic handling skills.)

The only way to gain these skills is to spend time in the saddle. You can do this practice on bike paths, on quiet residential streets, on quiet days or at quiet times of the day. The popular bicycle tours such as the Great Victorian Bike Ride are a great way to learn handling skills. It doesn't matter which way you do it; just get as much practice as you can.

2. *Take up a good road position*

Once you can handle your bike confidently, good road position is your next goal. A rule of thumb for round-town cyclists is to ride 'one metre out'. That means one metre out from the kerb or one metre out from the right-hand side of parked cars. This can be unnerving for a novice who might fear being hit from behind. (Fitting a mirror to your bike might help reduce this fear of the unseen.) Far more common are collisions at intersections and collisions when cyclists swerve suddenly. That is why you ride one metre out. Riding one metre out from the kerb means:

- a car coming from your left at an intersection will see you sooner.
- you will stay out of the gutters, the obstacles that build up in them and the poor surface close to the gutter which means you are less likely to swerve.
- When you ride one metre out from the parked cars you will avoid running into a door that is swept open suddenly, or swerving out into traffic to avoid it. One metre is only just enough. Car doors are surprisingly wide and sometimes stick out more than a metre. (Sometimes bike lanes are painted on the road surface too near to parked cars for safe riding. Make sure you have

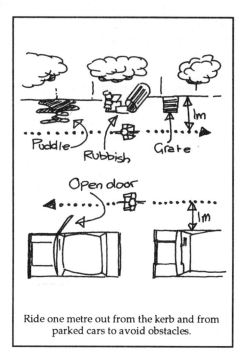

Ride one metre out from the kerb and from parked cars to avoid obstacles.

When a driver sees you on the road, they will go through the following process:

– notice a cyclist,

– estimate the cyclist's speed and direction,

– steer a safe course.

Then they will:

– look at something else. (This movement of their eyes could be a skilful scan of other parts of the road, a quick check of the mirror, or a careless look down at the radio. While they are looking away their car might have travelled 50 metres or more.) Eventually they will:

– look back at the cyclist.

If you are riding straight, then you will be safe for that period while they are looking away. Better still, when they look back, you will be where they expect to find you.

We can put the 'ride straight' rule the other way round: 'Don't swerve'. You could swerve and change your course just when the driver is not looking.

• Before you make any move to the left or right or make a turn, check behind you, then as quickly as possible set up another straight line to ride along.

• Before you dodge a pothole or obstacle on your straight line, check behind, move in or out as early as you can and set up a new straight line. If the obstacle can't be avoided – a pedestrian may have stepped off the kerb for example – then slow down or stop.

good road position whatever the bike lanes suggest.)

Good road position might mean that you need to be more than one metre out. If the kerbside traffic lane is too narrow, or about to get too narrow, for you to share with a car – such as at a single-lane roundabout – check behind and move to the middle of your lane to make sure you are not squeezed into the kerb.

If the traffic is too fast for you to take up good road position, then you should find an alternative route.

3. Ride straight

When you have good road position it is easy to follow the next rule: ride in a straight line. This avoids the 'swerving' collision and helps other road-users predict where you will be. My rule is: *Ride one metre out on an imaginary straight line at least 50 metres long.*

4. Look behind you

Check behind you regularly. A mirror is the best way to do this as it keeps your eyes on the road in front. Without a mirror you will have the biggest blind-spot of any road-user: a full 180 degrees behind your shoulders. All regular round-town cyclists should have a mirror (see Chapter 11).

Even with a mirror you will have some blind-spots so check first with your mirror and then take a quick look behind to confirm that the mirror has told you the correct story. You should be able to look behind without wobbling all over the place and you should do it quickly so you don't plough into something in front. Don't be afraid to pull over to the left and stop if you need to have a really long careful look behind you.

5. *Keep a safe braking distance*

Make sure you are a safe braking distance from any car in front of you. Bicycle brakes are much less effective than those on any other vehicle on the road. Chapter 7 discusses brakes in more detail.

6. *Stay out of blind-spots*

Stay out of other people's blind-spots. Cars can hide a bicycle to the left and to the right rear. Directly behind or in front of the car is usually safer.

• Right-side blind-spots. Some drivers check their outside mirror on the right, but if you are alongside the boot or right-side doors, you are probably in a blind-spot.

• Left-side blind-spots. Few drivers know what is happening on the left-rear side of their car and even fewer look out the left-side windows. Try not to be in a driver's left blind-spot when passing a road on the left: the driver might suddenly decide to turn left. Another left-hand-side problem is the passenger who throws open the door and jumps out of the car that has stopped at the lights. These people rarely look for cyclists.

7. *Communicate with other road-users*

Do all you can to increase your communication with other road users.

• **Use your road position to communicate.** Make sure you are in the correct lane. If, for example, you want to go straight ahead and the left lane is a left-turn-only lane, you should move right into the straight-ahead lane. If the traffic is going too fast in the straight-ahead lane, or there is no room for you to share the lane, then move to the right side of the left-turn-only lane to show that you want to go straight ahead. If the traffic is too fast for that, you might have to pull over and wait until the traffic clears before continuing.

• **Use hand signals to communicate when possible.** If you are going to signal, make it definite, even exaggerated. A good model is those exaggerated hand gestures the police use whenever they are communicating to road-users. They slowly uncurl their hands until the palm and fingers are flat. But don't take your hand off the bars if that will cause you to lose control. My favourite hand signal is a 'thank you' wave. I have a theory that if cyclists say 'thank you' a lot, we might get more consideration in the long run.

• **Use eye contact to communicate.** Try to catch the eye of drivers to make sure they have seen you. Search for their eyes through the windscreen, through rear-view mirrors and wing mirrors. It is surprising how well this works. It is almost as if there is something magnetic about the human eye that means they will notice your searching eye. Try to catch the eye of drivers who are waiting on your left or on your right at a Stop sign. Try to make eye contact with drivers coming in the opposite direction and planning to turn right. Pedestrians can be even less aware than drivers, so make eye contact with them too, when possible.

INTERSECTIONS
More than half of all bicycle and car collisions are at intersections, so here are some suggestions on how to travel through them safely:

Don't change your mind in the middle of the intersection
Think about your route before you set out. Visualise each of the intersections and how you will negotiate it. If you have sorted out your navigation before, you can devote all your attention to roadcraft when you are actually riding.

If you are not sure where you are going, be conscious of this and ride more carefully. Pull over if you need to check your navigation. Above all don't be unpredictable and pull out of a turn at the last minute. It is better to complete the wrong turn, stop and then backtrack.

Turning left
Turning left is the easiest way through an intersection.
 • Ride in the middle of the left-turn lane: this will stop left-turning cars cutting you off. They can overtake you once you are round the corner.
 • Watch out for cars coming from the right.
 • Watch out for oncoming cars turning right.
 • Don't forget the pedestrians; you must give way to them when you are turning left.

Going straight ahead
Going straight ahead through an

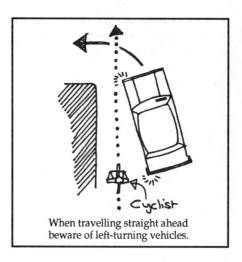

When travelling straight ahead beware of left-turning vehicles.

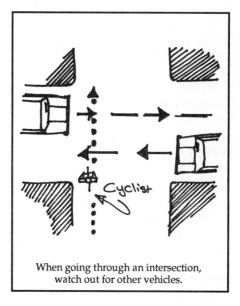

When going through an intersection, watch out for other vehicles.

intersection is more difficult. You need to keep an eye out for left-turning cars, cars coming from the right or left, oncoming right-turners and roundabouts.
 • **Left-turning cars.** Cyclists often grumble about drivers who do a left turn in front of them while they are trying to go straight ahead. But the left-turning car need not be a problem.

– Take up a road position that will communicate your intention. Usually this means riding in the middle of the kerbside lane. Don't hug the kerb: the cars won't see you, and if they do, they assume you are also turning left. In either case you are likely to be cut off. If the kerbside lane is a left-turn-only lane, take up a good road position and move into the straight-ahead lane as we described above. Alternatively, stop and wait for the traffic to clear.

– Try to avoid multiple left-turn lanes. These are often built at the entrance to freeways or major roads. Multiple left-turn lanes are really an oblique intersection and cars will come at you from behind and to the right. The best thing to do is to get into the straight-ahead lane or wait for the traffic to clear.

– Try to avoid high-speed, left-turn lanes such as off ramps from freeways and major arterials. These wide lanes allow cars to go fast into the corner and offer no protection to cyclists. One approach is to get out into the straight-ahead lane. Another solution – and this is what is recommended on freeways where cycling is permitted – is to ride up the left-turn lane as if you were turning left, then, when the traffic clears and where the left-turn lane is narrowest, cross to the other side and head back up to the road you want.

• **Cars from right or left.** Cars coming from the right or left also need to be considered when you are going straight ahead.

– Always check an intersection to the right and left before riding through it, even at traffic lights.

– Check the right side first, as those cars will reach you first as you enter the intersection.

– Check the left side as you get to half way.

– Don't rely on traffic lights to protect you: there is always one idiot who'll go through a red light.

– Cyclists should always stop when the traffic light is amber. If you ride through the amber light, you are exposing yourself to the drag-racing drivers who charge across as soon as the lights change. Use the pedestrian signal to estimate how long the lights have been green. If the pedestrian signal is flashing, the traffic signal is about to turn red. You will get to know the times and sequences of lights on a regular route.

• **Oncoming right-turners.** Watch out for oncoming cars turning right across your path.

– Try to catch the eye of drivers going in the other direction and wanting to turn right across your path.

– Slow down until sure they have seen you and that they are going to wait.

– When possible, try to cross the intersection alongside a stream of cars going straight ahead. This will protect your right side. Oncoming right-turners will often be ready to roar through a

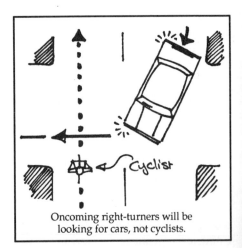

Oncoming right-turners will be looking for cars, not cyclists.

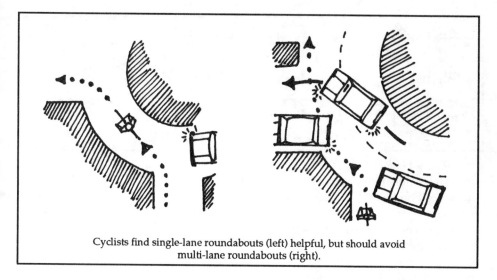

Cyclists find single-lane roundabouts (left) helpful, but should avoid multi-lane roundabouts (right).

gap in the stream of cars going your way, so try not to be in one of the gaps they are looking for.

– Don't enter an intersection behind or alongside a large vehicle that hides you from oncoming, right-turning traffic. The truck or bus that hides you might stop to turn, or speed away, and leave you exposed in the middle of the intersection to oncoming right-turners.

• **Roundabouts.** Single-lane round-abouts make an intersection much easier for cyclists. Priority is clear and you only have to watch out for one car at each entrance. But you do need to ride in the middle of the lane around the round-about otherwise someone will try to pass you on the roundabout or turn left on top of you. Use signals or body language to show which exit you are taking.

Try to avoid multi-lane roundabouts. They are designed for fast car travel and this is always bad news for cyclists. Not only will the cars be going fast, but you will probably have to ride past multiple exit or entrance lanes. There is no way to handle this safely except to wait for the traffic to clear.

Turning right

Turning right at an intersection is the most difficult traffic manoeuvre and there are three ways to do it.

• **Hook turn.** On busy streets, especially where there are traffic lights, I strongly recommend the two-stage hook turn.

– On the green light or when the road is clear, go straight ahead to the far side of the intersection.

– Stop and and turn your bike to face the new direction of your route.

– Wait until the lights go green for the new direction, or the road is clear.

– Head off in your new direction.

• **Reverse hook turn.** Sometimes it is appropriate to do a reverse hook turn.

– Dismount and walk across the intersection to the right.

– When the lights change, walk straight ahead.

– Remount and head off in your new direction.

• **Centre turn.** On a *quiet* street you can turn from the centre of the road. (If you are not sure if the street is quiet or not, do a hook turn.)

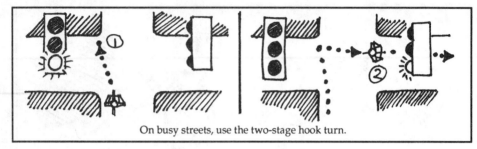

On busy streets, use the two-stage hook turn.

– Check behind you.
– Well before the corner, move out into a position that shows you intend to turn right.
– Watch out for other cars also making a right turn.
– Check oncoming cars and complete the right turn, making sure to give way to pedestrians.

Be alert

If you are riding around town, you must always be alert to the road surface, the weather, the light, and your own reaction time.

Watch out for poor road surfaces

A good road surface allows you to concentrate more on traffic conditions. But if the road surface is poor, you will have to concentrate more on staying upright and in the saddle. A skid or a fall can be painful in itself but is dangerous if it tips you in front of another vehicle.

Watch for surfaces that have been made slippery by gravel. (Chapter 7 discusses getting out of a skid.)

Watch out for bumps. Things that stick up include inspection covers, rails, expansion joints in bridges, a resurfaced section of road, lane markers and pedestrian-crossing markers.

When crossing rails, hoses or pipes, path edgings, even some driveway ramps, ride at right angles to the obstacle.

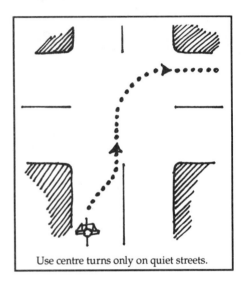

Use centre turns only on quiet streets.

Watch out for holes. A pothole can bump you out of the saddle and slotted drains can catch bicycle wheels.

Watch out in wet conditions

When it rains you will need to change the way you ride: there are seven times as many bicycle crashes in wet conditions. It is more difficult to ride safely in the wet because:

• Braking is more difficult. In wet conditions, even if you have alloy rims, it will take much longer for your brakes to work.

• Rain will make the road more slippery and your tyres will lose some grip.

• Rain will make things on the road much more slippery. Wet fallen leaves can cause skids. Lane marking and arrows painted on the road become like ice in the wet. Railway lines, tram lines and metal inspection covers are even worse. Skilful cyclists get in the habit of avoiding paint and metal in the dry so that the habit is there, already established, to help them in the wet. Watch out especially in the first rain after a dry spell: oil from cars builds up in dry weather and the first shower turns the road surface into a skid pan.

- In the wet, it is harder for other people to see you.
- It is also harder for other people to stop.

Watch out in poor light

Dawn, dusk and night-time are difficult times to ride as well. It is much more dangerous to ride at night. Low levels of light make it hard for careful drivers to see a badly lit cyclist – and not all drivers are careful. Make sure your lights and be-seen gear are effective. Chapter 11 discusses this equipment in more detail.

Use all your senses

Skilled cyclists maximise the use of all their senses. One advantage a cyclist has over most road-users is sound. On a quiet machine like a bike you can hear what is going on – better than a motorcyclist can, for example. Don't spoil this advantage by plugging into earphones. If you really like music on the move, travel by car or bus.

Staying away from alcohol and other recreational chemicals will help ensure your reactions are in tip-top shape. Alcohol reduces your ability to judge speed and distance as well as making it harder to concentrate. It can make you sleepy and it affects your sense of balance. It also increases your reaction

delay (see Chapter 7). Worst of all, it can give you a feeling that all is right with the world. This is not a good approach to riding in traffic. Tiredness, stress, sickness and being cold have similar effects. If you sense any of those performance reducers, you should compensate by riding more carefully, or not riding at all.

IMPROVING YOUR ROADCRAFT

Your bicycle roadcraft can always be improved. In fact all road users need to improve anticipation, increase concentration and check that they are doing the right thing. One tried and true way to achieve this is, as you ride along, to tell yourself the story of your trip, almost as if you were teaching roadcraft to someone else.

Tell the story of your ride

Your story could be something like this:
- Give Way sign; slow down, look both ways; into the gap of the median. This car coming along isn't indicating but it is slowing down and might want to turn. Wait for it to pass.
- Exhaust coming from that car: watch for it coming out of that driveway. Stop sign; get well over to the right for my turn but watch out for people sweeping in from the left and cutting the corner. Right foot high on the pedal ready to go: there's a good gap coming up here.
- Past these shops the driver may climb out of that delivery van, or a pedestrian might pop out on the far side: they run across the road to get to the bank. This is where there are all those potholes: move out to avoid that one in good time and set up a new straight line. The bus route here turns right so the bus will be trying to get

into the middle of the road. These lights coming up are difficult: the left-turn arrow stays on. Check behind and move into the straight-ahead lane.

• Lights changing the other way: get ready. Green for us; check right for the one who comes through on red. No-one doing it today. That station-wagon is looking for a park. Will I be able to move right? – no, the stream of traffic looks a bit thick at the moment. Uhuh, the station-wagon passenger is pointing; there we go, the station-wagon has pulled up and blocked my path. Well done, good prediction. I'll just wait for him to park and off we go again . . .

Telling your ride story to yourself will help you realise when you have done well and when you haven't and allow you constantly to improve your riding. This strategy works well, whatever vehicle you are using: even when you are not cycling but are driving a car, riding a motorcycle or being a back-seat driver. I am sure it will improve your cycling roadcraft.

CRASHES AND COLLISIONS

It is possible that you will have a crash when riding your bike. Fortunately most bicycle crashes do not involve cars; but a small proportion of bicycle crashes are collisions between a bicycle and another vehicle. Your roadcraft will help you avoid a crash or collision but you should be prepared.

• Make sure you have ambulance insurance.

• Carry a card with your name and address, the phone number of someone you want to be told if you are hurt and any special medical condition that might be relevant.

The standard rules for car collisions apply to bike-and-car collisions. If you are in such a collision and you are hurt or your bicycle is damaged:

• Give your name and address to the driver.

• Get the name, address and phone number of the driver.

• Try to get the names and addresses of some witnesses. Witnesses are important and often forgotten.

• You must report to the police all accidents that cause injury.

You might be able to get back on your bike after a crash or collision, but don't be too eager. Shock can be hard to recognise and it is difficult to judge its intensity. If you ride while in shock, you are increasing the chance of having another prang. It might be best to lock up your bike and use another form of transport. Even if you are okay to ride, check your bicycle very carefully before riding off on it. All sorts of things can get bent or knocked or cracked and it is dangerous to ride an unroadworthy bike.

If you do come off your bike in a crash, even if you were wearing a helmet, get a doctor to give you a check-up. Doctors can do a number of tests, including looking in your eyes to check for head injuries. Head injuries must be treated quickly and the symptoms sometimes aren't apparent to the head-owner for two or three days.

Chapter 6

BEGINNER RIDERS

CHILDREN AND BIKES

Can you remember your first bike? I
can certainly remember mine. It was a
second-hand, red-brown BSA. That bike
took a lot of punishment, and it was
probably relieved to be passed down
the family when I got a green Triumph
with three gears and a twist-grip gear
changer. Very swish.

I am sure we all remember our first
bike, or remember not having a first
bike, because bikes are a big thing in a
young life. First of all there is the tough
job of learning to ride and then the
satisfaction of being able to say 'Yeah, I
can ride a bike'. Once you are mobile,
the thrill of exploration begins; off to
the creek to bother the frogs or down to
the shop for lollies. Then there is the
thrill of independence and grown-
upness when you ride to school or
down to the pool all by yourself.

All this excitement means that it is
easy to help kids enjoy bikes. They will
love them without any effort from you.
Your contribution can be to help them

enjoy learning to ride; you can make
sure that, as they grow up, their bikes
fit them and are easy to ride; and you
can teach them to ride safely on the
road.

CHILDREN AS PASSENGERS

There are a number of ways to carry a
child about by bicycle. A trailer that can
hold one or two offspring and their
paraphernalia gives you the best
handling and them the most comfort.
But even though some trailers fold up
when not in action, they do take up
space, and they cost hundreds of
dollars. Trailers won't be available in
every bike shop either. Nor will many
of the passenger carriers easily
available overseas.

Most people end up using one of the
readily available, moulded-plastic,
child seats which cost around a
hundred dollars. Some seats attach to
the bike frame, and some of these have
suspension for passenger comfort.
Other seats attach to a rack which in

some cases allows you to unclip the seat easily. Rather than pedal a permanent seat to work every day, some people get another bike for child carrying. Some people don't mind the seat and use it to carry stuff when the child isn't on board. A daypack fits nicely into an empty child seat.

Children can sit in one of these seats as soon as they can hold their heads up confidently. You will know your child best, but I would be surprised if that was before six or seven months old. Most children will be too heavy and too big for the seat by the time they are four to five years old.

FITTING A CHILD SEAT

Most adult bikes will take a child seat, but the bike with a riding position where you lean forward a little and hold straight handlebars will give you the best control. It is easier to mount and dismount if the bike does not have a top tube in the frame. These open-top frames will flex a bit from side to side when the child is on board but this shouldn't be a big problem.

A child of up to four or five years can enjoy being a bicycle passenger in a properly designed child seat.

When you choose and fit a child seat, make sure:

• the seat is firmly attached to the bike. Use lock washers on the bolts that hold the seat to the bike to stop it rattling loose.

• there is a foot guard to keep tootsies out of the spokes. The guard should fit over the wheel behind the saddle, and in front of and underneath the child seat. Some seats have no guards but use straps to hold the child's legs into a foot slot.

• the seat has a pilot's safety harness: two shoulder straps and a lap belt that click together in a way that the Inquisitive One can't unbuckle.

• the seat has a high back and that the sides come up to form a three-sided bucket. This will help keep your co-pilot on board.

• your child has a light, foam helmet.

You might want to improve the rather basic padding in the seat and add some in-flight entertainment such as a furry animal on a string or something that rattles. (The string won't stop the item being thrown overboard but will stop it being lost. Make sure the string is short enough to keep the toy out of the spokes.)

BIKE-HANDLING WITH THE CHILD SEAT

A bicycle with a child on board is harder to handle than an unloaded bike. Make sure you have good handling skills before taking a passenger. You can practise handling the extra load by tying some phone books in the child seat.

• **Balancing and cornering.** The bike will be more unstable and will behave differently when cornering: it will be harder to lean and then, once the bike starts to lean, it will suddenly want to lean further.

- **It will take longer to brake to a stop** but, with more weight on the back, you can get more out of the front brake. (See Chapter 7 on braking.) One way to get your braking performance up is to ride more slowly.

- **Stopping and parking.** As soon as you slow to a halt and put your foot on the ground, the bike is going to want to tip over to one side. The main thing is not to lift the handlebars, as that will put the bike and passenger on the ground in a flash. Lean forward and keep a firm grip on the bars.

Don't lean your bike against a pole with the child in the back and let go of the bike: the front wheel will roll and the bike will fall over immediately. You can control the roll of the front wheel with an improvised handbrake, as was suggested when putting your bike on a train. Whether you use a handbrake or not, you should never walk away from the bike with your child still in the seat.

ON THE ROADS WITH A CHILD IN A SEAT

When you do go riding with the child, watch out for the excitement that occurs when your passenger sees a doggie or a red car. Vigorous wriggling will throw the bike about a bit but, with a steady pair of hands on the bars, you will be all right.

Look for quiet routes using back roads and parks as we discussed in Chapter 5. Footpaths are another option which we discuss below. If there is a busy road to cross or some other traffic problem, don't hesitate to walk and use the bike as a pusher. Even if you only pedal for half the journey to the shops or child-care centre, you are still doing better than a parent who has to walk all the way.

PREPARING TO LEARN TO RIDE

Learning to ride is a process that can start well before you get a child's first bike. Learning to ride well continues long after you can balance, pedal, stop and start. Chapter 7 has more on bike handling skills and Chapter 5 on roadcraft.

TRIKES, TRAINER WHEELS AND SCOOTERS

There are a number of popular children's toys that are good preparation for bike riding.

- **Punt-alongs.** The first bicycle-like toy that kids can handle is the plastic tractor or motorbike on which they sit and punt along with their feet.

- **Scooters** will help kids learn to balance and to corner on two wheels.

- **A good tricycle** is the best way to practise pedalling, braking and a bicycle-like riding position. To press children to ride a two-wheeler before they are ready is a mistake. Most youngsters learn to tricycle happily with no fear, and graduate confidently to a two-wheeler when they are ready. Good tricycles have chain drive to the rear wheel, gears and pneumatic tyres on decent-sized wheels. These trikes are a thing of joy and as pleasurable to ride as a bicycle – but they are hard to find. It is a mystery why manufacturers don't make a range of decent tricycles for kids. Even adults enjoy trikes; a local government councillor just down the road from me rides about everywhere on her trike.

If you hunt around, you will be able

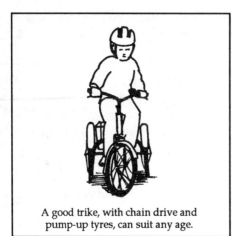

A good trike, with chain drive and
pump-up tyres, can suit any age.

to find a good trike but unfortunately
the most common junior trikes are
down the dinosaur end of bicycle
development. They have uncomfortable
solid-rubber tyres, vertical forks –
which means the trike is hard to steer in
a straight line – and no suspension. The
pedalling action through the front
wheel interferes with steering. The
machines have small wheels, no ball
bearings and no gears, which makes
pedalling such hard work that these
trikes usually don't need brakes. Most
of these flaws in pedal-powered design
were corrected in the early penny
farthings.

Despite these disadvantages, kids
love these trikes and they will ride
them, and treasure them, even after
they can handle a two-wheeler. Don't
let your kid miss out on a trike and if
you can find a decent one, so much the
better.

• **A bike with trainer wheels** may
help with practising pedalling and
braking. It also allows parents to buy a
wheeled thing for tots before they are
really ready to balance, because when
they are, the trainer wheels can be
whipped off and, voila, you have a real
bike. But don't expect the 'trainer'
wheels actually to train the child to ride
a two-wheeler.

Many parents believe that the
outriggers will teach their child to ride.
This method certainly worked for my
brother who, after some time on
trainers, walked in one day, asked Dad
to take off the trainer wheels, jumped
on and started riding the two-wheeler
around. But I know of many parents
who find that their child is frustrated
by the unwieldy and slow-moving bike
with trainer wheels. The riders also get
tired of being dumped on the ground
when they try to turn a corner.
Typically, riders will be 'high sided':
that is, they will turn one way – say left
– and the left trainer wheel will stop the
lean but throw the rider off to the right.

Some parents try to introduce a
learning element by raising the trainer
wheels a bit at a time, so that the bike
can be balanced while riding in a
straight line. But this often makes the
riders sway from side to side as they
ride along, bouncing from one support
wheel to the other, or else makes them
ride permanently canted over to one
side. It is Catch 22: if the riders *can*
balance, they don't need trainer wheels.

The plain truth is that a bike with
trainer wheels will not teach kids how
to ride a two-wheeler. A bicycle with
two supporting wheels is not really a
bicycle but a pedal-powered 'fourcycle'.
Fourcycling won't teach you to balance,
because when you are going straight
ahead you are already balanced; and it
won't teach you cornering because, if
you turn at any speed, you will tip the
whole thing over. Children might be
better off and happier staying on a
good, big trike until they are ready to
go straight to two wheels.

Choose a child's bike to fit that child's size and ability, not merely according to the three 'age' categories in which junior bikes are usually marketed.

GETTING THE RIGHT-SIZED BIKE

At some stage you will be ready to get hold of the First Bike. The most important thing is to make sure it is the right size. Anyone who is learning to ride and to handle a bike safely needs to have the correct-size bike. To do this you have to avoid two traps: economy and age.

The economy trap

Parents are often tempted to buy bikes that are too big, like buying oversize clothes that the kids can grow into. But you can't get away with this with bikes. A rider will find it hard to handle a bike that is too big and will be more likely to have a crash.

To get good value:

• Buy second-hand bikes.

• Use school networks to swap and trade machines with other parents with growing children.

• Buy a bike that is the right size now. If you must, let the child continue riding it even if it is too small. A bike that is a little too small is only inconvenient and inefficient, not dangerous.

The age trap

Children who aren't an average size for their age sometimes end up with the wrong size bike because shops tend to sell bikes by age and not by size. The shops use three common categories:

• **Two- to five-year-olds.** Bikes for these usually have 30-cm diameter wheels (12").

• **Four- to eight-year-olds.** Bikes for these usually have 40-cm diameter wheels (16"). They come in two frame types:

– a frame without a top bar, usually with curved forks and a longer wheelbase,

– a BMX-style frame with straight forks.

The step-through designs will probably only have one frame size. The BMX might come with a large or small frame and sometimes different-size handlebars. Bikes with 40-cm wheels will probably have trainer wheels.

• **Six-year-olds and over.** Bikes for these usually have 50-cm wheels (20"). Some have an open-top frame but most are built with a BMX-style frame. This is the standard wheel size for BMX competition for all riders up to adult and marks the start of the adult bike range which we discuss in detail in Chapter 8. In my opinion the single-gear BMX is the best thrash-about kids' bike ever sold as they are fun to ride and, when well-made, take quite a bit of punishment. They are not good for long distances and a BMX rider could get tired on a longer family outing.

For longer rides to school and bike-path exploration you should consider the mini-diamond frames with 55 cm (22") or 60 cm (24") wheels. These geared bikes are like mini versions of adult bikes and are excellent if they are the right size.

Small-wheeled 'shopping' bikes sometimes tempt people who imagine they can be used by all members of the family. These bikes are usually designed for adults and are not great for kids even though they can be made to fit.

The correct size

The solution to the age-and-size problem is to set the child on the bike and make sure the child can turn the pedals, reach the handlebars and can touch the ground easily. Check that the machine has an adjustable seat. (There is more detail on good bicycle fit in Chapter 9.)

If you are preparing a surprise bicycle present for Christmas or a birthday, there are a number of ways you can measure child against prospective bike. You can get the child's inside-leg measurement from a pair of their trousers; or cover up your measuring activities by starting a growth chart on the garage wall. Take a tape measure with you when you go looking for a bike.

BUYING A QUALITY BIKE

Your child will learn to ride more easily and get more good times out of a good-quality bike. It is also likely to last longer. Unfortunately there is not a lot of choice in children's bikes: a lot more effort goes into colours than into the performance of the machine. But here are five good features you can look for on a child's first bike:

• Check the bike has a **back-pedal** brake. Although these are much less effective than hand levers, young hands can have difficulty with levers.

• Look for a **low-geared bike**. Compare the gearing of the contenders by turning the pedals and seeing how often the valve of the rear tyre goes round for each turn of the pedals. The fewer times the valve goes round, the lower the gear and the easier the bike will be to pedal. The bike shop might be able to change the gear ratio for you. (See Chapter 8 for more on gears.)

• Look for a bike with **ball bearings**. Many junior bikes come without them. Ball bearings mean the bike will be easier to pedal, and might be an indication of higher quality overall.

• Look for a **sprung seat**, and for valves on the wheels which show the tyres are not solid rubber. Air-filled tyres make the bike much more comfortable.

• For beginner riders I would look for a bike with a **longer wheelbase**. Use a tape measure to compare wheelbase or stand the two contenders alongside each other, back axle to back axle, and see which one has the front axle further forward. The longer the wheelbase the better it will run in a straight line and the easier it will be to learn to ride.

You won't necessarily get it right first time. Once the bike has had a bit of use, your child might want to change some of the features. Don't forget that many things like pedals, handlebars, gears and saddles can be changed or adapted by the shop. Some kids like high bars, others prefer flat bars; some like gears, others prefer a single speed; some like back-pedal brakes and some don't, so it might take a bit of trial and error to find the most suitable combination of features. That, of course, is true for adults as well and is what Chapter 8 is all about.

A ROADWORTHY CHECK
Make sure your child's bike works properly. The brakes should work, the saddle and bars should not wobble and the tyres should be pumped up. You can use the quick check-list in Chapter 14 to make sure everything is okay. As kids get older they can do some basic mainten-ance on their bike. Nevertheless a careful parent will make sure the bike gets a regular bike-shop service or will run an eye over the bike every so often to make sure it has not become unroadworthy.

A GOOD HELMET
Before starting to ride, make sure the young rider has a light, comfortable helmet that fits well. (There is more detail on good helmet fit in Chapter 11.) Young riders will have crashes as they learn to ride and they will need this protection from the start. An early start to regular helmet-wearing will also help build a habit that will reassure you in later years when they are out on their own. Don't buy a too-large helmet that they can grow into. The association of helmets with discomfort and annoyance is not one you want to establish, nor will a badly fitting helmet do its job properly when it is needed.

I have seen young riders pushing over-sized helmets out of their eyes as they ride along: such helmets could even cause a crash.

LEARNING TO RIDE

THE RIGHT AGE
It is hard to know exactly when a child can learn to ride a two-wheeler. Everyone is different and everyone's circumstance is different. As a general rule, children can ride a two-wheeler by the time they are six years old. I know of physically adept four-year-olds who can thrash up and down the driveway on their bikes, and also of seven-year-olds having difficulty. Kids living on a quiet street will probably learn sooner than kids living near a busy street. Whatever the age, children must be ready to learn; don't force them.

LEARNING AS AN ADULT
I know of two adults who have successfully learned to ride, one in her thirties and the other in her forties. They faced a few barriers. The fact that they had never learned to ride a bike was related to an overall lack of confidence in sporty, physical things. They were out of the habit of try-try-and-try-again which kids are doing all the time; they were also out of the habit of falling over and getting a grazed knee. Overcoming these barriers took some mental effort and determination, but those things aside, the physical process of learning to ride was just the same as I describe below for young learners.

THE RIGHT APPROACH
If you are teaching someone to ride a bike there are four main things worth remembering:

- There is no right way to learn to ride a bike. There are a number of methods and all of them can work. Ideally you will choose the method that best suits the particular learner.

- Good teachers change the lessons to suit the attitude of the learner: some prospective riders will want to do it All By Themselves and others will want Lots Of Help. Sometimes the learner might reject your method and want to learn the same way that Jo next door learnt to ride.

- With bike riding you are trying to teach a sensation or feeling that is quite complex and, to use a hippy word, wholistic. Be patient with learners as they search for this feeling and don't bark out a list of instructions.

- Good teachers always back up a learner's efforts with encouragement, praise and rewards.

BALANCING GAMES

When you think that the time is right, introduce some balancing games to your bicycle outings. These three games might be enough in themselves for the person to learn to ride.

- **Scootering.** It is easier to balance a bike when you are coasting and your legs aren't pumping up and down. One bicycle game that helps learners is to scooter along with one foot on one pedal and the other pushing on the ground.

- **Skiing.** It is also easier to balance a bike that is moving quickly. Find a gentle slope, like a beginner's ski slope. If it is too steep you might frighten the rider and if it is too gradual the rider won't get up enough speed to stay upright. A mown grass slope is softer, but more difficult to steer over; it also needs to be steeper as the bike won't run as freely as on asphalt.

Lower the saddle so the rider's feet can slide along on the ground, before freewheeling down the slope with each shoe scraping on the ground. Practise a couple of passes with feet scraping, and then see if the rider can freewheel down the slope with feet up on the pedals. Two adults could be handy here, one as the pitcher and one as the catcher.

- **Punt along.** Punt along is another balancing game that takes a bit of spanner work to prepare. Lower the seat, take off the pedals, or get the bike shop to take them off for you. (See Chapter 14 for adjusting the saddle and removing pedals.) Then have the learner use the bike like one of those toddler's plastic punt-alongs. When learners are confident on the flat, see if they can punt and glide down a slope. Once they have got the feel of balance, you can put the pedals back on.

HOLDING THE SADDLE

At some stage the learner will be ready to try the real thing. Try holding the saddle of the bike and then walking or jogging beside the rider, not pushing but steadying any wobbles. Let learners gain confidence that they will stay up and that you won't let them fall over.

When the moment is right, you can provide moments of near solo-cycling by relaxing your grip on the saddle. As your grip loosens, the rider will feel the bike moving more from side to side. Let the rider learn how to cope with this movement before you take your hand away altogether.

Eventually you will be ready just to run alongside the learner with your hand touching the saddle ready to catch a big wobble. In the classic instance, after much practice, the rider looks

A beginner rider feels more secure with an adult alongside to steady the bike by the saddle if needed.

around at one point to see the teacher fifty metres behind. At that moment the child realises that he or she has Learned to Ride and you break out the chocolate biscuits.

Holding-the-saddle is a great way for the rider to feel all the cycling skills: pedalling, balance and cornering, at the one time. But the method asks a lot of the teacher. The runner has to be able to reach down to the saddle while running and has to be fit enough to stay alongside the bike and keep it upright while it is being ridden. It is almost certain that you will get tired of holding the saddle long before the learner gets tired of pedalling around. To some extent it is also a high-risk method because the rider might crash if you take your hand off the saddle too soon. Aside from scabs, a crash can cause a sudden drop in morale and trust which could set back the learning process. So I would recommend holding-the-saddle only when you consider the rider is well prepared and on the verge of learning to ride, possibly after successful sessions of the balancing games.

STARTING AND STOPPING

Starting and stopping are important learning-to-ride skills and often remain difficult even after the rider has got the hang of pedalling and balance. This is not surprising: they say that take-off and landing are the difficult bits of flying.

Starting

There are many ways to get rolling on a bike. But I've found this four-step method – by which the bike will take off in a straight line and be well under control – is the best to teach beginners and the best for regular riding.

1. Stand astride the bike.

2. With the left foot on the ground, raise the right pedal until it is at two o'clock and put the right foot on it. Beginners might find it easier to spin the pedal around by hand. If the bike has back pedal brakes, the bike might have to be wheeled forward until the right pedal is in the correct spot. Positioning the pedals can be frustrating: beginners find the pedals often refuse to do what they are told.

3. With the right foot on the pedal at two o'clock and the left on the ground, the rider is in the ready-to-start position. (For on-the-road riding this is the time to look around and see what the traffic is doing.)

4. Then the rider puts the bike in motion by doing three things at once:
   – pushing down on the raised pedal,
   – lifting their bum onto the seat and
   – lifting their left foot onto the left pedal.

Beginners might find this three-part sequence difficult at first. Often the bike runs out of momentum before they can:

– get their bum into position,
– find the left pedal,
– get the left pedal past twelve
o'clock in order to push the bike along.

Lowering the saddle will help them get seated. Practising on a slope will send the bike further on the starting stroke and give the rider extra time to find and turn the left pedal.

Stopping
Stopping is similar to starting.

• As the rider comes to a stop, she brings one pedal, say the right one, to bottom centre at six o'clock to support her weight.

• Then, just as the bike stops, the rider lowers the left foot to the ground. A perfect landing is when the foot hits the ground just as the bike has stopped and not before.

A beginner might find it hard to time the landing of the left foot; trying to put her foot – or worse, both feet – down too early, while the bike is still moving. This is like getting off a moving train, and it produces a distinctive stuttering, hopping motion that puts the bike out of control and can cause a prang, or bump the bicycle into sensitive parts. If the rider is having trouble stopping:

• Check that the brakes work and that the rider can operate them. (An early bail-out is sometimes a form of braking.)

• Get the rider to coast along without braking, with her weight on the pedal foot and the other foot shaving the ground.

• Tackle the fear of overbalancing by slow riding along a marked lane, as suggested below in the handling skills test. (See Chapter 7 for more on slow riding.)

YOUNG RIDERS AND TRAFFIC

PREPARING FOR ROAD RIDING
Children can control a bike and do all sorts of impressive bicycle feats and tricks long before they are able to ride safely in traffic on their own. The usual rule of thumb is that it is not until around nine years old that children have the physical and mental potential to be able to ride safely and confidently on the roads on their own. Before that age they lack the ability to concentrate for long enough. Perhaps more significantly, they can't make a number of judgements that are necessary for safe passage through traffic. For example, their judgement, from sight and sound, of the direction or speed of an oncoming car is not adequately developed. Nor have they developed peripheral vision: the ability to see things out of the corner of their eye.

During this time, before riders are ready for the road, it is a good idea to go riding with them on bike paths and then on quiet roads. Accompanied rides offer the opportunity to:

• develop bicycle handling skills such as braking and cornering (see Chapter 7).

• lay the foundations of good roadcraft. These skills are discussed in detail in Chapter 5 and include picking a route, being seen, maintaining good road position, riding straight, negotiating intersections, communication and knowledge of the road rules. (You can also build up this knowledge informally each time you go out together, even in the car.)

• work out low-stress routes to the milk bar, swimming pool, park or whatever are the regular destinations.

• judge when they are ready to ride unaccompanied.

RIDING ON FOOTPATHS

Many parents allow young riders to use footpaths as a stepping stone to riding on the roads, and many novice riders build up their confidence while riding on footpaths. As a result many people wonder if it is legal or not. The answer is generally 'No'. In Queensland and the ACT the law allows all cyclists to ride on footpaths. In other places it is technically illegal but police will only intervene if the rider is threatening pedestrians – for example in a shopping centre – and police can be sure of catching the offender. (The police are in a difficult situation with child cyclists as a child under ten cannot technically commit an offence.) But this situation will change as other States make footpath cycling legal, hoping to move some cyclists off the road and therefore reduce death and injury. Whether it is legal or not, I am sure cyclists will continue to ride on footpaths. The more important question is whether it is a good idea to ride on footpaths or not.

I think it makes sense if the path offers a shortcut or a refuge from a particularly busy road, but only as long as you don't upset pedestrians. Pedestrians don't like cyclists on their paths, especially if the rider is going fast. There is nothing more threatening to the not-so-sprightly, or to those with their thoughts far away, than an unguided eight-year-old belting around the corner on a bicycle. If you are going to let your children ride on the footpath, impress on them the need to give pedestrians priority wherever possible. The same applies to adults too, of course.

Nor should you be under the illusion that the footpaths are 'safe'. About a third of all cycle crashes occur on footpaths. People backing out of driveways or turning in from the road tend to be on the lookout for other cars, not cyclists on the footpath. A car being reversed out of a driveway is across the footpath before the driver can see along the path. Not many drivers turning into driveways will check the footpath before crossing it. If they do check the path, parked cars could hide a child cyclist coming along the path. Impress on your child and practise with them the anticipation and judgement they need to avoid these situations.

Footpath riders should take great care entering roads or crossing roads. The most common bicycle-motor vehicle crash type for young riders does not occur when the rider is using the road. It is the 'ride out' where the cyclist erupts onto the road, without looking, straight into the path of a car. Parents should ensure the young riders make a strong distinction between the footpath system and the road system. Adult riders should put on a different mental hat for each system and not sweep carelessly from one to the other.

RIDING ON THE ROADS

It is a big moment when the novice rider is ready to ride on the road. I recommend that you take this step as seriously as if learners were going for a licence, and in some formal way test both their handling skills and their roadcraft.

If you treat this step as a serious matter, then there is a good chance that the young rider will take the job of cycling on the road seriously. Your tests will gain status with the kids if you tell them that the tests are based on adult licence tests. You could back up your instruction with some outside help. Your local bike shop might know of a nearby Pedal Club. These groups turn bike-handling skills and road safety into a fun day out. Secondary schools, primary schools and private traffic-safety centres also teach bicycle road-safety.

• NSW residents can get a 'Bert' program and trailer full of bicycles at the local school for a week. The NSW police 'Cares' system teaches road rules through cycling round a transportable miniature road system.

• Victorian schools can get hold of the 'Bike Ed' program for primary students and 'Cycle On' for secondary riders and there are a number of trailers of bicycles for hire.

• The Queensland Department of Transport runs a bike education program in schools.

• In WA the police handle bike safety for primary students, while Bike West brings a three-hour bicycle education course to secondary schools and runs a school holiday program.

• In SA the Education Department teaches bicycle safety in schools.

• Tasmanian schools cover bicycle education as part of the health curriculum using the 'Bike Ed' and 'Out and About' courses.

• The NT offers 'Bike Ed' in all schools, runs bike safety centres in Darwin and Alice Springs and has trailers of bicycles available for rural and remote centres.

Your State bicycle group should be able to put you in touch with these other bicycle educators (see Appendix 5).

Handling skills test

Motorcycle riders in many States now have to pass a handling test before they are allowed on the road. This approach makes a good model for young pushbike riders. Handling is an important skill: most bicycle crashes are not with cars but as a result of going too fast or losing control. The test should be administered with good humour and encouragement. An outing or some treat would be appropriate as a reward for attempting and passing the test.

The rider is tested in a half-metre-wide lane which you could mark out with milk cartons or drink cans. The lane should be at least 50 metres long.

• **Starting.** The rider stands in the lane with one foot on the pedal, as described above, and starts riding without going outside the lane.

• **Normal braking.** First the rider has to ride along the lane away from the tester at a reasonable speed, do a U-turn at the end and head back down the lane. When the rider gets near the tester, the rider has to brake to a stop at a predetermined line.

• **Emergency braking.** The rider rides along the lane and does the U-turn in the opposite direction before heading back towards the tester. The tester then lifts an arm, or yells out 'Stop', and the rider has to stop as quickly as possible. (Chapter 7 discusses braking skills.)

• **Slow riding to test balance.** Motorcycle riders have to take at least 10 seconds to ride down an 18-metre lane, without putting a foot down or crossing the side lines. The cyclist should be able to take 60 seconds to ride 18 metres down the half-metre lane.

- **Look back and steer straight.** The tester stands at the end of the lane and, as the rider rides away, holds up one arm or the other. While steering a straight course down the lane, the rider should be able to turn his head to check which hand the tester is holding up.
- **Signal and steer straight.** The rider should be able to signal a right or left turn while steering a straight course down the lane.
- **Other handling tests.** Get the rider to help you devise tests such as weaving between a line of cartons or doing figure eights between three pairs of cartons, each four or five metres apart. This will give the rider a chance to show what they can do.

Handling skills - such as starting, braking, slow riding, looking back - can be tested in a half-metre-wide lane.

Negotiate a licence to ride on the road
Once the handling test is completed, you are ready to negotiate a 'bike licence' for riding on the road. Like the handling test, this approach is based on the adult licence test. A reward for negotiating the licence could be an outing, or permission to ride to a new destination or even a new bike. Explain to the rider that permission to ride on the road depends on convincing you

that he or she knows the road rules and will stick by the conditions of the licence. Make it clear that if the agreement is broken, you could restrict or withdraw the licence.

The agreement could be based on the following points:

- **Knowing and following the road rules.** The road rules should be learned, discussed and practised. Use the preparatory questions for car drivers or motorcyclists to test the rider's knowledge. For young cyclists two areas need special attention:

  – **Entering a road.** Most collisions between primary-school-aged students and cars are caused by riders going out into the road from a driveway, or over a kerb without looking, or by entering an intersection without looking.

  – **Turns.** Quite a few child-cyclist collisions with cars are when the cyclist swerves or turns right without warning or without checking if the road is clear. Right-hand hook turns (as described in Chapter 5) should be practised, tested and encouraged.

  I recommend refresher tests on the road rules, possibly each term or each year.

- **Parking** forms part of the road rules for cars, and many people would thank you if your child did not leave a bike sprawled on the footpath just outside the door of the shop.
- **Equipment.** Your licence could include an agreement that helmets will always be worn and bike is always in a roadworthy condition. You could agree that you will be told when something needs to be fixed.
- **Special conditions.** Your agreement could also include some special conditions such as:

  – No tricks on the road.

– Never ride on so-and-so road (a road you have both agreed is off limits).
– No riding after dark.
– Always lock the bike.

AN INVESTMENT IN THE FUTURE
You might think that all this work on handling skills, roadcraft and attitude is a bit over the top for something as simple as bicycle riding. But a bicycle is no different from any other vehicle on the road. Your hard work on bicycles will go a long way to protecting your children when they start to use motor vehicles and have to pass through that most dangerous period from eighteen to twenty-five years old.

Chapter 7

HOW YOUR BIKE WORKS BEST

In Chapter 6 we looked at learning how to balance, stop and start on a bike: basic skills that will get new riders up to the shops or see them through a short ride on the bike path, and enable them to say 'I can ride a bike'. In this chapter we look at the handling and the efficiency of your riding that makes a *good* bike-rider.

I wish you could be a good bike-rider by just reading this chapter, but the physical skills won't leap out of the book and weld themselves to your muscles. What I can do is suggest things to practise, and point out things you will feel or sense. Then, as you ride, you will be able to teach yourself. Don't be afraid to ask experienced riders for advice or to demonstrate something of which you are unsure.

Once you have got on top of these two groups of skills, they will become second nature and you will almost be unaware that you are using them when you ride. They will, however, be keeping you upright and enabling you to ride further or faster for the same effort.

HANDLING

Bike handling is the key to bike safety: around 80 per cent of all bicycle injuries are caused by handling errors. So if you are a good rider and can handle your bike skilfully, you are less likely to get into strife. The three main skills of good bike handling are: balance at low speeds, cornering and skid control, and effective braking.

BALANCE AT LOW SPEEDS

Bicycles are basically unstable. To be more stable a bike would have to be heavier, wider and go round corners more slowly. Novice riders find this instability easy to cope with when the bike is going fast but have trouble managing instability when they are slowing down, braking, coming to a stop or even starting off. A good rider will learn how to keep the bike upright at low speeds. The test in bicycle road-safety courses sets the target of an 18-metre ride in 60 seconds.

It is possible to develop this skill until you can balance at a complete stop. Sometimes you will see riders balance at traffic lights so as not to have to take their feet out of the pedals. Riders achieve this low-speed balance by shifting their weight from side to side. You can get some idea of the sensation if you stand on tip-toe on one foot and feel your body move, half intentionally, half unconsciously, so that you remain upright. You can see the same principle in action when a clown is riding a one-wheeled bicycle. The performer rocks the bike back-and-forth and side-to-side over the point-of-balance. You might see the clown balancing something on his nose and using the same small movements to keep it there.

As you ride around, practise riding more and more slowly to get used to this feeling of shifting your weight. You will find it easier to maintain your balance if you stand on the pedals. Eventually you will be able to stay upright while you are nearly stationary and your weight-shifting corrections will get smaller and smaller until it appears that you are almost still.

CORNERING

Beginners find corners difficult. It took me many tries to get round my first corner when I was learning to ride but, by steering and wobbling and hoping, I eventually made it. Novice riders who are quite happy riding in a straight line can still find corners difficult and frightening because they are not sure whether they are moments away from a crash. A good rider will know how to make the bike turn, how to avoid problems when cornering and how to correct a skid.

Shifting your weight
Novice riders are often under the misapprehension that to send a bike through a corner, you turn the handlebars, like turning the steering wheel of a car. But cornering on a pushbike is more a matter of shifting your weight: a feeling familiar to skiers, skateboarders, ice skaters, surfers and so on. The timing and amount of weight shift when cornering will depend on your speed and the shape of the corner: the faster you are going and the sharper the corner, the more you will lean. Once you are halfway through the corner, you will need to be ready to shift your weight again to bring the bike out of the lean and back to the vertical.

Actually you do turn the handlebars as well, but in the argument over which comes first, the chicken or the egg, I am going to argue that the weight shift comes first, allowing the bars to move and the bike to go round the corner. You can test this by walking alongside your bike holding the saddle. If, as you are walking along, you tilt the saddle towards you, the bike will turn towards you. You can resume a straight course by tilting the saddle back to the vertical. Because it is weight shift that starts a corner, it is possible to ride 'no hands' around a corner. In fact if it weren't so likely to cause a prang, I would recommend practising riding no-hands to improve your ability to feel how the bike handles. (What makes riding no-hands so dangerous is that the front wheel might hit a bump and throw you off the bike.) The moral is that the handlebars do not steer the bike except at very low speeds, and your hands are on the bars for bumps and balance rather than steering.

To improve your bike handling I recommend that, as you ride around, you practise consciously shifting your weight each time you corner.

The correct amount of leaning, steering or counter steering will take you smoothly through a corner.

Cornering by counter steering

Good riders do use the handlebars to help them with corners but it is done in a strange way, known as 'counter steering'. By pulling on the bars in the opposite direction, as you are leaning into a corner, you will actually increase your lean and send the bike closer to the inside of the corner. For example, if you lean into a left-hand bend and, while you are leaning, *gently* pull the bars to the right, the bike will dip even further to the *left* and take the corner more sharply. This is hard to believe but it works. Motorcycle racers use this technique on every corner.

Counter steering is also useful for a very sharp turn or an emergency dodge. If you are travelling in a straight line and want suddenly to dodge left: lean to the left and pull the bars to the right. The bike will make a sharp turn to the left. You will need to practise this a lot on imaginary obstacles to prepare your reflexes for a real situation.

Learner motorcyclists have to show they can counter steer to corner and dodge before they get their licence and a good bicycle rider will practise and develop these same counter-steering skills. On a pushbike though, don't pull the bars too hard when you are counter steering.

How much to lean or counter steer

How much you lean or counter steer will depend on the shape of the corner. Corner B in the diagram is sharper than Corner A, which means that, at the same speed, you will have to lean or counter steer more through B. Alternatively, if you don't want to lean any further in Corner B than you did in Corner A then you will have to slow down for B.

Novice riders tend to ride through corners following a line parallel to the outside and inside of the bend, shown by the solid line in Corner C. But there are alternatives to this route. The fastest line through Corner C is shown by the

Your speed and line have to be judged correctly when corning.

broken line. This new line turns the corner into a shallower curve. A speedster can use this line to go faster through the corner; cautious riders can maintain their original speed but use the same line to reduce the amount they need to lean.

In real situations, the fastest line is not always the best line. Out on the road, someone might be coming the other way so it is obviously not a good idea to cut a right-hand bend or swing wide on a left-hand bend. The same cornering forces will be enticing the other road user onto your side of the road. Nor, if you are out on the road, should you be crossing traffic lanes just to get a good line through a corner. Usually the best line is a compromise.

When you are out riding, practise adjusting your speed, your lean and your line through corners.

Cornering problems
Novices often fear leaning their bike through a corner, thinking that it will skid and dump them on the ground. But a bike can lean a long way before it becomes unstuck. It is unlikely that you will ever force the bike to lean so far over, or to go so fast through a corner, that the centrifugal force alone will lift the bike off the ground and dump you on the road. But leaning over does make you more vulnerable to a number of things which you should look out for:

• **The pedal crank.** Make sure the inside pedal crank is up high when you corner. A bike can lean quite some way if the inside pedal is up at 12 o'clock. But if the inside pedal is down at 6 o'clock, you can't lean very far before it hits the road. You can test this by standing next to your bike and tilting the bike towards you with the pedal set at 6 o'clock and then at 12 o'clock. Get into the habit of lifting the inside pedal as you start to lean to go round a bend.

• **Tyres.** Make sure your tyres are pumped up tight so that they are hard to squeeze. Tyres with a very low pressure can distort when you lean into a corner. A high pressure in the tyres will give you the most lean and the fastest cornering. Surprisingly, tread pattern doesn't seem to make much difference to bicycle cornering.

• **The angle of the surface.** Check if the road is angled the correct way. You are less likely to fall off on well-banked corners because the banking absorbs some of the centrifugal force. The fastest cycling corners are banked like the tracks of a velodrome. You might have even seen circus cyclists ride around a vertical wall. Unfortunately, it is not unusual for a suburban street corner and especially a bicycle path to be banked the *wrong* way, tilting to the left when you want to lean to the right, for example. Slow down if the corner is banked the wrong way.

• **Bumps on the surface.** Check if the road is bumpy. If the surface on a corner is bumpy and you are leaning over, a wheel could be thrown in the air and lose grip. Slow down if there are bumps like potholes, rails or tram tracks in the middle of the corner. Watch out for the bump or bullnose on driveway and footpath ramps. Some local governments have been far-sighted enough to drop this unecessary and bicycle-dumping design.

• **Slippery surface.** Check if the road is slippery. Dry weather and a clean surface gives you the most friction. Slow down if the surface is slippery. Gravel spread across asphalt makes a very slippery surface for cornering, so does rain. Watch out especially when it rains after a dry spell: the water mixes with oil on the road to make a very slippery surface. Rain also makes road-paint, metal inspection covers and leaves extremely slippery. If you ride over wet road-paint or a metal inspection cover while cornering, you will be on your bum in an instant. Motorcycle riders and skilled cyclists try to avoid these obstacles in the dry so that it is second nature to avoid them in the wet. Three cheers for South Australia which uses non-slip road paint.

SKIDS

Anyone of the above problems could cause your bike tyres to lose traction in a corner and start to skid. But a slide is not necessarily the start of a crash, especially for a good rider who has learned how to correct a skid.

A rear-wheel skid

• **Practise, to prepare your instinctive reactions**. In the same way that advanced motorists practise skidding, so a skilled cyclist will find a suitable place to practise rear-wheel skids. When I was young we spent a lot of time trying to achieve impressive rear-wheel skids. We used to ride fast, lean into a turn on gravel and then jam on the back brakes. And this system still works today. When you know what it feels like as the back wheel breaks away, and what it feels like to bring the bike back under control, you will be better able to do it in an emergency.

• **Be ready for a skid**. If you decide to ride fast through a corner that could produce a skid, or are riding in slippery conditions, prepare yourself mentally. If

the skid begins, you will be more ready to take action.

• **Stop braking**. The chances are that you started the skid by putting on the brakes.

• **Stop cornering** and steer 'into the skid' by turning the handlebars in the direction the back wheel was heading.

Then, all being well, you will swing back upright and the skid will stop.

Rear wheel slides to right

Steer 'into the skid' to correct a rear-wheel slide.

Front-wheel skids

These are frightening and usually so sudden that there is not a lot you can do. Fortunately front-wheel skids are also rarer than rear-wheel skids.

When you are in the skid, the solution is similar: stop braking, steer into the skid and hope. If you want to practise controlling a front-wheel skid, and it is a dangerous thing to practise, you could try riding over a bump like a garden hose at a narrow angle.

The best policy is to avoid front-wheel skids. One important technique is to ride over bumps at right angles. Cross all path edges, footpath ramps, driveway gutters and rail tracks at right angles.

Skid avoidance

We know that rally drivers, racing motorcyclists and film stars all skid every time they drive round a corner. But pushbikes, unlike motor vehicles, gain no advantage from skidding as they don't have the power coming out of a corner to make a slide worthwhile. All a skid does on a bicycle is 'wash off' speed. So probably the best strategy is to avoid them altogether. There are three basic anti-skid principles:

• Read the road. Analyse the situation by looking at the angle or bank of the road, and for bumps and slippery surfaces. Then, if necessary,

• brake before you lean into the corner so that you

• enter the corner at a non-skid speed.

If you do have to brake while leaning through a corner, get out of the lean, get the bike upright, do your braking and then get back into leaning. That needs to be done quickly and takes a lot of skill and practice.

EFFECTIVE BRAKING

Bicycles brake badly. A hundred years of effort in bicycle design has been directed to making them go faster and not very much to making them stop. As a result bicycles today probably have worse brakes than any other vehicle on the road. (Chapter 8 looks at types of brakes and wheel rims.)

A good cyclist will ride with better-than-average anticipation so as to brake in time. This takes us back to the theme of roadcraft which we looked at in Chapter 5. A bicycle's poor braking performance also means a good cyclist

will be careful about speed. If you ever hear yourself saying 'I couldn't brake in time' what you meant is 'I was going too fast in that situation'. A good cyclist also knows how to brake quickly and is aware of factors that make braking take longer.

How to brake quickly

There are two rules to follow to get the best braking out of your bike:

• **Emphasise the front brake.** You probably know that if you brake sharply with the front wheel you can fly over the handlebars and off the bike. To avoid this short, sharp flight, many people brake only with the back brake. But it takes at least twice as long to stop a bicycle on the back brake alone than the front alone. This is because as the weight of the bike and rider is thrown forward by braking, the rear wheel lifts off the ground, which makes it harder for it to contribute to the braking effort.

The same shift of weight that makes the back wheel a bad choice for braking makes the front wheel a good choice: the bike's forward momentum squashes the front tyre harder onto the road. Unless you emphasise the front brake, it will take you much longer to come to a stop. In good conditions, around three-quarters of the braking job is done by the front brake. If the surface is slippery you might need to go easy on the front brake so you don't induce a front-wheel skid.

• **Don't lock the wheels.** The second rule of bicycle braking is don't grab the brakes and lock the wheels. If you lock a wheel it stops rotating.

– Lock the front wheel and the bike turns into a pendulum that will pivot over the front axle and dump you on the ground.

– Lock the back wheel and you will produce a rear-wheel skid where the bike keeps moving, dragging the stationary tyre along the ground. Some people think that this sort of pencil-eraser method of stopping is the most effective. But that is not so. Although a skidding wheel does begin to slow the bike down, you can slow down more quickly by allowing the wheels to rotate.

• **The best technique for braking** combines the fundamental rules described above. A good rider will squeeze the brakes harder and harder, especially the front brake, always easing the pressure just before the wheels lock up. If you do lock up the wheels, let go the brakes and start squeezing again. What you are looking for as you squeeze is that magical spot where the brakes are on as hard as can be, but not quite enough to lock up the wheels. This gives you the fastest stop. The anti-lock brakes that are appearing on some cars and motorcycles have a computer and other bits of gear that find the magical spot for the motorist. It is worth doing a bit of practice to turn yourself into an anti-lock braking system.

Six things that make braking take longer

• **Reaction time and braking distance.** Car drivers, when they go for their licence, are taught that there are two components to braking: reaction time and braking distance.

– Reaction times vary according to the person and the circumstance. The fastest human driving reactions in a race, for example, can be as quick as 0.2 seconds. But lack of fitness, cold, tiredness and sickness can extend your

reaction time to longer than 1.0 seconds. The usual rule of thumb is that the time between seeing the danger and starting to apply the brakes is about 0.8 seconds. Perhaps it is more accurate to call this the *reaction delay*.

– Braking distance increases dramatically with speed. If you double your speed, braking distance could increase three to four times. Let's look at two examples. If you are travelling at 15 kph, or 4 metres a second, on your bike, you will travel 3.2 metres before you touch the brakes. Depending on your braking technique and how good a braking system you have, your braking distance could be another 12 metres, perhaps 15 metres altogether in this case. If you are going faster – say 30 kph – the reaction delay means you will travel around 6 metres before starting to apply the brakes (6 metres is across an average room) and then with your extra braking distance it could take you over 40 metres to stop.

• **Surface.** Your braking distance will also depend on the road surface. Dry concrete is best for stopping quickly. Loose or slippery surfaces, such as gravel or wet asphalt, will mean you take longer to come to a stop. Wet road-paint or wet metal are as slippery as ice and not only will prevent you stopping but could also throw you into a skid. Braking is another reason always to ride on the best surface.

• **The weight** you are carrying will increase your braking distance. Allow for this when you are carrying extra weight, such as camping gear, school books or a child.

• **Heat** can also affect the performance of your braking system: hot rims and hot brakes all take longer to work.

'Brake fade' from an overheated braking system doesn't happen riding around town but it can happen on a long, steep descent. (It is to reduce brake fade that cars and motorbikes have gone over to disc brakes. Discs don't grab any better but they stay cooler longer.)

• **Wet weather** is a braking hazard. Car drivers are taught that cars take longer to stop in wet weather. So do bikes. In technical terms the coefficient of friction – that is, how sticky the road is – goes down by half in wet weather. In other words the road is twice as slippery for everyone. Bikes are further disadvantaged because their brakes are not protected from water and so will not work as well. You can assume that your braking distance will double in wet conditions. You can improve wet-weather braking by lightly squeezing the brakes every so often to dry the rims.

Wet-weather braking is really bad with steel rims. These rims go round up to thirty times before they dry off and the brake pads begin to grip. If you have steel rims, don't go riding in the rain. If you ride in the rain, it is well worth using a bike with alloy rims as they dry off twice as quickly.

• **Cornering.** Your bicycle will only brake well if it is upright and travelling in a straight line. If you are leaning into a corner and you brake heavily, you are more likely to skid and fall off than to slow down. Brake before you lean.

EFFICIENCY

Since you have to put in physical effort to make the bike go, it is worth knowing the way the bike works most efficiently. When you learn to ride efficiently, you ride with less effort over the same distance, a longer distance for the same effort, or faster over the same distance. The two main factors in cycling efficiency are: riding position and pedalling style.

AN EFFICIENT RIDING POSITION
Many cyclists, especially novices, like to sit up when they are riding a bike, as if they were sitting on a bar-stool having a drink. This riding position feels familiar, it gives recreational riders a better look at the view and in traffic helps you keep an eye on what is going on. (See p. 96 for more on 'Riding Position'.) But if you are going to spend more than half an hour on your bike, it is worth considering a riding position where you lean forward. This will gives you two efficiency advantages:

Leaning forward is efficient as it reduces 'wind resistance' and builds the pedalling muscles.

- **Increased muscle power.** Bending over while you pedal uses more and stronger muscles to drive the pedals. Bending over also allows your arms to contribute to the effort. You might have seen pictures of runners in the old days starting their sprint races standing up. These days Olympic sprinters start from a crouch with a curved back and with their feet against starting blocks. Bending over as you pedal gives you a similar advantage.

- **Reduced air pressure.** The other reason that cyclists, especially racers, ride leaning forward is to reduce the air pressure that they have to pedal through. You won't notice it, but when you are riding at about 15 kph the lower air pressure behind you starts to pull you backwards. It takes a lot of work to resist this pull of air pressure. At 30 kph only twenty per cent of your effort is spent propelling the bike, the rest is spent pushing nearly 500 kilos of 'wind resistance' out of your way each minute. That is like struggling past five big footballers. Each increase in speed takes a greater increase in power from the cyclist. A cyclist pedalling along at 30 kph who suddenly doubles the power going into the bike will only go 10 kph faster.

The problem of air pressure – or wind resistance, as it is popularly known – gets worse when the wind gets up. A head-wind, for example, will slow you down by increasing the air pressure at the front of the bike. If you start out at 30 kph and a 15-kph head-wind springs up, it will knock you back to about 20 kph. If you want to keep going at 30 kph, you will have to double your power output. Cross-winds have a similar effect. Optimists will be pleased to know that a 15-kph tail-wind will bump you up from 20 kph to 35 kph for free.

Perhaps the most dramatic illustration of the effect of air pressure is to compare the various world records for cycling. The world-record speed for someone on a racing bike is around 60 kph. Lying down in a streamlined shell a cyclist can get up to 100 kph. On the other hand, behind a moving vehicle, a cyclist can ride at over 240 kph. The difference between these speeds reflects the different air pressure that each rider has to pedal through.

There are a number of things you can do to minimise the air-pressure problem.

– **Train** until you become fitter and stronger.

– **Ride behind another cyclist.** In some races riders 'draft' others by riding in the low-pressure zone behind the lead rider. This is rather like following a rude and beefy friend through a crowd and takes about a third less effort. A group of cyclists drafting each other in turn can ride up to 5 kph faster than a single cyclist. Some bicycle races, such as the time trial or triathlon, don't allow you to use the low-pressure zone. You can still get some benefit from the low pressure as far away as five bike-lengths behind another rider or from passing trucks, but don't get caught doing it. These benefits are available to ordinary cyclists who can help each other by taking turns out in front.

– **Wear smooth, tight-fitting clothing.** Some racers wear shiny, one-piece body suits, but all wear some form of body-hugging gear. Nor do racers stop at clothes: they wear short hair and shave their arms and legs. Ordinary cyclists aren't so desperate for increased efficiency and so don't need special clothes. But if you ride in a billowing shirt, dress or cape you might have to work around 10 per cent harder.

– **Ride an aerodynamic bike.** The bike itself is responsible for a third of the air-pressure problem, a significant amount in races, which are measured in fractions of a second. For this reason, competition bikes are designed to reduce air pressure, usually by hiding the cables, reducing the number of spokes, streamlining the tubes and redesigning all the bits that bolt on. All this work and expense can make a 5 per cent difference or about half-a-dozen seconds' advantage in an hour's riding. So you can see that an aerodynamic bike, rather like a racing spoiler on the family car, will not make a great difference to the ordinary rider.

Which brings us back to riding position. Your body is responsible for two-thirds of the air pressure and one of the best ways to reduce your contribution is to bend over the bars. The low riding position used by competition cyclists, such as in triathlons, can cut air pressure by a quarter.

AN EFFICIENT PEDALLING STYLE
The most efficient way to pedal a bike is a combination of a correct and secure foot position and a good pedalling action while you spin the pedals at a good speed.

Feet
Efficient pedalling is based on correct position, correct direction and good grip.
 • **Position.** The ball of your foot should be above the pedal axle. Some people pedal with their instep centred

on the pedal as if climbing a ladder, but the instep is not suited to pedalling. The saddle height adjustment discussed in Chapter 9 is based on pedalling with the ball of the foot.
 • **Direction.** Most people should pedal with their feet pointing straight forward. If your toes naturally point slightly inwards or outwards, then your foot direction should reflect that.
 • **Grip.** The more secure your feet are on the pedals, the more efficiently you will pedal. A hard-soled shoe will ensure that your pedalling effort is not dissipated by a spongy sole. Racers use stiff-soled cycling shoes which are fixed to the pedals to provide optimum position, direction and grip. Pedal options are described in Chapter 8, cycling shoes in Chapter 11.

Turning the pedals
Imagine we are looking side-on at a pedal going round, and that the crank is the hour hand on a clock. All the power in a pedal stroke comes from 12 o'clock to 7 o'clock and most of that power from 2 o'clock to 5 o'clock. For that reason novices often think of pedalling as an up-and-down action like operating a foot pump or pushing your foot down to open the lid of a pedal bin. But it is more useful to think of pedalling as a three-part circular motion: push, scrape and lift. As you pedal, these three parts are combined into one smooth motion.
 • **Push.** You begin the power stroke as your foot comes up to 12 o'clock by pushing the pedal away, as if you were trying to push it to the front of the bike. This action gets the pedal round to 3 o'clock.
 • **Scrape.** Then you start to scrape your foot backwards like a bull pawing

the ground as the crank goes from 3 to 7 o'clock. That is the end of the power stroke.

• **Lift.** Ideally you will lift your foot during the upstroke from 7 to 12 o'clock. This lifting action doesn't add more power but it makes sure that the foot going up is not making extra work for the foot on the other side. No riders can get power from the upstroke but they can stop themselves losing some on the other side.

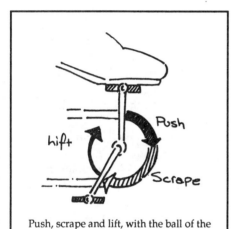

Push, scrape and lift, with the ball of the foot above the pedal axle.

PEDALLING SPEED

Some bike riders seem to enjoy forcing the pedals around. You can see these riders – men especially – pedalling as if they were lifting heavy weights at the gym. But the longer you ride, the more obvious become the disadvantages of slow, strong pedalling.

First of all, pushing hard on the pedals can stress your joints. Many tough young men and women have damaged their knees by pedalling slowly and putting heaps of effort into each pedal stroke. Slow pedalling is also poor long-term energy use. If you heave on the pedals like a rower, you are asking the muscles to contract for a

long time on each pedal stroke. That uses a lot of energy which the muscle has difficulty replacing quickly. A short muscle contraction uses less energy and that makes it easier for the body to replenish the muscle. So if you want to ride for a long period, you should only ask the muscles for a little bit of oomph on each pedal stroke. Using the right gear makes pedalling up or down hill easier on the muscles.

Efficient pedalling is a rhythmic activity more like running or bouncing a ball and is best done fast and at a steady speed. If you watch experienced cyclists, you will notice that whether zooming along the flat or crawling uphill, they will – as much as possible – maintain a steady pedalling speed and allow their road speed to go up and down. Professional racers in long races turn the pedals as fast as 110 revs each minute, nearly two revolutions each second. That is the upper limit for well-trained cyclists. Pedalling much faster than this becomes counter-productive as more and more energy is spent rotating the legs and less on turning the pedals.

The optimum pedal speed for a long time in the saddle seems to be between 80 and 100 revs a minute. Somewhere in that range will be your best pedalling speed. As you ride, check the sweep hand or second-counter on your watch and count the number of times one foot makes a pedal stroke in 15 seconds. That will give you an idea of your pedalling speed. (Competition riders use a bike computer that continually monitors pedal speed.) If you find that you pedal slowly at the moment, don't try to go to 110 revs all in one go. Start on the slow side at 60 or 70 and work upwards.

BEST GEAR USE FOR EFFICIENT PEDALLING

For years and years all bikes had one gear and even today, when many bikes have a cutlery drawer full of gears, there are junior bikes, adult bikes and racing bikes that still have only one gear. This is because, for many riders, one gear is all they need. If your bike has one gear and you are never in the saddle for more than half an hour at a time and you are happy with your cycling, it is not worth getting more gears or learning about gears.

Another large group of riders would find that an old style three-speed gear would be enough for their riding needs, (see Chapter 8 for a comparison of gear systems). I think it is a pity that today, both these groups of riders are probably using multi-geared ten, fifteen, twenty -one or even twenty-four speed bikes. The glut of gears is unfortunate because there is nothing that is more daunting to a novice, or non-mechanically-minded rider, than the subject of gears and nothing that is as likely to cause confusion or unhappiness when out riding than a tangle of uncooperative gears. So I am going to start with some advice on how to deal with a bike full of gears when you only really use one or two. Then we will go on to discover how gears can make longer stints in the saddle more efficient and enjoyable.

A BEGINNERS' GUIDE TO GEARS

The following suggestions will take you step by step towards using all the gears on your bike. If you are happy with one gear, I recommend avoiding the subject altogether. If you want to know more, investigate the four levels of know-how given below. Many riders can stay happily on Level 1; others will find that going to Level 4 will significantly help their riding.

Don't expect to grasp everything about gears all at once. Ride your bike around for a period of time at each Level until you become confident and are keen to know more. For those who find a descriptive explanation of gears hard to grasp, I suggest you ask a friend who knows about bikes to demonstrate how gears work in practice, perhaps on a ride together.

Avoiding gears altogether

The way to avoid knowing about gears is to get a bike shop or a knowledgeable friend to set your bike in the middle gear. Leave the gear lever alone and go off and enjoy the thrill of cycling.

Level 1: Finding middle gear on a multi-gear bike

The following steps will enable you to set a bike in its middle gear.

• **Examine your gears** to find out what sort of gear system you have. If there is one sprocket at the front and one at the back, and the rear hub is the size of a soft-drink can, then you have hub gears – probably three altogether – which you change through a lever on the handlebars.

You can spot a derailleur system by the multiple sprockets on the rear wheel or by an arm which holds the chain and hangs down from the rear axle. (Chapter 8 has more on the difference between the two systems.)

• **Investigate the levers.** On a derailleur bike the levers could be on the down tube, stem, or handlebars. Support the bike (see Ch. 14, p. 161) so that you can turn the pedals and simultaneously move the gear levers back and forth.

Three-speed gear levers generally are in low (the uphill) gear when the lever is near the bars.

The lowest gear on a derailleur bike is when the chain is on the smallest sprocket at the front and the biggest sprocket at the back. The chain is moved – and the gears changed – by two levers: one moves the chain between the front sprockets, the other moves it between those at the rear. Turn the pedals, move one lever at a time and watch what happens. The lever pulls a cable which moves an arm which pulls or pushes the chain off one sprocket until it is hooked by another sprocket. This method of 'de-rail-ing' the chain from sprocket to sprocket gives the system its name.

I don't know what your levers will do – there is little consistency among bikes – but you might find that the right-hand lever moves the chain at the rear and that moving the lever forward moves the chain to the bigger sprocket and a lower (or uphill) gear. Watch what it does and make a mental or written note: right, forward, lower. Do the same for the other lever.

• **Set the gears in the middle.** Whatever system you have, move the levers until you are in the middle gear. This is easy on a three speed. On a derailleur bike move the chain to the small cog at the front. If you have three front sprockets, move it to the middle sprocket. Move the chain to the middle sprocket at the back. If you have six rear sprockets, move the chain to sprocket three or four. If you only ride short distances, leave the bike in this gear and go on to the next chapter.

Level 2: Changing gear
With hub gears it is possible to change gears while pedalling or when you are stopped, simply by moving the lever. If you are pedalling when changing gears, ease up the pressure on the pedals while the sprockets are sorting themselves out. Back-pedalling after moving the lever can help the sprockets settle into their new position.

The challenge with derailleur gears is getting all the derailing and re-railing right. An unsuccessful gear change can produce lots of crunching and banging; it can take so long that you slow right down; or it can fail completely, leaving you in the wrong gear. If you are new to derailleurs, I recommend that you ignore the front sprockets and use only the ones at the back.

To make a successful derailleur gear change, there are four things you need to do:

1. Remember which lever to move and which way to move it. Use the mental note you made in Level 1.

2. Keep pedalling: the sprockets and chain need to be moving for the chain to find a new home.

3. Pedal gently while changing: taking the pressure off the pedals takes the tension off the chain and allows the derailleur to bend the chain towards the new sprocket. Pedalling gently also allows the chain to get seated properly on the teeth of the sprocket. If you put the pressure back on the pedals before the chain is properly seated, there will be a mighty crunch as everything slams into place.

4. Change early for uphills: if you need to change down to climb a rise, change *before* it becomes difficult to pedal. When you are pedalling uphill you will be putting tension on the chain and it will be too late to make an easy change. It doesn't matter if your

downhill change is late as it is easy to pedal lightly when coasting downhill.

Level 3: Using the front sprockets

When you are confident moving the chain between the back sprockets, you might want to use the ones at the front. A generalisation is that a larger front sprocket will give you more downhill gears on the three smallest rear sprockets, and a smaller front sprocket – on a three-front-sprocket bike – will give you lower gears on the three largest rear sprockets.

The process of changing front sprockets is similar: remember which lever to move, keep pedalling and pedal gently: it is easy to knock teeth off the front sprockets by putting the pressure on before the chain is seated. Don't try to change front and back sprockets at the same time.

Level 4: Understanding what is happening

What you are doing when you change gears is changing the relationship (ratio) between the number of times the pedals go round and the number of times the rear wheel goes round. The fewer times the wheel goes round for each turn of the pedals, the lower the gear. A lower ratio means that less push is required on the pedal to make the wheel go round. A common ratio on bicycles is 1 to 2 where one turn of the pedals produces two rotations of the back wheel. This ratio can be achieved by a 40-tooth front sprocket turning a 20-tooth sprocket at the rear.

Front sprocket: 40

Back sprocket: 20

Ratio of front to back: 1:2

With a 40-tooth front sprocket turning a 13-tooth sprocket at the rear, each turn of the pedals would rotate the rear wheel three times. In practice, if you kept pedalling at the same speed and changed from the 20-tooth sprocket to the 13-tooth sprocket, you would go faster. The more the wheel goes round for each turn of the pedals, the higher the gear.

Front sprocket: 40

Back sprocket: 13

Ratio of front to back: 1:3

Conversely a 40-tooth front sprocket turning a 26-tooth sprocket at the rear would rotate the wheel one-and-a-half times every time you turned the pedals. Assuming you pedalled at the same speed, the bike would go more slowly but would be easier to get up a hill.

Front sprocket: 40

Back sprocket: 26

Ratio of front to back: 1:1.5

As an illustration, let's follow Achilles and Helen as they go for a ride on their bikes. Apart from the gears, their two bikes are exactly the same. (Remarkably, both Achilles and Helen also weigh the same, have the same level of fitness, strength and cycling experience.) As they ride along they are pedalling at the same rate – 70 pedals a minute – using a 40-20 gear. But then the road starts to go up a hill, which makes it difficult for them to keep pedalling at the same speed.

Helen has a bike with a low gear (40-26) so she changes down and keeps pedalling at the same rate. Achilles is pedalling slower and slower until he can't pedal any more. For a short time he stands up on the pedals and turns them with his weight. Finally he has to get off his bike and push it to the top of the hill.

Helen waits for Achilles at the top of the hill and again they set off together. Soon the road leads downhill and both riders find that their pedalling isn't doing anything. Achilles, who has a high gear (40-13), changes up, keeps pedalling at the same rate, and starts to go faster. Helen spins the pedals but soon finds that she can't turn them fast enough to make the bike go faster. So she coasts down to the bottom of the hill where Achilles is waiting for her.

You can imagine that if you had been riding with these two on a bike with a single 40-20 gear you would have been walking up the hill with Achilles and coasting down the other side with Helen. On the other hand, if you had three gears – 40-13, 20, 26 – you could have ridden up the hill and gone fast down the other side.

The story of Achilles and Helen gives you a clue to the great advantage of gears. The further or faster you ride, the more you will want to stay in the saddle and use your energy efficiently by pedalling at a steady speed. The more gears you have, and the more appropriate the set of gears is on your bike, the more time you will spend pedalling at your optimum pedal speed, whether riding on the flat, downhill or uphill. Without the right gears you will have to vary your pedalling speed as the road goes up and down and that will use up your energy more quickly. In extreme cases you will have to get off and walk, like Achilles, or coast downhill like Helen.

You can see why people who do a lot of riding have traded their three-speed bikes for ten-speeds and the ten-speeds for twenty-four-speed bikes. But even these people, on a short ride around town, will use only a couple of gears even if their bike has twenty-one available.

Chapter 8 looks at how you can make sure you get a set of gears that suits the riding you do.

Chapter 8

WHAT KIND OF BIKE FOR YOU?

A BEWILDERING VARIETY

There is a bewildering variety of bicycles on sale, as you might discover when you walk into a bike shop. Some examples of these different designs are shown on the opposite page. Some bikes are obviously different; others look similar but can be made of different alloys and metals and be fitted with different grades of components.

Though there are different manufacturers, different model names and different features on all the models, most bikes made today use a frame manufactured by one of the handful of big frame factories in Taiwan or Japan. This frame is then kitted out with components from one of the half dozen component manufacturers like the big Japanese company Shimano. There are exceptions to this rule: you will find a homegrown product in many countries, from the exotic frames made in the

United States, through indigenous European brands like Raleigh, Bianchi and Gazelle, to the historic Chinese Flying Pigeon.

But even though, in Australia, the chances are you will be riding a Taiwanese frame with Shimano components, you still have to make a choice from the wide range of style, quality and price, from just over $100 to well over $3 000. It is not surprising that most bike buyers are a bit confused.

Manufacturers try to simplify the problem of bicycle variety by selling half-a-dozen 'types' of bicycle. You have probably heard of names like 'mountain bikes' and 'BMX bikes' and 'racers' and 'ladies' bikes'. If retailers always sold the same basic set of bikes, then things would be less complex. But, every couple of years, like fashion designers, the bike makers and sellers release a new type of bike. The new

All bicycles are variations on the same basic machine, as bike catalogues show.

type is promoted as 'the best sort of bike' and the customer is given to believe that all previous efforts at bike design fell a long way short. You might have noticed some of these changes yourself. Years ago the standard bike had three gears, big wheels, thick tyres, and straight handlebars. That was replaced by a bike with ten gears, smaller wheels, narrower tyres and bent-over handlebars. That type of bike gave way to one with even more gears, even smaller wheels, fatter tyres and straight bars. Now the fashion seems to be swinging back to larger wheels and narrower tyres again. The different permutations and combinations of features used by different manufacturers can be very confusing.

Some bicycle books try to list the types and explain the differences between them. But I bet that, however long the list, you will quickly find a type of bike that isn't in the book. I am going to suggest three ways to sort out the complexity of bike buying.

• Ignore it. Don't worry about what is the *best* type of bike to get or use: just get one you like the look of. A bike is a bike, and as long as the pedals turn and the wheels go round, it will give you the thrill of cycling.

• Ask questions at a couple of specialist bike shops. Tell the sales staff about your needs and they will be able to tell you about the current models and what their strengths and weaknesses are. Then you can make your decision based on their advice. (There are many other good reasons for going to a specialist and these are listed in Chapter 10.)

• The third way is to understand the principles of how to judge a bicycle for yourself. This is easier than learning the details of all the types on sale, and the advantages are considerable. When you know how to judge a bike, you will be able to weigh up the pros and cons of any bike you see, new or old, fashionable or unfashionable. This will give you a clearer idea of what you want and you will be able to talk the language of the bike shop. (Chapter 6 looks at buying bikes for kids.)

The more bikes you buy, the more useful this knowledge will be. It is not just bike enthusiasts who buy a lot of bikes: a couple with three kids could have five bikes in the shed and the kids will probably need at least another two bikes each before they finish growing up. You can use your bicycle judgement to see if you need to modify your current bike, replace it or enjoy it as it is.

Bicycles differ from each other in one or other of five basic characteristics: frame, wheels, drive train, riding position and braking system. Within each of these the bike designer can trade off things like speed or comfort, weight or strength, quality or price. We shall look at each characteristic in more detail below, but a checklist summarising the five main features is given at the end of this chapter. You might want to refer back to Chapter 2 for the map of the names of parts.

FRAME

The frame of a bicycle should suit the rider's physical proportions and the main use of the bike: easy riding, off-road or competition.

At the beginning of *The Hound of the Baskervilles*, Sherlock Holmes is able to describe the character and behaviour of a doctor by studying his walking stick. In a similar way it is possible to describe the character of a bicycle by looking at three characteristics of the frame: the pro-portions, the shape, what it is made of.

COMPARING DIFFERENT-SIZED FRAMES

Model	A	B	C	D	E
Top tube length (cm)	57.0	56.0	56.8	58.2	57.0
Seat tube length (cm)	56.0	57.2	45.7	45.7	48.3
Wheelbase length (cm)	99.2	102.0	105.0	106.0	105.0
Chainstay length (cm)	41.0	44.0	42.5	42.5	42.5
Crank axle, from ground (cm)	27.0	27.5	30.2	30.2	30.5
Top tube , from ground (cm)	82.0	82.3	76.3	76.3	77.2
Fork rake angle	40°	45°	45°	45°	45°
Head tube angle	73.5°	73°	72°	71°	71°
Seat tube angle	73°	73°	73°	73°	73°

THE PROPORTIONS OF THE FRAME
Frame proportions are usually published in manufacturers' catalogues similarly to this table, which describes five bikes, A-E.

• **Size of rider.** As we shall see in Chapter 9 the frame should be the right size for you in both height and length. The five bikes on the chart come in four different heights (seat-tube length) and roughly three different lengths (top-tube length). Models C and D have the same frame height but different top-tube lengths. If you have proportionally longer arms it would be worth trying Bike D.

A quick way to spot the difference in frame height between two bicycles is to look at the *head tube*. A bike with a long head tube is for a tall person.

• **Off-road use.** The ground clearance of the frame (measured from crank axle to the ground) will also tell you whether the bike is intended to be used off the road or not. A typical bicycle, like A and B on the chart, will have a

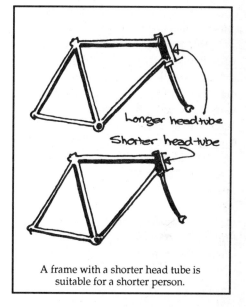

A frame with a shorter head tube is suitable for a shorter person.

ground clearance of around 27 cm. This reflects the conventional length of the pedal cranks and allows the bike to be pedalled while going round some corners. Bikes that are going to be ridden over rocks and logs often have a larger clearance, up to about 32 cm. If you are going to ride off the road you might try E which has a ground clearance of 30.5 cm.

(If the manufacturer raises the ground clearance, then it is hard to compare frame height by measuring the seat tube. In this case top-tube height from the ground would be a more useful measurement. A further complication is that some frames have a top tube that angles down from the head tube to the seat tube. In this case you have to estimate – perhaps by stretching a piece of string between top tube and seat tube – what height a horizontal top tube would be.)

• **Wheelbase.** Bikes with the same frame height and length can be built with short or long wheelbase, such as C and D on the chart on p. 79. Wheelbase affects steering and spring:

– **Steering.** A short wheelbase gives you 'quick' handling and switches easily from one corner to another. Competition bikes usually have a short wheelbase. A long- wheelbase bike runs easily in a straight line but takes longer to react to corners. Bike D would be more relaxing to ride on a long straight road.

– **Spring.** For a hundred years designers have tried to build bicycles with active suspension, like the telescopic forks or sprung rear-axle you find on motorbikes. The problem with active suspension is that it has always been expensive, heavy and inefficient. (Each time you push the pedals on a bike with active suspension you lose some of your push as the bike bounces on the springs.) Now bike designers appear to have solved the problem of weight and if you have a deep bank account, you can buy lightweight bikes with active suspension which are fun to ride. The designers have not yet solved

the problems of cost and loss of pedalling power, but maybe that day is not far away.

The moral is that most us will be riding bikes that get their suspension from the flex in the frame and forks. (The saddle and wheels can also contribute to a softer ride.) A bicycle with a long wheelbase is more comfortable as its slightly longer tubes and chainstays, and its shallower angles, give the frame a bit more spring. A short-wheelbase is not as comfortable to ride because the tubes are shorter, more vertical and less springy. But even without active suspension, the more you move towards comfort the more you sacrifice efficiency. On a long-wheelbase bike some of the push from the pedals is lost as the frame flexes, so bike C will put more pedal power onto the road than D.

If you are considering competition you will probably look for a bike with a shorter wheelbase because power and quick steering will be more important to you than comfort. On the other hand if you are going for a leisurely holiday ride you would look for a long-wheel-base bike with more comfort but a bit

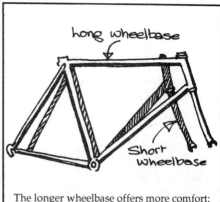

The longer wheelbase offers more comfort; the shorter wheelbase, more power.

less power. The traditional ladies' bike usually has a long wheelbase which is partly why it is so comfortable and easy to ride.

A quick way to spot the difference in wheelbase is to look at the gap between the seat tube and the rear wheel. On a short-wheelbase bike the front of the rear wheel is close to the frame, the back of the front wheel is close to the frame and the head tube and seat tubes are nearer to being vertical. Another method is to check the bend in the forks, straighter forks indicate a shorter wheelbase.

- **Forks.** Another clue to the bike's performance is the bend at the end of the forks. For most of their journey down to the wheel the front forks follow the angle of the head tube. But as they approach the wheel axle, they bend forward. This bend is called fork rake. Generally the rake will reflect the design of the rest of the frame. A big bend at the end of the forks will complement the spring and steering of a long-wheelbase bike. On some frames the forks can be bent up 65 cm out of straight. A small

bend will complement a short wheelbase. Bike A on the p. 79 chart is probably a racing bike as it has a short wheelbase and small fork rake. Some bikes come with forks that are almost straight – BMX bikes, for example.

- **Frame angles.** Another way of assessing the spring and handling of a bike is by looking at the angles of the seat tube and head tube (see Chapter 2). This difference is harder to spot just by looking but the seller should know what the angles are, or at least be able to look them up. When the seat and head tube stand nearer to the vertical, the angle will be greater or steeper and the bike will probably have a shorter wheelbase. The more the designer tilts the top of the seat tube and head tube to the rear, the more the angles are reduced and the more likely the bike is to have a longer wheelbase. As you can see from the chart, the tubes on bike A stand nearest the vertical and, model by model, the angle of the head tube tilts away from the vertical. Long-wheelbase bikes usually have seat-tube angles of 72° - 73°. Short-wheelbase bikes are

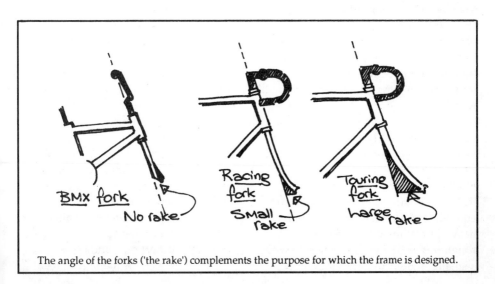

The angle of the forks ('the rake') complements the purpose for which the frame is designed.

usually built with angles of 73° - 75°. As you can see, the categories overlap. Here are two descriptions from a bicycle catalogue describing bikes with different frame angles:

The 72° angles soften the ride without sacrificing efficiency.

The stiffness and low-flex of the frame, the steep angles (73°) *and short wheelbase provide you with the dynamic response and precision handling of the most expensive racing bikes.*

As you might have realised by now, neither wheelbase, nor fork rake, nor tube angle, is, on its own, the deciding factor in a bike's performance. Each feature relates to the other and together they are indicators of the designer's intention for the bike.

THE SHAPE OF THE FRAME: POWER OR CONVENIENCE

The shape of the frame tells you how stiff and strong it is and how much it has been adapted for convenience. Common options are:

- **A diamond frame.** The traditional 'diamond' shape with front and rear triangles is widely used as it provides a stiff frame that resists distortion when you push on the pedals. (If a bike frame bends as you pedal, some of your effort is going into twisting the frame and not into propelling the bike.) The frame will want to twist more if you are pedalling hard, have a child passenger or a pair of loaded panniers. The diamond design also works quite well at resisting shock from the wheels.

- **The flattened diamond.** The traditional diamond frame is not strong enough for off-road bikes that receive heavy punishment from jumps or rough tracks. These bikes are built with a smaller flattened diamond. These

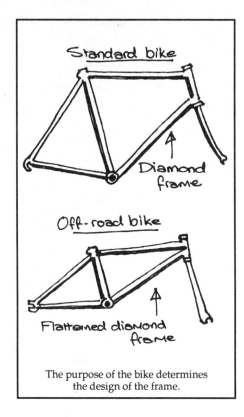

The purpose of the bike determines the design of the frame.

frames are stronger and stiffer than the typical diamond but not so comfortable to ride. The low top tube is also less likely to bite a rider who is bounced forward off the saddle.

- **Small diamond frames.** Short people have trouble finding a diamond frame that is low enough for them to straddle. It is more difficult to design a diamond frame below a certain size because, if the top tube is lowered and the wheels remain the same size, there is nowhere to put the head tube. But there are successful diamond frames made for shorter people – they often carry a smaller wheel at the front – but they are not easily available. (This is probably because there are more short women than short men and bikes tend to be built by men for men.) As a result,

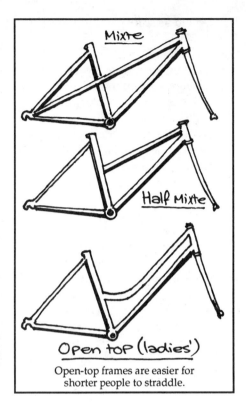

Mixte

Half Mixte

Open top (ladies')

Open-top frames are easier for
shorter people to straddle.

short people are drawn to the open-top frame or one of the compromises such as the *mixte*, the *half-mixte* and the flattened diamond.

• **The open-top frame.** There are many frames designs that leave out the top tube, sacrificing some pedalling efficiency for other benefits. Traditionally women were encouraged to go for such bikes as they are easier to pedal wearing a dress and easier to get on and off in a decorous manner without swinging your leg in the air. But unless you do ride in a dress, there is no necessity for women to ride a bike without a top tube and these days many women prefer a diamond frame. Women who are riding regularly in triathlons, for example, will always choose a bike with a stiff diamond frame.

Leaving out the top tube makes it easier to design a bike that will fold up. Folding bikes come into their own on public transport as, inside their carry bag, they can sneak onto the train or bus despite a bicycle ban and without paying for a ticket. Some people keep a 'folder' in the boot of the car which allows them to park away from the congestion and ride to their destination. There is a contradiction in folding bikes: the better they are at folding, the worse they are to ride and vice versa. I don't know anyone who uses a easy-folding bike regularly and I do know a number who have tried and given them up. If you are thinking of trying a folder, borrow one or buy second-hand to see if it will do what you want.

• **A compromise.** Two common designs make a compromise between power and convenience. The *mixte* has a tube that runs from the head tube to the back axle. The other common design doesn't have a name but could be called a *half-mixte* as the top tube starts at the head tube but stops at the seat tube on its way to the back axle. I recommend either of these if you are after convenience or are too short for a diamond frame.

MATERIAL OF THE FRAME
The quality of the materials and the skill in the construction of the frame are major influences of the cost of the bike and what it will be like to ride. As a general rule, the more you pay for a frame the more likely you are to get a frame that is lighter, stiffer, stronger, more resilient and more responsive. How much it is worth spending on the frame to increase quality is a matter for your judgement and bank account.

- **A basic frame.** The frame of a basic $200 bike is usually made out of pipes formed by cutting a flat sheet of mild steel, rolling it and then joining the seam. These pipes are welded by machine, and the fork crown is stamped out of a piece of metal. The basic bike frame is not light or stiff or resilient but it is cheap.
- **A better frame.** A better bike frame will have two improvements: it will be made of a nickel-steel alloy that has been drawn into a seamless tube.
- **A 'good' frame.** A good frame will be made from tubes of chromoly: a light and strong steel alloy made with chromium and molybdenum, or sometimes manganese and molybdenum. Sometimes the chromoly tubes are made lighter still, by a process called *butting*. Butted tube walls are made thick at each end, where they are under stress, but are thinner in the middle between the joins.

These steel alloy frames are more expensive but are lighter, which is worth a lot in competition. More importantly they are more responsive and therefore more of a pleasure to ride. 'Responsiveness' is a vague word used to describe the difference that you feel when you ride a bike with a quality frame. You might have experienced a similar difference between two pairs of runners or two stereo systems. If you get the chance to compare a basic and a good bike, you will be astonished at how different the 'good' frame feels. But the jump in quality could add up to $500 to the price of the complete bike.

- **An exotic frame.** Light and responsive bikes can also be made out of exotic materials such as aluminium. You can usually tell an aluminium frame by the large-diameter tubes. As frame-builders search for the perfect frame, they have produced frames made of various plastics, glass-reinforced nylon, Kevlar, carbon fibre, and titanium. Each of these exotic materials has its own advantages and disadvantages but the high price of these bikes makes it all rather academic. High-quality steel remains the dominant frame material as it is still the best value for money and the easiest to repair.

There are differences between the 'feel' of steel and the various exotic frame materials, and strong subjective opinions about which is best. As the frames get more expensive the differences in feel become more subtle. Anyone can feel the difference between a basic frame and a good frame but it takes experience to be able to feel the difference between a $1000 frame and a $2000 frame and the extra dollars will not necessarily buy you any advantage: it is possible that the price difference could be due entirely to the price of the exotic materials or the complexity of their manufacture and assembly.

WHEELS

The most significant factors in the choice of wheels are: weight, size, rims and tyres, and are usually determined by the kind of regular use the rider will make of the bike. Observing the wheels of a bike is like observing the feet of an animal: are you looking at a camel that can trudge through sand, a horse for the high road or a greyhound for quick getaways?

WEIGHT AND STRENGTH

The big trade-off in wheel design is between weight and strength. A wheel needs to be strong and the usual way to add strength is to add weight. But a wheel also needs to be light so that the bike is easy to move forward. A heavy wheel takes more effort to swing around than a light wheel and therefore has slower acceleration.

Look for the compromise that suits you best. Off-road cycling needs a heavier wheel that emphasises strength. City cycling requires reliability and therefore probably also emphasises strength. A road racer will want both durability and lightness. A track racer sprinting on a polished wooden velodrome will have the lightest wheels. The weight and strength of a wheel are largely decided by three things: spokes, hub and rim.

• **Spokes.** A typical bike wheel is held together by spokes. Exceptions include children's tricycles which have cheap metal wheels, small-wheeled children's bikes with one-piece plastic rim and spokes, and expensive racing bikes which use lightweight solid wheels to reduce air pressure. Metal spokes remain the best compromise between strength, weight and cost. The spokes can vary in number, length and gauge:

– **Number.** Most wheels have 36 spokes of medium-carbon steel coated with zinc. Competition wheels are sometimes made with as few as 24 light-gauge spokes whereas a tandem rear wheel might have 44 heavy-duty spokes. Chrome-plated or shiny nickel-chrome alloy spokes look better than zinc spokes but are more brittle.

– **Length.** Spokes vary in length to fit different hub and rim diameters.

– **Thickness or 'gauge'.** Most wheels are built with 2-mm-gauge spokes but the gauge can vary from 1.4 mm to 2.6 mm. These gauge differences are easily seen if you compare a couple of bikes at the bike shop.

Bikes can also differ in their spoke pattern and assembly:

– **Pattern.** You can see radial spoking on some small-wheeled bicycles and track bikes. On these wheels the spokes radiate from the hub to the rim like hands on a watch. They are uncomfortable to ride as there is no spring in the wheel. (Cobb and Co used radial spokes on their coaches but they put springs between the wheels and the passengers.)

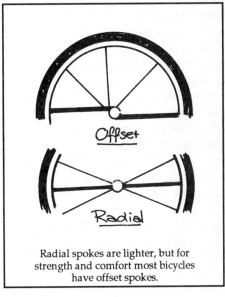

Radial spokes are lighter, but for strength and comfort most bicycles have offset spokes.

In most bicycle wheels the spokes take off from the hub at an angle, forming not a straight line across the clock face, but a long-armed sideways Z from one side of the rim to the other. These offset spokes are better than radial spokes at turning pedalling into motion, as the spoke forming the top of the Z can tow the wheel around clockwise. An offset pattern of spokes is also more comfortable. When the wheel goes over a bump the arms of the Z bend, dissipating the shock. The amount of spoke offset or angle is reflected in the number of other spokes each spoke crosses on its way to the rim. Most bicycle wheels are 'three cross': that is, the spoke crosses three others on its journey from the hub to the rim. Three-cross wheels are stiffer than four-cross.

– **Assembly.** Whatever type of spoke or spoking pattern that is chosen, the result depends on the skill of assembly, and the more you try to reduce the weight of the wheel, the more important it is to build it properly. On an ideal wheel all the spokes are at the same tension and as tight as they can be without distorting the rim. This gives the wheel its best chance of surviving the twisting force that the drive train puts into the wheel and the distortion from bumps in the road. Uneven spoke tension will put more stress on the tighter spokes and they will be more likely to break. A top-quality racing wheel will be completed by someone with years of experience who will check each spoke with a tension gauge. Once upon a time a bike shop I knew used a tension gauge on every spoke of every wheel they sold. Very few of their customers came back for wheel repairs. Today most wheels are assembled by machines that zip up half-a-dozen spokes at a time and produce a wheel that will cope with average use.

This variation in the skill of assembly makes it possible for a light wheel that is well built to be stronger and less likely to break than a heavy wheel that has been zipped together by a machine. You can make a quick check of spoke tension by plucking the spokes like the strings of a harp. If they are at equal tension, they should all play the same note.

• **Hubs.** The heaviest hubs are made of steel and use a nut on each side of the axle to secure the hub to the frame. An alloy hub is lighter and can usually be identified by the quick-release lever instead of nuts. The size of the hub flange can influence the performance of a wheel. If the hub has a high flange, the wheel uses shorter spokes and is therefore stiffer. Low-flange hubs need longer spokes and therefore give a softer ride.

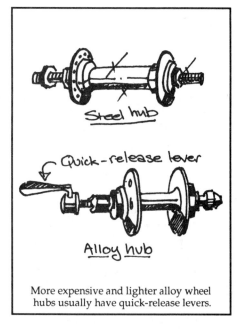

More expensive and lighter alloy wheel hubs usually have quick-release levers.

• **Rims.** Rims come in different widths and, in general, a narrow rim is lighter. The cheapest and heaviest rims are made of shiny chrome-plated steel. Lighter rims are made of a duller non-reflective alloy which is more expensive but just as strong. These alloy rims also have the great advantage of better braking characteristics (see Chapter 7). You will easily be able to spot the difference between these two types.

SIZE

The second option in wheels is between big wheels and small wheels. In general, larger wheels have more spring in them, are easier to pedal at low speeds and go over bumps more easily. A smaller wheel with shorter spokes will be harder and stronger than a larger wheel. Most adult bikes come with wheels that are:

• **65 cm** (26"). Bikes that are ridden off-road tend to use these wheels for extra strength and because they allow a more compact frame.

• **67.5 cm** (27"). This old British standard is giving way to its near metric equivalent below.

• **70 cm or 700c**. Most adult bikes are standardising on this size used by competition riders.

There are no new bikes in Australian bike shops these days with the easy-rolling 28" wheels that used to be on 'ladies' bikes'.

As we have seen in Chapter 6, kids' bikes start with 30-cm wheels and go up to 40 cm, and to 50 cm, the standard BMX wheel size.

Some adult bikes come with small wheels ranging from 50 cm to 55 cm to 60 cm. Folding bikes have small wheels. Shopping bikes tend to have small wheels too, as a bike is easier to handle if the weight of groceries is lower to the ground.

TYRE WIDTH AND PRESSURE

Tyres come in a range of widths and pressures, which are usually written on the side of the tyre. These two features tell you how much work it is going be to pedal the bike. The higher the pressure and the narrower the tyre, the less power it will take to move the machine. As you lower the pressure,

you lose efficiency but you gain comfort and you can gain traction. Here are some of the common choices:

• Track-bike tyres are run at up to 200 pounds per square inch (psi) (1400 kPa). Not surprisingly, running a tyre at high pressure increases the risk of a burst tyre.

• Racing bikes have tyres about 1 cm wide which hold over 100 psi (700 kPa).

• A typical bike will have tyres that are 2.5 cm wide and carry around 70 psi (500 kPa), double the average pressure for a car tyre. These tyres will have about three times the rolling resistance of a racing tyre.

• An off-road bike will have tyres up to 5.7 cm wide with pressures of around 45 psi (300 kPa) and sometimes as little as 25 psi (200 kPa) when being ridden through sand or loose dirt. Running a tyre at low pressure increases the risk of the rim mashing the tube onto the ground and causing a puncture.

Unlike cars, bicycle braking and cornering is not significantly influenced by tread, but a tractor-style tread will grip better on a loose surface.

WEIGHT IN TYRES AND TUBES

The tyres and tubes fitted will influence the weight of the wheels. A knobby tyre is wider and carries a lot more rubber and is therefore heavier than a tyre with little tread. A thorn-proof inner tube is much heavier than a typical inner.

Competition cyclists traditionally use a completely different wheel and rim design from a typical tyre on an alloy rim, which makes their wheels about half a kilo lighter. Rather than the car-style, U-shaped rim and tyre, racers use cylindrical or tubular tyres on a rim with a rectangular cross-section made of the lightest alloy. The inner tube sits, like a sausage roll, inside the roll of the tyre and is pumped up through a Presta valve (see Chapter 14). The tyre casing is made from cotton, silk or synthetic belting, covered with a thin slick of rubber for grip. Tubular riders enjoy easy pedalling on these light, high-pressure tyres but they also have to fix more punctures. To repair a puncture on a tubular you have to unstitch the side of the sausage roll to reach the inner. This is a complicated manoeuvre which explains why tubular riders carry a spare tyre around with them. You can often see spare tubulars rolled up under the saddle of racing bikes.

DRIVE TRAIN

The drive train is all the bits, from the pedals to the gears, that drive the bike forward. When choosing the drive train on a bike you need to assess the pedals, cranks and gears. Your choice will reflect the time you spend in the saddle and the importance you place on cycling efficiency. A round-town bike will have a simple drive train, but a bike intended for longer rides will have special pedals and multiple gears chosen to suit the terrain and the fitness of the rider.

PEDALS

Pedals differ in weight, in how they hold your foot, and in how well they support your foot. As with other bicycle parts, lightweight pedals are made of aluminium alloy; cheaper and heavier ones are made of steel.

Short-distance bikes have one of the following types:

• **Rat-trap pedals.** The worst of all pedals are made of thin metal plates topped with a serrated edge like a rat trap. These pedals cut into soft-soled

shoes and offer neither comfort nor efficiency. They are less common these days on new bikes, but if the bike you want is fitted with them, I recommend that you ask the shop to change them for another type.

• **Platform pedals.** Wide platform pedals are the best general-purpose pedals as they support the balls of your feet. These pedals are cheap and emphasise comfort and convenience. But, because they won't hold your feet in the correct position, they are not the most efficient.

Long-distance bikes use the more efficient pedals with a *cleat*, or bracket that locks the pedal to the bottom of your shoe.

• **Toe clips.** The traditional way to bind your shoe to the pedal is with a cleat on the cycling shoe and toe clips with a strap. The cleated shoe fits onto the narrow ridge of the pedal and then, by tightening the strap on the toe clip, you lock the shoe and your foot firmly in place. Toe clips come in different lengths to suit different-sized feet. The disadvantage of this system is that it takes time to learn how to get your feet into toe clips: they are hard to get out of and the straps can hurt your feet. Many riders use toe clips with ordinary shoes and without cleats. This keeps the ball of the foot over the pedal axle, but the narrow ridges of these pedals can be uncomfortable to push with ordinary shoes.

• **Click systems.** The most efficient and comfortable pedals click into a matched pair of shoes. A few years ago the people who make ski bindings realised that cyclists are very like skiers in their need to lock their feet into one position and so they designed bicycle versions of their systems. These increasingly popular click systems provide all the efficiency of a traditional system but, by doing away with the toe clip and strap, are much more comfortable. They are also much easier to get in and out of. Not surprisingly, they are quickly replacing the traditional system. Competition versions of these systems have a large cleat under the shoe, not unlike the traditional toe-clip cleat. This makes you walk like a duck and sound like Fred Astaire. New designs hide the cleats within the sole of the shoe so you can walk normally and silently. These systems are clearly the best, and clearly the most expensive, as you need to purchase special pedals and shoes. (There is more on pedalling efficiency in Chapter 7 and on special cycling shoes in Chapter 11.)

CRANKS

The cranks connect the pedals to the front gear sprocket, and vary in weight and length.

- **Weight.** Lightweight cranks are made of aluminium alloy, and cheaper ones of steel. Alloy cranks are pushed onto the crank axle. Steel cranks are usually wedged on with a cotter pin. See Chapter 14 for more on how cranks are attached.
- **Length.** Cranks can be 165 mm to 175 mm long. Most bicycles come with standard-length cranks of 170 mm. Longer cranks give you a leverage advantage going uphill but you won't be able to spin them as quickly as standard cranks. It is also easier to bump them on the ground if you pedal round a corner. People with shorter legs might find shorter cranks make riding easier and more enjoyable.

GEARS

The main choice with gears is between simple systems that are convenient for short distances and the complex derailleur system that offers substantial benefits on longer rides. Once you have a derailleur system, it is possible to adapt it so that the set of gears matches what you use the bike for and your level of fitness.

Choosing a gear system

- **Single gear.** There are single-gear childrens' bikes, 'ladies" bikes and even some competition bikes. A single gear is fine for short trips such as riding to the station or up to the milk bar. Single-gear bikes are reliable and, with no gear-changing mechanism, little can go wrong with the drive train. They also often have a chain guard which protects your clothes from the greasy chain.
- **Hub gears** have a number of advantages and, for a round-town bike, they are a natural choice. Despite being mechanically complex they are simple to use. As we saw in Chapter 7, hub gears can be changed when you are stopped or on the move. Hub gears can go out of adjustment but are usually easy to readjust (see Chapter 14). Because the moving parts are protected from rain and dirt, hub gears take longer to wear out. The chain also lasts longer and, with a spring clip on one chain link, it is easy to remove, clean and lubricate. Bikes with hub gears can also be fitted with a chain guard.

Where hub gears lose out is in the number of gears they offer: you can only get three, five or, at most, seven gears into a hub. These days they can also be more expensive than a cheap derailleur system.

- **Derailleur gears** are found on most bikes. A five-speed derailleur has one sprocket at the front and five at the back, a ten-speed has two front sprockets and five at the back, an eighteen-speed bike has three sprockets at the front and six at the back. The current limit seems to be three at the front and eight at the back.

As we saw in Chapter 7, you will ride most efficiently if you maintain a steady pedalling speed and change ratios to suit the terrain. So the further or faster you want to pedal, the more ratios you will want to have available and therefore the more likely you are to want derailleur gears. On short trips few people use all the ratios on a derailleur bike and many riders would probably be better off with a simpler hub-gear system.

Derailleur systems are mechanically simple but it takes time to learn how to operate them (see Chapter 7). Even when you know how to work them, a poor derailleur system can be slow to change, and a good system that is worn or out of adjustment can be unable to move the chain, will let the chain slide around on top of the sprockets, will change sprockets when you don't want it to and can throw the chain off the sprockets altogether. In these situations the derailleur system is a pain. Riders put up with the problems of derailleurs because they provide a lot of gears and because you can swap the sprockets until you have a set of gears that suits the riding you do.

Easy-to-use derailleur systems
Bike manufacturers have worked hard to reduce derailleur problems. The various new chain-and-teeth designs, click-to-change gear levers and derailleur-arm geometries have made the systems easier to use, reducing the frequency of derailleur problems. It is worth checking the derailleur system on the bike you are considering. Check if it has:

- **a quality derailleur system?** By and large, a quality derailleur system will work more quickly and reliably than a cheap one. While your chain is leaving one sprocket and moving to another you can't make the bike go forward, so the faster your derailleur system, the less time you are in pedalling limbo. This is obviously important in competition but it is also relevant to riders tackling a hill where a slow change will reduce climbing speed and momentum.

Derailleur systems rise in price and quality in a similar way to frames. Generally, expensive frames have top-quality drive trains, but because the frames are made by one company and the drive trains by another, you could find one brand puts an average drive train on a good frame while another puts a good drive train on a moderate-quality frame. The bike shop should be able to show you where the derailleur system you are considering sits in the range. The Shimano component range laid out in Appendix 3 shows how derailleurs come in a range of types (for racing, off-road use and for budget bikes), in a range of quality (400, 500, 600), as well as how models are superseded every so often.

Once you buy a particular drive-train system, you will have to stay with it: components such as chain, sprockets and derailleur arms are not usually interchangeable with components made by another company, nor are they always compatible with components from other systems made by the same company.

• **a click system?** Click systems are the easiest derailleurs to use. The traditional derailleur, which is quickly becoming obsolete, requires the rider to ease the lever just the right amount until the new gear engages. This technique takes a bit of time to learn. With a click system the rider simply moves the lever from click to click and the derailleur moves the chain just the right amount to put the chain on the next sprocket and into the next gear.

• **easy-to-reach levers?** Traditionally gear levers are fitted on the downtube (this position keeps the gear cable short which was important for the old-style derailleurs) but this is the hardest place to reach. If you have racing-style drop bars, get levers that go in the end of the bars, or on top of the bars near the stem or next to the brake levers. The latest brake levers for racing bikes use the same lever for brakes and gears. Straight bars usually have the gear levers in an excellent position right near the handgrips or even in a twist-to-change handlebar grip.

Choosing your set of derailleur gears
The perfect bike gearing would be infinitely variable, providing just the right gear for each slope. Unfortunately this sort of gearing is not available. Cyclists have to choose a fixed number of gears: the number depends on the 'size' of the derailleur system, and this set of gears can be made up in many combinations of front and rear sprockets.

Some sets are suitable for fit triathletes while others are more suitable for uphill, or load-carrying riding. To assess the suitability of your bike's gears, you need to describe and analyse them.

• **Gear description.** To chose between different sets of gears, you need to be able to describe and compare the individual gears in the set. The way to do this is to look at the *metres travelled* for each turn of the pedals in each particular gear. For one turn of the pedals, we can calculate:
Metres travelled = Wheel diameter x Front-to-rear-sprocket ratio (see p. 74) x Pi.

This calculation has been done for a normal 70-cm-diameter wheel for each sprocket combination and is laid out in chart form in Appendix 2. As you can see from Appendix 2, bicycle gears range from the lowest – about 2 metres for each pedal rotation – to the highest, used by racing cyclists – about 10 metres per pedal.

• **Gear analysis.** For your own bike you can do a chart showing how far the bike will travel when used with each of the different combinations of front and rear sprockets. Count the teeth for each front and rear sprocket. (Sometimes the number of teeth is stamped on the sprocket.) Below is given a blank sprocket-gear chart (Chart A). It has space for three front sprockets and eight rear sprockets; your bike might only have one or two at the front and five at the rear. Enter the number of teeth for each front and rear sprocket of your bike in the designated areas in Chart A. Follow the example given in Chart B for a typical ten-speed bike (70-cm wheel, two front and five rear sprockets). Now fill in the metres travelled, using the chart in Appendix 2.

You can calculate the metres travelled on the lowest gear of the ten-speed – 42 front and 28 rear – by calculating the ratio 42/28, or 1.5, and then using this formula:
70 cm (Wheel diameter) x 1.5 (Ratio) x 3.14 (Pi) = 3.3 metres – or read it from the Appendix 2 chart, row 42, column 28.

A. BLANK SPROCKET GEAR CHART – FOR YOUR BIKE
(Distance travelled in metres)

				Rear sprockets (no. of teeth)				
Front sprockets (no. of teeth)		✕						
								✕

B. SPROCKET GEAR CHART – TEN-SPEED BIKE
(Distance travelled in metres)

		Rear sprockets (no. of teeth)				
		28	24	20	17	14
Front sprockets (no. of teeth)	52	✕	4.8	5.7	6.7	8.2
	42	3.3	3.8	4.6	5.4	✕

The number of metres travelled, 3.3 metres, has then been entered on Chart B, placed below 28 and in line with 42.

Don't worry if your wheel diameter is not 70 cm. A 65-cm-diameter wheel will be very little different and you can still use the Appendix 2 chart to approximate the metres travelled.

Now you can carry on and fill out the blank Chart A for your bike. For different front-rear sprocket combinations for a 70-cm-wheel bike, the distance is calculated already in Appendix 2.

Chart B, for this ten-speed bike, gives you an idea of the strengths and weaknesses of its set of gears.

– High gears (8-10). The highest gear is about 8 metres. This would help you go fast downhill. But for ordinary riders it is not much use as it is very hard to turn an 8-metre gear at 70 pedal revolutions a minute. Most standard bikes have too many high gears, missing out on useful middle and low gears.

– Middle gears (4-7). Most of the gears on this bike are middle-range gears which would be useful for ordinary riding.

– Low gears (2-3). There are no low gears on this ten-speed bike. The lowest gears are usually found on bikes with three front sprockets. These low gears are well worth having if you are going for a long ride in hilly country or if you are carrying a load. Most standard bikes don't have enough low gears.

- **Limits to gears.** Apart from the limitation of the number of sprockets, any set of derailleur gears will be limited by the ability of the chain to bend, and by duplicate ratios. These limitations mean, in practice, that a ten-speed will only be a six-speed.

  – Chain bend. In Charts A and B two combinations have been left blank because you will wear out the chain very quickly if you ride with it on the outside front sprocket and the most inside rear sprocket or vice versa.

  – Duplicates. You might notice that different gear combinations give roughly the same metres per pedal. On the ten-speed the 52-24 is much the same as 42-20 and 52-20 is much the same as 42-17. These two duplicate ratios mean that the bike has six useful gears.

- **Range and steps.** The limitations on gears mean that your set will be a compromise between two factors: range

and steps. 'Range' describes how high and how low your set of gears will reach: 3.3-8.2 on the ten-speed. This bike is neither a specialist hill climber nor downhill speedster. 'Steps' describes the jumps between the ratios on a set of gears. The steps on a ten-speed between the gears get bigger as the bike is going faster: the 0.5 step between the bottom two gears is good but the 1.3 and 1.5 metre steps at the top would make it hard to keep a steady pedalling speed. The Gear analysis Chart C puts this information on the ten-speed in one place.

Chart D is a blank gear analysis chart for you to fill in the details of your bike. Refer to Chart A, and in the two 'Range' boxes write your highest and lowest gear. In the 'Useful gears' and 'Duplicate' boxes write the gears you have in ascending order. By subtracting one useful gear from another you can work out the step between each gear and record it on the last line. A step of 0.5 is about right. (Some people like to tape a list of their useful gears to the handlebars while learning the gears on a new bike.)

C. GEAR ANALYSIS CHART – TEN-SPEED BIKE

Useful gears	3.3	3.8	4.6	5.4	6.7	8.2
Duplicate ratios			4.8	5.7		
Range	3.3	8.2				
Step to next gear	0.5	0.8	0.8	1.3	1.5	

D. BLANK GEAR ANALYSIS CHART – FOR YOUR BIKE

Useful gears	___	___	___	___	___	___	___	___	___
Duplicate ratios	___	___	___	___	___	___	___	___	___
Range	___	___					___	___	___
Step to next gear	___	___	___	___	___	___	___	___	___

Different sets of gears

There are many different sets of gears. Some sets come with high and low gears – a wide range – so that you can buzz up and down big hills. But a wide range will have big steps between the gears which will make it difficult to maintain steady pedalling up and down smaller hills. When the gears are close together – small steps – so you can pedal steadily while riding up and down small hills, you only get a narrow range which makes either climbing or descending a problem. At the two extremes a racer will fit higher gears with small steps, while a loaded cycle-camper will use lower gears with small steps. The only thing you can't get is a wide range with small steps.

As an illustration, let's imagine the Three Musketeers are each choosing a set of five gears for their bikes: 2 is low and 10 is high, just like in real life.

Athos choses 2-5-6-7-10. This is a wide range including both the highest and lowest gears. He will be able to climb the steepest hill in 2 and belt down the steepest slope in 10. He can keep pedalling steadily on small undulations as there are small steps between the three middle gears. But on medium ups and downs the big steps from 2 to 5 or from 7 to 10 will leave him stranded in a gear that is too high to pedal at his chosen speed, or force him to drop his road speed suddenly and pedal in the bottom gear.

Aramis choses 3-5-6-8-9. The range is neither high nor low. It won't get him up the biggest hills and it won't go as fast as Athos' bike. Nor will it go as well on the small undulations as Athos' bike because of the uneven steps between the middle gears. But there will always be a gear somewhere near what he wants. (This is similar to the gearing on the ten-speed bike – Chart C.)

Porthos has a light bike and is a very fit cyclist, so he choses 5-6-7-8-9. The range is high but he has been training for years and can pedal 'big' gears at a high pedal speed. The small steps between the gears will work well for his next triathlon. (This is similar to the gearing on the triathlon bike – Charts E and F.)

E. SPROCKET GEAR CHART – TRIATHLON BIKE

(Distance travelled in metres)

			Rear sprockets (no. of teeth)					
			21	19	17	15	14	13
Front sprockets (no. of teeth)		54	✕	6.2	7.0	7.9	8.5	9.1
		42	4.4	4.9	5.4	6.2	6.6	✕

F. GEAR ANALYSIS CHART − TRIATHLON BIKE

Useful gears	4.4	4.9	5.4	6.2	6.6	7.0	7.9	8.5	9.1
Duplicate ratios				6.2					
Range	4.4	9.1							
Step to next gear	0.5	0.5	0.8	0.4	0.4	0.9	0.6	0.6	

G. SPROCKET GEAR CHART − UPHILL BIKE

(Distance travelled in metres)

		Rear sprockets (no. of teeth)				
		32	26	21	16	13
Front sprockets (no. of teeth)	42	✕	3.6	4.4	5.8	7.1
	36	2.5	3.0	3.8	4.9	6.1
	26	1.8	2.2	2.7	3.6	✕

H. GEAR ANALYSIS CHART − UPHILL BIKE

Useful gears	1.8	2.2	2.7	3.0	3.6	4.4	4.9	5.8	7.1
Duplicate ratios			2.5		3.8			6.1	
Range	1.8	7.1							
Step to next gear	0.4	0.5	0.3	0.6	0.8	0.5	0.9	1.3	

D'Artagnan, from Gascony on the edge of the Pyrenees mountains, choses 2-3-4-5-8. The others will all leave him behind on the downhill, but he will have little trouble negotiating the foothills or the steepest mountains with this low range and the small steps between the lower gears. (This is similar to the gearing on the uphill bike – Charts G and H.)

Let's look at three real-life examples:

– **A specialist triathlon bike**. A set of gears for a triathlon bike might look like Charts E and F.

This is a fast bike and you would have to be fit to ride it. It has nine useful gears between 4.4 and 9.1. The steps don't average much above 0.5 and there is only one duplicate ratio.

– **A specialist uphill bike**. A set of gears for a specialist uphill or load-carrying bike might look like Charts G and H.

This fifteen-speed bike will go well up steep hills. In bottom gear the pedals will turn faster than the wheels. The bike won't break any land-speed records as the top gear is only 7.1 metres. There are only three duplicate ratios and ten useful gears. The steps are mostly around 0.5.

(Most bikes like this one with three front sprockets will need a large-capacity rear derailleur. Derailleur capacity is measured by calculating the difference between the front sprockets and the biggest and smallest rear sprocket and then adding the two answers. In this case 42 minus 26 = 16; 32 minus 13 = 19; 16 plus 19 = 35. So the rear derailleur will need a capacity of 35. The triathlon bike has a capacity of 20.)

– **A hub geared bike**. The ratios in a hub gear change from make to make not to mention variations in the front and rear sprockets. But on a typical three-speed bike with a 42 front and 18 back sprocket, bottom would be around 3.5 metres, middle would be 5 metres and top around 6.5 metres. These big steps in a narrow range show that the hub gear is best suited to around-town use.

Choosing your own set of gears
It takes some time in the saddle and some work with pen and paper before you will know what characteristics you want your set of gears to have and what the limitations are of the gearing you have. Once you know what you want, you can ask the bike-shop specialist to help you adapt your gearing to suit. You will need their advice because not every maker produces a complete range of sprocket sizes and, even if they do, it can be hard to find the sprocket size you want.

Most people settle for an easily available combination which they have found, after a bit of trial and error, suits most of their needs. But let me warn

you that it is possible for the quest for the perfect gearing system to take you all your life.

RIDING POSITION
The three basic riding positions are: sitting up straight, leaning right forward and a compromise between the two, leaning forward a little (as pictured on p. 68). Most bikes can be adapted to offer any of the three positions but usually riders choose a preferred position and get a bike that has been designed to suit that one. Frames built for competition make it easy to set up a leaning-right-forward position and shopping bikes are built to be ridden sitting up straight.

• **Sitting straight up: bars high.** Traditionally bikes were ridden sitting up straight. The traditional ladies' bike usually has an upright riding position with a wide saddle, and handlebars that point back towards the rear of the bike. The traditional gents' bike was similar. It had drop bars that were turned around so they stuck up like bulls horns and you stuck your Gladstone bag in between the bars. For this riding position the saddle is usually set lower than the bars. It feels familiar, is comfortable for short distances, and gives good visibility.

• **Leaning right forward: saddle high.** Competition bikes are designed to tilt the rider right forward. The further or the faster the cyclist has to ride, the more they lean right forward. This position reduces air pressure, allows more muscles to be used in pedalling and distributes the cyclist's weight between arms and bum, adding some natural suspension to the bike. (See p. 68 for more on 'Efficiency' of riding position.) Drop bars that curve down and point to the rear, or time-trial bars that curve forward, allow riders who are in the saddle for a long time both to get down low and to find a number of different hand and body positions.

Many bikes are set up this way, with hard, narrow saddles set higher than the bars. But leaning right forward is uncomfortable, at least at first. It is unnerving for the beginner and it is not so good for looking at the view. If the bike you want is set up this way, but you don't want to lean right forward, ask the shop to change the bars and adjust the bike to suit you.

• **Leaning forward a little: saddle and bars level.** More and more bikes these days offer a compromise riding position which tilts the rider forward a little way onto a set of straight bars that are level with the saddle. Compared with sitting up straight, this position allows more muscles to be used in pedalling, reduces air pressure to some extent and distributes some of the cyclist's weight between saddle and bars. It also maintains good visibility. This riding position is ideal for short rides. Straight bars can be adapted for longer rides with bar extensions or replaced by bars that allow the rider to lean further forward and change their hand position. (See 'Riding and handlebars' below.)

MODIFYING AN EXISTING BIKE
Your riding position can be modified, to some extent, by moving the handlebar stem or seat post up or down. Chapter 14 describes how to adjust them. Both stem and post usually have a maximum height marked on them. If you lift either post or stem too far out of the frame they might break or pop out while you are riding. If you want the

bars or seat up higher than the mark, you can usually buy an extra-long stem or post. If have tried these adjustments and you still can't set up the riding position you want, you might have to get another frame. Whichever riding position you choose, it should take account of the most efficient saddle height described in Chapter 9.

RIDING POSITION AND SADDLE
Your choice of riding position will influence which saddle you choose. If you have chosen an upright riding position most of your weight will be on the saddle, so look for a wide, well-padded, sprung saddle. Consider a slip-on cover made of sheepskin or filled with gel. If you have chosen to lean right forward, then you are probably more interested in speed. In

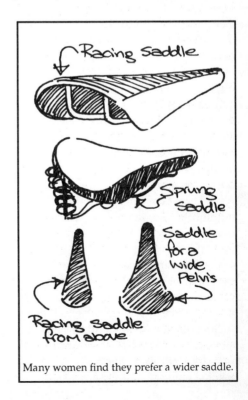

Many women find they prefer a wider saddle.

this case your saddle should be pretty firm so it doesn't dissipate your pedalling effort, and will be as narrow as possible so as not to interfere with your thighs as they go up and down. Many women find they prefer a wider saddle that accommodates the larger gap between their pelvic bones.

Saddles are made of all sorts of stuff. Plastic is used on cheap bikes and kids' bikes. This makes these uncomfortable saddles largely kid-proof and rain-proof. More expensive and more comfortable plastic saddles are padded with foam of different thicknesses and then covered in a skin of real leather or leather-like plastic. Leather-covered saddles don't get as hot and sweaty as the plastic models. Heavier leather saddles are still popular among high-mileage cyclists. When new these are as hard as a plastic saddle but, like shoes, they do eventually adapt to your shape. They can lose this carefully gained shape if they get soaked.

Drop bars offer a choice of efficient riding positions for longer rides.

RIDING POSITION AND HANDLEBARS

Your choice of riding position (see Chapter 7) will also influence which bars you choose. There are basically two types of bars: racing-style drop bars or straight – or near-straight – bars. Either sort of bar can be bought in aluminium alloy or steel, depending whether you want light weight or a lower price.

• **Drop bars**. Riders who want to lean forward will look for drop bars, which are usually ridden with the crook of the hands between thumb and first finger on the brake-lever hood. These bars get you down low to reduce air pressure. They also offer different positions for your hands: down on the

bottom of the bars, in the curve of the U shape, over the brake levers, behind the brake levers and the most upright position next to the stem. This allows a change of scenery for tired hands and wrists. Time-triallers and triathletes are allowed to compete with bar extensions and adaptions that offer further variety and greater streamlining. Drop bars make the bike more difficult to control and feel odd to many riders as your hands are always sideways. If you are riding in traffic with drop bars you will have to make an extra effort to keep your head up. Crash statistics suggest that riding in traffic with your head down over ultra-low triathlon bars is quite dangerous.

• **Flat bars.** Riders who want to sit up more will use flat bars that run at right-angles to the frame or curve back towards the rider. These bars give a

Flat bars offer a more upright
riding position for short rides in traffic
or over rough ground.

feeling of confidence and stability to
beginners. They also give riders more
control when negotiating obstacles on
rough tracks. They are more
appropriate for riding in traffic as, with
these two riding positions, your head is
up higher. Flat bars do become a
problem on a long ride as they increase
air pressure and offer few alternative
hand positions. This last problem can
be overcome by fitting extension bars or
bars that curve round in an oval,
providing, in effect, two parallel
straight bars.

Some bikes are sold with very wide
flat bars. These extra wide bars offer
extra control but they can make it hard
to get through narrow gaps.

BRAKES

Braking is not something that bikes do
well, but some bikes do it better than
others. Probably the weakest link in any
braking system is the technique of the

rider, which is discussed in Chapter 7.

The most important choice about
brakes is whether to buy alloy rims or
steel rims. In dry weather there is little
difference in braking performance
between the two. Wet alloy rims take
twice as long to stop as dry rims. But
wet steel rims will take four to six times
as long to stop. If you anticipate riding
in the rain, and the bike you like has
steel rims, check the cost of swapping
to alloy rims. It is easy to spot alloy
rims as they have a dull lustre unlike
the reflective surface of chromed steel.

As well as looking at the rims you
can judge a bike's braking performance
by looking at the type of brake calipers,
the type of levers and the quality of the
brake pads.

CALIPERS

When you pull on the brake lever, the
brake cable pulls a pair of pivoting
calipers that grip the rim with the brake
pads. These pivoting calipers come in a
number of designs:

• **Centrepulls and sidepulls.** Most
bikes come with centrepull or sidepull
brakes. With sidepull brakes the brake
cable pulls one caliper from above and
one from the side on a single pivot. On
centrepull brakes one cable pulls up on
both calipers. Quality sidepulls are
favoured by competition cyclists as
they are the lightest type of brake.
Cheap sidepulls can be hard to adjust.
Generally, centrepull brakes are better
on budget bikes.

• **Cam-operated centrepulls.** The
most powerful centrepull brake pulls a
cam up between the calipers. They are
so powerful they are usually fitted only
to the rear wheel.

• **Cantilever.** The best general-
purpose brakes are cantilever brakes,

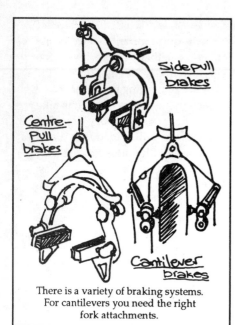

There is a variety of braking systems. For cantilevers you need the right fork attachments.

lot to do with it: a quality pair could set you back ten dollars. Some good pads emphasise low-heat braking. These soft-compound pads are relatively sticky and only require gentle pressure to work at slow speeds. But if they are used heavily, for example on a long descent, they will fail and smear themselves around the rim. Hard-compound pads require more squeeze power but will not fail when they are hot.

LEVERS
The type of brake levers you use will depend on the type of bars you have selected.

- **Horizontal levers.** The brake levers that are easiest to use pivot horizontally on flat bars.
- **Vertical levers.** Drop bars have levers that pivot vertically. These levers are hard to use until you build up strength in your hand.
- **Horizontal levers on drop bars**. There are quite a few riders who have drop bars but want a more upright riding position. Manufacturers seek to help

which pivot on bosses on the forks. Cantilevers are the simplest and the most powerful of the common types of brake. Unfortunately, they can be fitted only to bikes with the right forks.

- **Other types.** In the past, adult bikes used to come with back pedal brakes. Kids' bikes still have them, which is a good thing as young kids' hands are not strong enough to operate brake levers. Some bikes and many tandems come with car-style drum brakes inside the wheel hub. Drum brakes are heavier but brake powerfully and work much better in the wet. Disc brakes have been tried on bikes but they offer no advantage.

BRAKE PADS
Most bikes are sold with cheap brake pads. A cheap and easy way to improve your braking performance is to buy a 'better' set of pads. It is harder to define what a good set is, though price has a

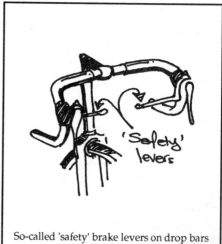

So-called 'safety' brake levers on drop bars can, in fact, make braking even less effective.

them by fitting a second pair of brake levers that run parallel to the top of the bars. I think these so-called 'safety' levers are ineffective and dangerous.

If you have a bike with drop bars and you want a more upright riding position, change to flat handlebars.

THE MAIN FEATURES OF A BICYCLE

Here is a quick checklist of the main considerations in choosing a bike.

Frame
- Size
  - height
  - length
- Handling characteristics
  - short wheelbase
  - long wheelbase
- Power or convenience
  - a diamond frame
  - a convenient frame
  - a compromise
- Performance
  - mild steel
  - quality steel-alloy
  - exotic materials

Wheels
- Weight and strength
  - Heavy strong wide wheels
  - Lightweight narrow fast wheels
- Size
  - Smaller wheels: 65 cm diam.
  - Larger wheels: 70 cm diam.
- Rims
  - Alloy
  - Steel
- Tyre width and pressure
  - 1 cm wide at over 100 psi
  - 2.5 cm wide at 70 psi
  - Up to 6 cm wide at around 45 psi

Drive train
- Pedals
  - click pedals
  - toe clips and cleats
  - platform pedals
- Gear system
  - hub gears
  - derailleur gears
- Number of gears
  - 1 to 24
- High gears
- Low gears
- Range and steps
  - a wide range with big steps
  - a narrow range with small steps

Riding position
- Sitting up straight
- Leaning right forward
- Leaning forward a little
- Saddle
  - width
  - covering
- Bar shape
  - drop
  - flat

Brakes
- Wet-weather braking: alloy rims
- Type
  - centrepull
  - sidepull
  - cantilever
  - backpedal

Chapter 9

FITTING YOUR BICYCLE

A well-fitting bike makes it easy to enjoy your cycling. A bike that doesn't fit you properly will take more effort to pedal, can be more uncomfortable and, if the bike is too big, can be dangerous.

Bikes, like clothes, come in different sizes. Just as you have to make one or two body measurements to get the right-sized pair of jeans, so you have to for bikes.

In the first part of the chapter you will find out how to measure your bike, how to measure yourself and how to make sure that the bike you have, or the bike you are going to buy, is the best size. In the second part we shall look at finer adjustment. In the same way that you can turn up a pair of jeans or the cuff of a shirt, bikes can be adjusted to make the machine fit your legs and arms more precisely.

For both these jobs it is worth seeking the advice and assistance of a specialist bike shop. Chapter 10 goes into the benefits of finding a helpful bike dealer.

THE BEST FRAME SIZE

Bicycles differ in many ways but it is the frame that decides the size of the bike. Not the wheels or the handlebars or the pedals, just the frame. The frame that is the right size for you will:

• match your leg length so that you will be able to pedal efficiently;

• match the top half of your body, so that when you ride you are not balled up like an echidna or stretched out like a lizard drinking.

The first dimension is 'frame height' and the second dimension 'frame length'. When manufacturers and salespeople say 'bike size' they are usually referring to only the frame height. The usual way to measure the height of a frame is from the centre of the crank axle to the centre of the top tube. The length of a frame is measured from the centre of the head tube to the centre of the seat tube. For a bike without a top tube, you measure where the top tube would be. There is more on atypical frame shapes in Chapter 8.

Top-level competition cyclists go to a lot trouble to make sure their bike frames match their bodies and riding styles and there is much debate over the scientific and intuitive prinicples that will produce the best match. We will start with a quick way to tell if a frame matches your body. When you come to change your bike for something better or more suited to you, then it is worth doing more detailed measurements for body and bike. Like the best clothes, the best bicycles are tailor-made for each rider, but we can afford to ignore these complex measurements as most of us use an off-the-rack size.

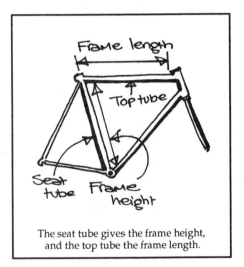

The seat tube gives the frame height, and the top tube the frame length.

A QUICK CHECK FOR FRAME HEIGHT AND LENGTH

These two quick checks should be made whenever you are buying a bike and especially when buying a child's bike. If the bike you are looking at passes these two tests you might want to skip from here to the section on finer adjustment.

• **Height.** A quick way to see if a frame matches the length of your legs is to straddle the top tube. Take off your shoes and stand over the bike and see if you can put your feet flat on the ground. If the top tube is trying to cut you in half, the frame is too big. There should be at least a 2.5-cm gap (about the diameter of a 20-cent piece) between the top tube and your pelvic bone. You can still use this system on a bike without a top tube if you stretch a piece of string horizontally across the gap where the top tube would be.

Bike riders who ride on rough roads look for a frame with a large gap between top tube and saddle, sometimes up to 10 cm (about the length of a standard audio-cassette). This allows the way-off-the-beaten-track rider to fit a long seat post, and to move the saddle down low for steep descents. Unless you are doing that sort of riding, you don't need a top tube this low.

• **Length.** A quick way to see if a frame matches the length of your upper body is to put your elbow on the front of the saddle and reach forward with your fingers. You should be able to touch the handlebars. If your fingers fall short by a long distance, the frame is probably too long. If your fingers go beyond the bars, then the frame is probably too short. This is not a precise measure as the saddle can be moved backwards and forwards and the handlebars fitted to a long or short stem.

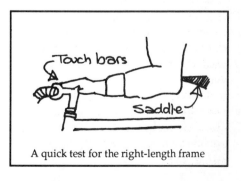

A quick test for the right-length frame

BUYING A BETTER BIKE: MORE DETAILED MEASUREMENTS

When you are upgrading your bike it is worth investigating the matching of your body to the bike more closely. There are four measurements to make: two on the bike and two on your body. Knowing these will increase your chance of making a satisfactory purchase.

Measuring your bike

• **Height**. Measure the frame height by running a tape measure along the seat tube from a horizontal line through the centre of the crank axle to a horizontal line through the centre of the top tube. (This measurement assumes that the manufacturer has built the crank axle at the standard height of 27 cm from the ground. As we saw in Chapter 8, some bikes come with a higher crank axle and some with a lowered top tube.)

• **Length.** Measure the frame length along the top tube from the centre of the seat tube to the centre of the head tube. If your bike doesn't have a top tube, measure the distance along a horizontal line from the top of the head stem to the top of the seat tube.

Frame height and your body

Frame height is based on the length of your legs, usually the *inseam* or *inside-leg measurement*. (Later in this chapter this measurement is also needed to adjust your saddle height.) Here are two methods that cyclists use to measure inseam. It is a good idea to get someone to help you as it is difficult to do accurately on your own.

• **Method One**. Stand in your socks against a wall on a hard floor, with the outside of your feet at each end of a 30-cm (12") ruler. (The ruler

approximates the distance between the pedals.) Put something as high as possible between your legs, like a book or T-square and, holding it level, mark this height (i.e, of your pelvic bone) on the wall. Then measure from the mark to the floor.

• **Method Two.** Lie down on a hard floor and put your feet, again with the outside about 30 cm apart, against the wall. Then put the book or T-square as high as possible between your legs and mark that spot on the floor. This method might be easier on your own as you can wriggle away from the mark without moving the T-square.

When you are on the bike your inseam will run from the top of the saddle, down the seat tube, along the crank to the pedal axle. But we can't just subtract these distances from your inseam because your leg should always be slightly bent at the bottom of the pedal stroke. So we use a rubbery-figures formula to reduce Your Inseam Measurement (YIM) until we get the ideal frame height of your bike.

There is some debate over what is best formula. The simplest calculation multiplies YIM by 0.66 or two thirds. Another approach is to subtract 22.5 cm - 27.5 cm from YIM, depending on your overall height: 22.5 if under 175 cm, 27.5 cm if over 182 cm, and 25 cm for those in the middle. (Off-road riders usually subtract another 5 cm from the result of these calculations.)

As you can see from Chart A on the next page, these calculations give a different result and therefore only an idea of the frame height rather than a precise figure. Someone with an inseam of 75 cm could use a frame between 47.5 cm and 52.5 cm, depending on their total height.

CHART A: FRAME HEIGHT RELATED TO INSEAM

YIM in cm	YIM times 0.66	YIM less 22.5 cm	YIM less 25 cm	YIM less 27.5 cm
60	39.6	37.5	35	32.5
65	42.9	42.5	40	37.5
70	46.2	47.5	45	42.5
75	49.5	52.5	50	47.5
80	52.8	57.5	55	52.5
85	56.1	62.5	60	57.5
90	59.4	67.5	65	62.5
95	62.7	72.5	70	67.5
100	66.0	77.5	75	72.5

Frame length and your body

Frame length is based on the length of your arms - your 'reach'. One way of measuring it is to sit against the wall with your arm above you, the back of your hand against the wall and your thumb at right angles to the fingers as if you were stopping the traffic. Measure the distance from the base of your thumb to the floor. Half of that distance is the approximate ideal length of the top tube on your bike.

BUYING OFF-THE-RACK SIZES

Most bikes, like clothes, come off the production line in a limited number of off- the-rack sizes based on average body measurements. This means that you probably won't find the ideal sizes that you have just worked out in the manufacturer's categories. For men of 'average' size this won't be a problem. But women can have difficulty finding a bike that fits well since many bikes are made to fit male body proportions. It will be easier to get a good fit if you understand how the off-the-rack sizes work.

Frame height from the manufacturer

Most manufacturers build each model of bike in a number of frame heights.

WHIZZO FRAME HEIGHTS

Mens'	Ladies'
17.5"	17.5"
19.5"	
21.5"	

YODEL FRAME HEIGHTS

Mens'	Ladies'
19"	18"
21"	
23"	
25"	

ZIPPO FRAME HEIGHTS

20"
22"
24"

Let's look at three examples above from a bike catalogue. (The model names have been changed to protect their identity.)

You can see that your choice is limited:
• The Yodel offers the most number of frame heights but doesn't go as low as the Whizzo.

- If you need a high frame and want a Whizzo then you could be out of luck.
- Someone who wants a Zippo the same size as the second smallest Yodel will also be disappointed.

You will also notice that this company still measures frame height in inches. Some shops and catalogues speak metric but some still speak imperial. A shop near where I live has a ticket on each bike showing the frame height, but half the tickets are in metric and half in imperial. We'll use metric consistently from now on; there is a conversion chart at the end of the book. Here are the same three bikes with metric frame heights:

WHIZZO FRAME HEIGHTS

Mens'	Ladies'
43.75 cm	43.75 cm
48.75 cm	
53.75 cm	

YODEL FRAME HEIGHTS

Mens'	Ladies'
47.5 cm	45 cm
52.5 cm	
57.5 cm	
62.5 cm	

ZIPPO FRAME HEIGHTS

50 cm
55 cm
60 cm

Looking at the 'Frame height related to inseam' chart (A, previous page), you can see that:

- a small person with an inseam of 70 cm will need a frame possibly between 42 and 47 cms and will be looking at the smallest Whizzo or the smallest Yodel. But the smallest Yodel might be too big. The small person could try the middle-sized Whizzo but that also looks a bit big.
- A 70-cm-inseam person wanting an open-top frame could try either the Whizzo or the Yodel.
- The Zippos will fit someone with an inseam from around 75 cm to 90 cm. But someone with an 80-cm inseam will have to decide whether to go up to the 55-cm frame or down to the 50-cm frame. One thing that might help them to decide is the length of the frame.

Frame length from the manufacturer
Most production-line bikes come in a set combination of height and length. But some manufacturers offer frames that vary in both height and length. Sometimes their catalogues will give you the top-tube dimensions. Here are two bikes as described in a catalogue (the terminology is not always consistent: here 'frame size' means height and 'top tube' refers to frame length).

TOURE ALPHA

Frame size	Top tube
47.5 cm	52.8 cm
52.5 cm	53.7 cm
57.5 cm	54.7 cm
62.5 cm	56.2 cm

ROAD ALPHA	
Frame size	*Top tube*
47.5 cm	53.7 cm
52.5 cm	53.7 cm
57.5 cm	53.4 cm
62.5 cm	53.4 cm

The Toure Alpha gets higher and longer at the same time whereas the Road Alpha can get higher without getting longer.

When in doubt about fit

If you like a particular bike but are not happy with the fit, I suggest you:
- try a different model by the same maker;
- try a similar model from another manufacturer.

If you have a relatively long reach, you might have to look at a slightly higher frame in order to get a longer top tube. If you have a relatively short reach, you might have to choose a lower frame that has a shorter top tube. You can see that there is a bit of judgement and a bit of compromise involved in getting the right-size frame. Don't be afraid to ask the staff at a specialist bike shop to help you.

FINER ADJUSTMENT

Once you have the best frame size for your body, you are ready to make the fine adjustments to the saddle and handlebars so that you can ride in an efficient and comfortable position. (Chapter 7 and Chapter 8 discuss choosing a riding position.) These adjustments can be done within half an hour, but many riders keep fiddling with them for a few months until the bike feels just right.

SADDLE

You are after two things with saddle adjustment: efficiency and comfort. It sounds a bit puritanical, but the one to emphasise is efficiency. With your saddle at an efficient height not only will you go find the job easier but you are less likely to stress your body, harming your back or knees, for example. Comfort is more subjective. Many riders come to find the efficient position to be the most comfortable. Unfortunately it doesn't work the other way and a position that is comfortable to a beginner is not always efficient.

You can do three things to put your saddle in the most efficient position:
- make it higher or lower by adjusting the seat post,
- move it nearer to or further from the bars,
- make it level or tilt it up or down at the front.

A quick way to set saddle height

To check saddle height: sit, leg straight, heel on the pedal at the lowest point.

Set the saddle so that your leg is straight when your bare heel is on the pedal at the bottom of the pedal stroke. The heels are used as a measure so that when you come to put the balls of your feet on the pedal, your leg will be bent just the right amount.

• Change the saddle height by loosening the seat-post bolt and moving the seat post up or down in the frame. (Chapter 13 talks about the tools and technique needed for this process.) The aim is to get the saddle as high as it can go with the balls of your feet on the pedals.

• Make sure you have not set the saddle too high with this test. With someone holding the bike, pedal backwards, with your heels on the pedals. (Sit evenly in the saddle, or the leg length test will be inaccurate.) If your hips rock from side to side when you pedal backwards, the saddle is too high. Adjust it down a few millimetres, until you can confirm that your hips stay level when pedalling backwards.

If all has gone well, the length of the head tube should be about the same as the length of exposed seat tube under the saddle. If the saddle is right down next to the frame, then the frame is probably too big for you. If the seat post sticks out like a telegraph pole, you might have to get a bigger frame or a longer seat stem.

Mathematical ways of setting saddle height

Research into competition cycling has come up with a couple of formulae for saddle height based on the inside-leg (or Your Inseam Measurement – YIM) described on p. 104. As with frame measurement, there is some debate about which formula is best.

• **Method one** says put the crank in line with the seat tube at about 7 o'clock and set the saddle so the *distance from the pedal axle to the top of the saddle* is YIM multiplied by the magic number 1.09 (burst of power) or 1.07 (longer stints in the saddle).

• **Method two** says set the saddle so the *distance from lowest part of the top of the saddle to the centre of the crank axle* measures YIM multiplied by the magic number 0.885 (burst of power) or 0.883 (longer stints in the saddle).

If you are using cleats to lock your shoes to the pedals, you will probably have to raise the saddle a touch more, as the cleats on the bottom of your shoes might make your legs 'longer'.

SETTING SADDLE HEIGHT (in centimetres)

YIM	*Method one* Pedal axle to saddle top		*Method two* Crank axle to lowest point on top of saddle	
	YIM x 1.09	**YIM x 1.07**	**YIM x 0.885**	**YIM x 0.883**
60	65.40	64.20	53.01	52.98
65	70.85	69.55	57.53	57.40
70	76.30	74.90	61.95	61.81
75	81.75	80.25	66.38	66.23
80	87.20	85.60	70.80	70.64
85	92.65	90.95	75.23	75.06
90	98.10	96.30	79.65	79.47

If you use the formulae to check your current saddle setting and find that you want to raise the saddle, don't put it up all the way in one go: let your muscles adapt bit by bit to the new height.

Measuring how far forward to set the saddle

Once you have the saddle at the right height, you can adjust its fore-and-aft position with two vertical lines. As a general rule, racers find that 'further back' is better.

Use a plumb line to measure the distance between the front of the saddle and the crank axle. The saddle should be between 4 cm to 9 cm further back.

Another method is to sit on the saddle with the cranks pointing backwards and forwards at 9 and 3 o'clock. The front – or at least the centre – of your knee should be directly above the pedal axle. To check it you can sticky-tape a plumb bob to your knee.

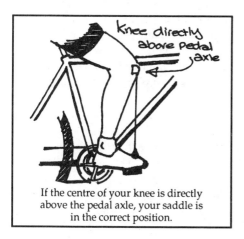

If the centre of your knee is directly above the pedal axle, your saddle is in the correct position.

Saddle tilt

All saddles can be tilted up and down. This allows you to set it horizontal to the ground, at whatever height the seat post is. I recommend that you start with your saddle horizontal and then experiment with other positions if you need to. Some riders find they prefer their saddle tilted slightly up at the front.

HANDLEBARS

Reaching to the bars

Your handlebar position is based on your saddle position, which is why we are doing this one last. Whatever type of handlebars you have chosen, they need to be in easy reach and that is usually defined by the length of the stem. You can test your handlebar position in a number of ways:

• Put your elbow on the front of the saddle and reach forward with your fingers. The tips of your fingers should just reach the bars.

• Sit on the saddle with one hand on the bars in what is, or will be, your normal riding position. Let the other arm dangle until it is its 'natural' length. Then, keeping it relaxed, swing it up to the bars. It should arrive at the place on the bar that you would normally hold when riding.

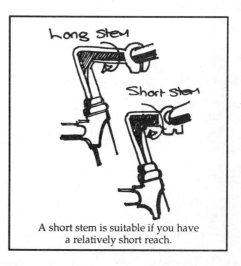

A short stem is suitable if you have a relatively short reach.

If the bars are too near, you can replace the stem with one that has a longer top section. If the bars are too far away, you can fit a 'shorter' stem, but stems don't usually come shorter than 8 cm. You can move the saddle towards the bars, but that will upset the efficient position you organised earlier. If the saddle-to-bar problem is significant, you might have to try another frame size.

Height of the bars

The height of the handlebars depends on the riding position you have chosen (Chapters 7 and 8).

• If you are sitting straight up, put the bars higher than the saddle.

• If you are leaning forward a little, set the bars the same height as the saddle.

• Racers, who lean right forward, usually set their bars about 2.5 cm to 8 cm lower than the saddle.

Handlebar height can also be influenced by the shape of the stem. On most stems the top section is horizontal and the handlebar bolt is level with the stem bolt. But the top section of some stems is angled up from the stem bolt to the handlebar bolt. Track-racing stems are angled down from the stem bolt to exaggerate the forward riding position.

Width of the bars

The width of the bars should be roughly the same as the width of your shoulders. Your bike shop should be able to provide the right bars. Drop bars, for example, come in a variety of widths from 38 - 44 cm, a number of depths from 12 cm to 15 cm, and a number of lengths from 7.5 cm to 10.5 cm. If you have flat bars that are too wide you could hacksaw them to the right width.

POSITIONING YOUR FEET ON THE PEDALS

The adjustment of cleats, toe clips and click pedals (see Chapters 7 and 8) is usually a matter of trial and error. The idea is to centre the ball of your foot over the pedal axle and to have your foot facing fore and aft. If your toes naturally point slightly inwards or outwards, then your adjustments should take that into account.

Toe clips come in a number of lengths. Yours should allow the ball of your foot to be over the pedal axle.

RECORDING THE RESULTS

When you are satisfied with the adjustment of your bike, make a note of the measurements. Then if your bike is pinched, or you borrow someone else's, or buy a new one or fit a new part, you can immediately adjust everything to suit you.

Some people like to mark the stem and seat post, just where they leave the frame, to indicate the correct height. Then if you have to lower the saddle or bars for some reason, to take them on a plane for example, it is easy to restore them to the correct position.

Chapter 10

BUYING A BIKE

WHERE TO BUY

Many people buy new bikes from the sports section of a big department store because the bikes are more competitively priced there. But price is only one consideration. Bicycle shops offer a range of other advantages that provide overall better value.

- **Assembly.** One advantage the bike shop has over the department store is mechanical skill. Bikes come to every retailer in pieces, in a carton. The retailer then assembles the pieces and the bike is wheeled onto the showroom floor. In a bike shop, the assembly is more likely to be done by a skilled bike mechanic. It is unlikely that the department store will have a skilled bike mechanic on staff. (Whomever you buy a bike from, it won't do any harm to run through the quick check-list in Chapter 13.)

- **Experts.** Another advantage that the specialist shop has is cycling experience. When you go to buy a bike you will want to compare the makes and models and talk about the main characteristics of the bikes. This discussion will be more successful with an experienced cyclist and you are more likely to find an experienced cyclist at the specialist shop.

- **Fitting.** A good specialist shop will take time to fit you properly with the right-sized frame. (This is discussed in detail in Chapter 9.) The specialist shop might even have a sizing machine, which looks like a bicycle frame on a stand. You sit on the sizing machine and the saddle is raised and lowered, and the handlebars moved back and forth. Then, when all is well, you read off the sizes on the scale. The people at a specialist shop will also help you with fine adjustment and be prepared to help you if you come back once or twice to get the fine adjustment just right.

- **Adaptability.** In a good bike shop, the staff will be able to help you adapt the bike you want to buy. For example, they might change the gearing, vary the riding position, fit alloy rims, install better brake-blocks, change the handlebars or swap the saddle. They will also offer a wider range of accessories, such racks, bags and mudguards. These changes and accessories might be unavailable at a department store.

• **Service.** Once the dollar is in the till, the difference between a specialist shop and a department store becomes even more obvious. All bicycles need a tune-up after you have ridden them for a while. Many specialist shops offer you the opportunity to bring your bike back after a couple of months for a free service and that will give you another chance to make changes or improve the fit. Department stores can usually organise repairs and maintenance but will send the bike off somewhere else to get it fixed, possibly to the local specialist shop! Bike shops usually give quicker service to people who have bought from their shop. One shop I know goes even further and will only work on 'their' bikes.

Over time you should be able to build up a relationship with a good bike shop. They will come to know you, they will remember your bike, they will offer advice, discuss the pros and cons of the latest accessories and will put you in touch with other cyclists in the area doing your sort of riding. In return they hope you'll buy things from them and maybe one day upgrade to a better bike. If you are planning to stay with bikes or think you will spend a reasonable amount of time on your bike, it makes sense to start this relationship with a specialist shop, preferably not far from your home.

BUYER BEWARE

There can, of course, be problems you might encounter in buying from a specialist shop. In some shops your choice will be limited; they might only sell bikes from one manufacturer, for example. Nor will bike-shop advice always be completely impartial: like the department stores, bike shops are also trying to sell bikes to pay the rent. Some shops are interested only in looking after one type of rider - racers, for example - and are not very welcoming to cyclists who don't fit their expectations. Nor are bike shop staff always well-informed or full bottle on customer service. Mechanical service is more important in some shops than others. Shops make money from the sale of bikes and, to some extent, the sale of accessories, but make little from maintenance, so some shops try to do as little maintenance as possible. One shop I know makes sure they frighten away customers who want any service beyond the first obligatory one. If you have had bad service at a bike shop, it might have been intentional.

Not all small shops that sell bikes are worth supporting. Sometimes a toy shop or a track-suit shop adds bikes to its range of products but offers no specialist advice or service to the cyclist. These shops are small versions of the department store. On the other hand, don't dismiss a shop just because it sells fishing rods or toys as well as bikes. They could still offer good service and advice and just be flogging furry rabbits to help stay in business.

PRICING BIKES

You can pay anything between $100 and $5000 for a bike. The price and the quality both go up in jumps.

• **The cheapest bikes** are the bargains at the department store for around $100-$150. These basic bikes will get you started on the thrill of cycling, but very cheap bikes can be hard to adjust, hard to maintain and easy to break.

• **A better bike** will cost around $350-$550. The increased price will give you much more than three times the quality; for example, you will get a much better saddle, alloy rims and a better-quality frame. The bike will be more pleasurable to ride and will probably go longer between services.

• **A quality bike** can cost from $800-$1000. These bikes cost twice as much but there is twice as much quality; the bike will probably be lighter, have a more reliable drive train, a good frame, lighter wheels and good brakes. A quality bike will feel noticeably different to ride and will give you reliable service and riding pleasure for a long time.

• **A top-quality bike** can easily cost over $1000 but at this level the price jumps become bigger than the quality jumps. In other words, a $3000 machine will probably be better than a $1000 bike but not three times better. In this price-bracket you are also starting to pay for exclusivity, innovation, fashion and cachet, all of which can add to the price without adding to the quality. Competition riders will be interested in these more expensive bikes as the expensive features help them shave a few seconds off their time.

Most cyclists climb these quality steps one at a time, starting with the basic bike, and trading up when they become aware of the limitations of the bike they have. Beginner cyclists would be unwise to spend $1000, as they would be spending more than they need to get a good bike, and would be

paying for features and characteristics that they might not ever want.

Obviously, how much you spend will depend on how much you earn and what other financial commitments you have, but it will also depend on how much cycling you do. One good way to help fix the budget for your new bike is to estimate the hours you'll spend in the saddle. The longer you spend in the saddle, the more you will want comfort, efficiency and safety and the more it will be worth paying for those benefits. You could, for example, allow yourself $10 for each hour you spend in the saddle in your bicycle's first year. If you go riding with the kids on average for a couple of hours once a month - that is 24 hours riding a year, then you could put $240 towards a new bike. If you are riding to work for twenty minutes, three times a week, or over 100 hours a year, you could think of spending $1000 on a bike. If you are going on a nine-day holiday ride and will be in the saddle for seven hours each day, you could spend $600. A triathlete who completes 200 hours of training during the racing season could spend $2000.

Although price alone will not guarantee quality, you're much more likely to get some quality if you can leave the bargain-basement bikes behind. If your bike budget comes out at around $200, it might be worth looking for a second-hand bike or taking the old treadly down to the bike shop to see what they can do about reviving it. If you are wavering between two price categories, I suggest you emphasise quality. In the end if you want to sell the bike, you will find that a higher-quality bike is easier to sell.

Don't forget that extras (see Chapter

11) could double the cost of a basic bike. At least allow in your budget for the essentials, such as a good helmet and lock.

SECOND-HAND BIKES

There is no reason why you should always buy a new bike. Second-hand bikes are often good value. The ideal purchase is a quality bike that the owner has replaced with a better model. The worst second-hand buy is a cheap bike that wasn't great when it was new.

The main disadvantage of buying second-hand is that it can take a long time to find what you want. This time should probably be included in your estimate of cost. The quickest way to find a good second-hand bike is to go to a specialist shop. There is a good chance that they will have some used bikes for sale and they will be able to comment on the bike's quality and tell you what sort of condition it is in.

Bikes can be found at jumble sales, garage sales, street markets and on the noticeboards at universities and colleges. But it could take you a long time to find the right bike this way and so most people look in the classified advertisements in the newspaper or one of those papers specialising in second-hand sales. Bike magazines also carry classified ads.

SIFTING THE CLASSIFIEDS

When you scan the ads look first for the correct-sized frame (Chapter 9). Make a short-list of bikes with your frame size, and then ring up each owner before deciding which of your short-list you want to visit. Get as much significant information as you can over the phone. Ask about the five main characteristics discussed in Chapter 8: the frame, the wheels, the gears, the riding position and the brakes. Confirm the price. After that you can worry about things like colour.

Unfortunately the classified ads are often a mine of useless information. Sellers often try to describe the bike by telling you the maker and model name. This shorthand works for motor sellers - 'XC Falcon' or 'Honda VF 1000 R' give you a clear idea of what is for sale - but pushbikes are so varied that this sort of information is nearly useless.

Most bikes combine a frame from one factory with components from one of a number of component manufacturers. Generally components will match the frame for quality and age. Theoretically, if you know the component manufacturer's product history, you can get a good idea of how old the bike is and what sort of quality it was when it was first sold. (The Shimano company courteously supplied this book with the product history for their components and it is given in Appendix 3. This will help you judge second-hand Shimano-equipped bikes.)

IS IT A LEMON?

Eventually your persistence will pay off and you will find yourself standing in front of a bike that looks the goods and is the right price. It is important to confirm that the bike is structurally sound: that the frame and forks are not damaged. If the bike is basically sound but not in top condition, don't worry too much: most things can be fixed or replaced when you get the bike serviced. If you can get the seller to agree, take the second-hand bike to the local bike shop for a quote on getting the bike roadworthy and use this in your negotiations about price.

The problem you don't want to buy is a bent or broken frame or forks. These problems can also usually be fixed but the price is much higher. Bent forks could cost $100 to straighten out.

- **To check if a bike has bent forks or frame**:

– Ride the bike. A bike with a straight frame and forks should run true. If the bike swerves all over the place like something from the Fruit Fly Circus, something is wrong.

– Run alongside the bike holding only the saddle. Again, the bike should roll in a straight line. It is dangerous to do this test by riding no-hands.

– Ride the bike through some water onto a dry surface. See if the rear tyre mark runs in the same track as the front tyre mark when the bike is going straight ahead.

– Your eye is also a reasonable guide. Look at the bike from head on, and from the rear, to check that it is straight.

– To check for frame distortion, run your finger around the down tube and top tube where they meet the head tube. If you can feel a bulge or crinkled paint, the frame might have distorted. Sometimes on a bent frame you can see a crack, especially near where the tubes meet each other.

- **To measure frame and fork alignment**:

– Fork. Take off the front wheel (see Chapter 14) and drop a plumb line through the centre of the fork crown (see Chapter 2). The blades of the forks should be equidistant from the centre.

– Frame. To check for side-to-side frame distortion, run a piece of string from the back axle round the top of the

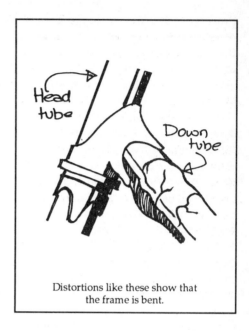

Distortions like these show that the frame is bent.

head tube and back to the other back axle. The seat tube should be the same distance from the string on each side.

GET A RECEIPT
Finally, when the deal is done, make sure you get a written receipt when you buy a second-hand bike. It should say something like:
31 February 1999. I have sold such and such bicycle [and here you could use the frame number, or you could use the name and colour] *to Alfred Deakin for $5500 which I have received.*
[Signed] *Henry Parkes.*

The receipt proves that you have paid the seller and the bike is yours. If the bike has been stolen, the receipt can help protect you from being charged as a receiver of stolen goods.

SELLING YOUR BIKE
When you come to sell a bike, the easiest way is to ask a bike shop if they will sell it for a commission. This

process can take months or just a few days. The bike shop will help you set the price; they will also want it high so that their commission is higher. They will advise you whether it is worth doing any work on it before you sell.

If you are selling – or buying – a bike by advertisment, make sure the important information is there: frame size, wheel size, number of gears, riding position (which you could describe by the type of handlebars) and braking system. Useful ads, for example, would contain something like the following information:

- *50 cm diamond frame, 65 cm wheels, knobby tyres, 18 speed, flat bars, cantilever brakes . . .*
- *45 cm mixte frame, 68 cm wheels, 12 speed, drop bars, centrepull brakes . . .*
- *52 cm diamond frame, 700c wheels, tubulars, 12 speed, sidepull brakes . . .*
- *BMX , 50 cm wheels, one speed, back pedal brake only . . .*

You could then add other information such as special features, extra bits, brand names, mechanical condition and the colour.

Chapter 11

ACCESSORIES AND NECESSITIES

New bicycles are badly equipped. Like cars, they come with brakes and somewhere to sit but, unlike cars, you will need to pay extra for basic safety-gear such as lights and a mirror, not to mention a pump and some way of carrying luggage. Here is a short-list of the most necessary 'accessories':

- Helmet
- Mirror
- U-lock
- Lights, front and rear
- Be-seen gear
- Bell
- Rack and luggage-carrying gear
- Pump
- Mudguards
- Computer (useful for speed and distance)

 Your cycling wardrobe should include, besides tops and bottoms: firm-soled shoes, gloves and wet-weather gear. (See 'Cycle clothing' below.)

BIKE ACCESSORIES

HELMET

These days helmets are compulsory in Australia but for the last ten years or more, ever since they started to make wearable helmets, it has been stupid to ride a bike without one. The doctors who lobbied for the compulsory-helmet law estimated that three-quarters of cyclist fatalities could be avoided and severe head injury reduced if riders wore helmets.

 Your helmet must fit your head and be buckled on securely if it is to do its job.

 Make sure the shell fits snugly on your head. Buckle the helmet up and then try to pull it forward over your eyes or wobble it from side to side. If the helmet wobbles a lot, or you can pull it forward, try another size. If the shell is uncomfortably tight, try another size. The adjustable pads inside helmets are for comfort rather than changing size. Sometimes one brand of helmet will suit your head better than another. Try a few different brands until you find the best fit.

• Make sure the helmet is done up securely. A good helmet will have two straps on each side that meet at a strap-holder under your ear. The helmet should then buckle up under your jaw. Every so often you will need to adjust the straps so that the strap-holder sits in the right place and the chin strap is tight enough. Loose straps or an undone buckle could allow the helmet to move just when you most need it.

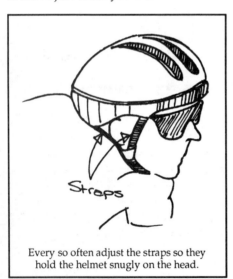

Every so often adjust the straps so they hold the helmet snugly on the head.

• Your helmet should be lightweight and have good ventilation.

• Add to your visibility on the road by getting one in a bright colour such as yellow or white. But don't hesitate to buy a black helmet if it means that you or your child will feel less daggy wearing it: a helmet of any colour that you wear is better than one you leave at home.

• Helmets can lose their ability to protect your head. Many hours of ultra-violet light will weaken your helmet. Helmets are designed to survive only one big thump: if you drop your helmet onto hard surfaces, you can reduce its effectiveness. Always treat your helmet gently: put it down the right way up so it will not roll and crash onto the floor; do not dump heavy things on top of it. I prefer the kind of helmet with a hard outer shell as it is more durable. Every two years, or more frequently if it is worn a lot, change your helmet for a new one.

LIGHTS AND BEING SEEN

One day, perhaps, new bikes will be sold complete with an easy-to-use, reliable, lighting system. At present, however, your new bike will not be legal for night-time riding unless you add a white front light and a red rear light. If you ride at night, dusk or dawn, you must use lights. If youngsters are delivering newspapers early in the morning, for example, it is most important that they have a good lighting system.

Front and rear lights

Out in the country, and away from cars and street lights, use your front light to see where you are going. Aim your front light so that the pool of light hits the ground some distance in front of your wheels. But if you are riding in traffic, the main purpose of your front light is to let other people on the road know you are there. Cyclists fear being hit from the back but but front-on collisions are more common. For this reason aim your front light at the eye level of the car drivers.

Your rear light is also there to let

other road users know that you are there. Brake lights on cars these days are now fitted much higher so that they can be seen and, for the same reason, you should fit your rear light as high as possible. Ideally the rear light should stay on whether you are stopped or moving. I strongly recommend flashing, red tail-lights, which are visible from a long way away. You might want to fit two.

Bulbs and lenses
I'd recommend a light with a bright halogen bulb, because these are brighter than standard bulbs. The shape of the light reflector behind the bulb can vary from product to product and so can the lens. Some lights throw a beam of light rather like water shooting out of a hose: most of it goes straight ahead and some sprays to the side. Other lights are more like a watering can spraying light all around. Ideally you want a light with a good straight beam that also sprays a bit to the side for the cars coming from the left and right. Your local bike organisation should be able to recommend a particular brand of light.

Powering the lights
• **Battery**. If you are an occasional night-rider then battery lights are probably the go. They are usually a bit cheaper than a dynamo system. Some battery lights bolt onto your bike but most are a temporary fit with a clip or strap. Strap-on lights are attractive to people who like to keep their bike looking swish or need to do a night-time training ride but don't want to carry the lights during a competition. Battery tail-lights are also good because they remain illuminated even when you come to a stop.

Unfortunately, battery lights need a lot of remembering: to bring them with you so you don't get stuck without lights, to take them off so they don't get pinched, to buy new batteries if they are getting low and to carry a back-up set or recharge renewable ones.

• **Dynamo**. Dynamo lights are usually more expensive than battery lights but they can't be forgotten and, for regular night-time riders, they will be much cheaper than throw-away batteries. But they do have problems:
– You have to pedal to turn the

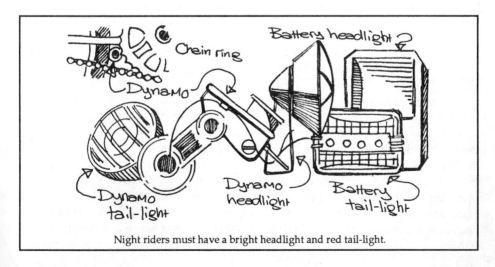

Night riders must have a bright headlight and red tail-light.

dynamo as well as the wheels, which means pedalling is harder work. The hardest to pedal is the old-fashioned bottle-shaped dynamo which runs on the sidewall of the tyre. The barrel-type dynamo, which runs on the tread of the tyre, takes less pedal power and is less likely to get in the spokes. The most convenient and free-running dynamos are – or rather were, since they are rare – the hub-dynamos built into the wheel, but you have to pedal this dynamo all the time.

– Power output from dynamos is variable. The lights get dimmer as you slow down and go out completely when you come to a stop. Some barrel dynamos tend to slip when the tyre tread is wet and stop providing power to the lights. Few dynamos have a voltage regulator and, so if you get up a good speed, they can blow out your light globes.

• **Other possible power sources**. You don't have to be Albert Einstein to work out that the best sort of light would combine a dynamo and a battery. Unfortunately dynamos with a battery back-up cost an arm and a leg to buy. Electrical hobbyists could put one together for you. A cheaper and less complex, do-it-yourself solution is to fit your bicycle with a permanent, rechargeable battery. Electrical hobby shops sell rechargeable batteries about the size of a paperback book that will run two six-volt lights for three hours. You will need to connect up a switch for the lights and a recharger socket to refill the battery. This system costs a bit more than a dynamo, requires a bit of soldering and does mean you have to carry around a one-kilo battery. But it does give you an easy-to-use, reliable lighting system.

BE-SEEN GEAR
If you are riding on the roads, it is a good idea to wear something that is bright during the day and reflective for night riding. There are a number of safety shirts, jackets, sashes and vests available from bike shops and industrial safety shops.

If you are a daytime-only rider you could use a bright T-shirt or fluorescent cycling shirt. Orange or yellow are the best colours for daytime. Other fluorescent colours, like green, work well and white is okay.

Regular night-time riders should get some back-up for their lights. Your lights will mean that motorists will notice something in the darkness; then you want them to recognise that 'thing' as a cyclist. Define your shape with reflective material. It would help if there were a standard vest that all cyclists wore. Some bright daytime vests come with night-time strips of reflective material and so will do double duty. The best night-time-only gear is made either of the yellow material that firefighters use or the silver used by the police. If your riding position has you leaning right forward, then a bum-flap of reflective material might be better than a vest or sash. You can buy ready-made reflective gear such as sashes, trouser clips and wrist bands; and you can get cloth or tape which will sew on to clothing, bags and backpacks. Some night riders add reflective tape or stickers to their helmet and to the bike.

Once you have lights and some visibility gear that makes you recognisably a cyclist, consider fitting top-quality reflectors. Unfortunately the reflectors that come with new bikes have little value.

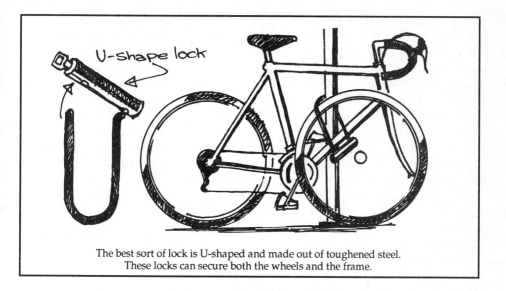

The best sort of lock is U-shaped and made out of toughened steel.
These locks can secure both the wheels and the frame.

MIRROR

If you are riding around town, you need a mirror (see Chapter 5). Without a mirror a cyclist has the biggest blind-spot of any road user: a full 180 degrees behind your shoulders. You can buy mirrors that fit onto straight handlebars, drop bars or even your helmet.

LOCK IT OR LOSE IT

Thousands of bikes are stolen each year in Australia, especially new ones. But most bikes that are stolen were not locked up, so if you lock your bike you have gone a long way to protecting it.

Your bike is most likely to get pinched from your house; from the front yard, back yard or from an unlocked shed. If your bike is inside the house or locked up in the garage or shed, it should be reasonably safe. If you are leaving it outside, lock it to the balcony, patio rail or fence.

A cheap simple lock will protect your bike for a short period. But the longer you leave your bike, the better the lock you need. If you have a valuable bike or you are parking it where it is likely to get knocked off, you will also need a good lock.

A U-shaped lock made out of toughened steel is the best sort of lock. These locks weigh about a kilogram but will hold out against any everyday tool like bolt-cutters, hacksaws or pliers. Be wary of cheap U-locks that have copied the shape but have not bothered to toughen the steel. U-locks are so good that you should be careful not to lose your key. Make sure you put the spare in a safe place.

Where to lock up

When you are locking up in town, look for somewhere with lots of passers-by and, if it is night-time, try to park in the light of a street light. Make sure the baddies can't get your bike by lifting it up and over the pole, or by breaking the tree you have locked it to. Don't annoy people by parking your bike in everyone's way.

Moveable bits left on your bike, like

pumps and battery lights, could well disappear by the time you get back. Take them with you. If you have a quick-release front wheel and you are leaving your bike for a long time, you might want to take off the front wheel and put the lock through the back wheel, frame and front wheel.

After the Great Bike Robbery

If your bike is stolen, there is no chance of getting it back unless you know its frame number as well as details such as colour, maker's name and the size of the wheels.

Each bike frame has a unique number, like the engine number on a car, stamped on the drop-out of the rear axle or underneath the crank axle.

Bicycle-user groups, service clubs and the police organise bike-registration days and engrave another number onto the bike. This extra number could also help to trace your bike and might deter thieves. If you have reported your bike stolen and know these numbers, then you have a chance of getting it back. Without this information it is a lost cause. One quick way to keep a record of the other features is to take a photo of the bike.

Insurance companies hate covering bicycles for theft because they get pinched so often and so easily. Some companies will sell you an add-on policy to the contents insurance on your house to cover theft away from home. Don't assume your insurance covers theft: check when you buy or renew a policy that it covers your bike. You might need to shop around to get cover at a reasonable price. Your travel insurance might cover the theft if the bike was pinched from you on holiday.

BICYCLE BELL

State road laws say you must have a warning device like a bicycle bell or horn. This is an old law from the days before cars came with air conditioning, stereos and sound proofing. These days a bell is useless for warning cars. But they are very useful for warning pedestrians on a bike path, especially because the ringing bell is a distinctive bicycle sound. Use your bell from a fair distance away: walkers can get quite a shock if a bike bell goes off suddenly just behind them.

CARRYING A LOAD

Bicycles are usually sold without any way of carrying things. Many cyclists wear a small backpack but if you put a lot of weight on your back you will raise the centre of gravity and make the bike unstable. You can also damage your back. Where possible let the bike carry the weight.

All loads

Anything you carry will affect your balance and cornering so make sure the load is:

- **tied down tight**, so no part of it can creep out and wrap itself around the spokes and gears, bringing you to a sudden stop. Securing the load will also stop it shifting while you are cornering.
- **down low rather than up high**. Putting weight up high raises the centre of gravity and increases the instability of the bike. The advantage of panniers is that the load is moved down towards the wheel axle.
- **balanced.** Any load must be balanced over each side, or you will have trouble riding in a straight line and could lose control of the bike in a corner.

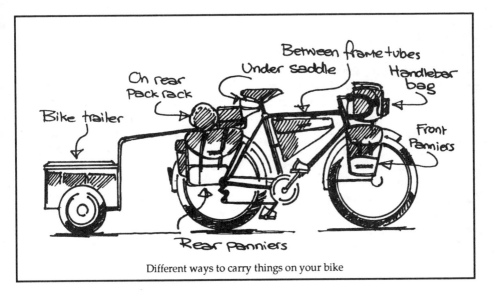

Different ways to carry things on your bike

• **at the front rather than the rear**. If possible, carry heavier weights at the front. What with you in the saddle, bicycles already have more than enough weight on the back wheel. Panniers alongside the front axle have a double benefit: they move the weight down and to the front.

Six places to carry a load

• **Rear rack**. A convenient place to carry things is on a rack above the back wheel. A good rear rack has two arms and two legs: one leg on each side bolts onto the frame near the rear axle and one arm on each side bolts onto each seat stay. Cheaper racks have two legs but only one arm. With regular, heavy use the single arm can weaken and break.

Rear racks are both high up and at the back, and therefore not ideal for heavy things. On a bike holiday you would put something light like your sleeping bag on the rear rack. For round-town riding is possible to get bags, baskets and lockable boxes to go on top of the rack. (Chapter 6 talks

about child seats on the rear rack.)

• **Rear-wheel panniers** are the most popular way to carry loads as they are usually large, at a convenient height and detach easily. For a small load you can ride with just one pannier, but any substantial load should be spread evenly between the two panniers so that the bike is balanced.

The extra weight of rear-wheel panniers will make the bike harder to handle and can contribute to spoke failure in the rear wheel. A bike with heavily loaded rear panniers will also be hard to lean against a single post. A good tip is to lean the bags rather than the frame against the post.

• **Handlebar bags and baskets** are very convenient for carrying a few things back from the milk bar. I especially like the look of the old-fashioned cane handlebar-baskets. Touring cyclists often use a handlebar bag for cameras, purses, sunscreen and sunglasses. You can get a similar sized bag, called a saddle-bag, that hangs behind the saddle.

Things can bounce out of an open-top basket and, because the handlebars are up high, bags and baskets are really only good for light things. Posties do put a heavy load in a front basket but steering these bikes is quite difficult.

- **Front panniers** are mainly used by long-distance tourists. Because the weight is down low at the front, these bags actually make the bike more stable, though less manoeuvrable. A load shared between front and rear panniers takes some of the stress off the rear wheel. The disadvantage of front panniers is that you have to bend a long way to get things out of the bags.

- **Between the frame tubes**. There is a spot between your knees that can be used for carrying a few things. This space is usually reserved for thin things like water bottles, fuel bottles, pumps and locks. You can get, or make, a triangular pannier that hooks on between the frame tubes. In some countries cyclists use a narrow pair of saddlebags that hang over the top tube. The top tube is also a good place to strap long, thin things like a cardboard poster roll or cricket bat.

- **Trailer.** Probably the best way to move heavy or bulky stuff by bike is with a trailer, as it leaves the bike's balance and cornering performance untouched. Some trailers are just a large, plastic crate on billy-cart wheels. These are good for carrying groceries over short distances and cost less than $200. You can find stronger and more sophisticated trailers with larger spoked wheels which will carry camping equipment or tools but these are more expensive.

There are also trailers specially designed for carrying children.

PUMP

Valves

Before you buy a pump for your bike you need to work out what sort of valves your bike has. There are two common possibilities:

- **Schraeder (or car valve)**. Most bikes now have the same valves as cars. These valves are strong enough to hold twice the pressure you will ever need in a bike tyre. They are also convenient as they can be pumped up with a bike pump, a car foot pump, a 240-volt compressor or a service-station air hose. (Be careful if you do use a service-station air hose: the gauge will probably be inaccurate and the compressor will be powerful enough to blow the tube apart.) I recommend fitting all your family bikes with Schraeder valves.

- **Presta (or racing valve)**. These valves were developed for racing tubular tyres but some ordinary bikes come with them. They can be pumped up only with a bike pump. It is not worth using these valves unless your competition bike runs on tubulars and you want to swap to another set of wheels for training. In this case it makes sense to standardise on Presta valves.

- **Woods (or bicycle valve)**. If your bike was bought some time ago it might still have these valves. They can be pumped up only with a bike pump.

Bike pumps

There are three common types of pump. They will all work on your tyres but you must have the correct connection.

- **Cheap hand-pump**. These are cheap and portable. The pump-valve connection is a flexible hose that must be matched to suit the valve. These pumps are hard work and you will not

Most bikes have Schraeder valves, like cars; others have Presta or, occasionally, Woods valves.

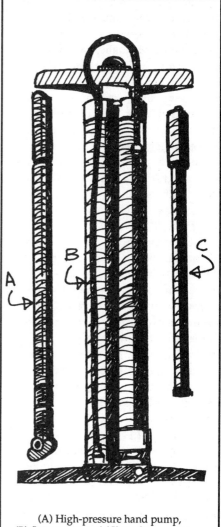

(A) High-pressure hand pump, (B) floor pump and (C) medium-pressure hand pump

be able to pump your tyre up hard. They are really only good for on-the-road repairs.

• **High-pressure hand-pump**. These portable pumps are still hard work but will pump the tyres to a higher pressure. The end of the pump fits over the valve and sometimes can be locked onto the valve. Sometimes the whole pump has to be changed to match the valve but most can have the end adapted to suit Schraeder or Presta valves.

• **Floor pump**. More expensive floor pumps are the easiest to use and usually come with an accurate pressure gauge and a connection that can be swapped to suit Schraeder or Presta valves. If you are cycling regularly, it is well worth getting a floor pump. Floor pumps can't be carried on the bike.

(See Chapter 13 for details of how to pump up your tyres.)

MUDGUARDS

Mudguards are a good idea for regular riders in rainy conditions. If you don't ride when it is raining, you don't need them, but when you ride a bike without mudguards in a light shower you get drenched by the front wheel, and the rear wheel flicks a wide muddy stripe up your back. Mudguards get leaned against things, bumped into things and generally bashed around so, when you are buying, look for mudguards that can twist and recover their shape and are not likely to chip. Some plastic ones are bendy but do chip; some metal ones resist chipping but, once bent, they stay bent. Metal mudguards are very good at rattling. Good-quality mudguards cost more but will take much longer to deteriorate.

Not every bike needs mudguards. Competition bikes don't carry them because they increase air pressure. Off-road riders don't use mudguards because on a muddy track they become mud collectors and bring the bike to a clogged, sticky halt.

COMPUTER

Bicycle 'computers' do a lot more than tell you the speed you are going. They all have different features - some will tell you your altitude! - but most can tell you current speed, fastest speed so far, current distance, total distance so far, the time, and the time since you started. These features can be a lot of help on a long-distance ride. Athletes use the computers that count heartbeat and pedal cadence.

CYCLE CLOTHING

Cynics would say that special cycle clothing is just tradition and fashion but there are some sound principles of efficiency, safety and comfort in cycle clothing. The following items are worth considering if your rides go longer than half an hour:

SHOES

If you were to buy only one bit of cycling wear, I would suggest cycling shoes, as they offer efficiency and comfort. In a good cycling shoe the sole will be hard and stiff, possibly with a steel shaft running inside it, so that all of your foot contributes to the pedalling action and no push is lost through a soft

sole. Some shoes go one step further and lock onto the pedals, either with toe-clips or a click system like a ski-binding system. Chapters 7 and 10 have more on this.

Of your everyday shoes, some will be better for cycling than others. Next time you are in a bike shop pick up one of the display cycling-shoes and feel the stiffness and hardness of the sole. That will help you choose the best of your shoes to ride in. Running shoes, for example, don't make great riding shoes as they are designed to be bendy and spongy.

Stiff-soled cycling shoes offer efficiency and comfort.

GLOVES

Cycling gloves make the handlebars more comfortable and give you something to wipe the sweat away with. Cycling gloves have also saved many a grazed palm during a fall.

– Warm-weather cycling-gloves have no fingers, padded palms and an open back for ventilation.

– Ordinary gloves are okay for cycling in cold weather but will wear out quickly on the palms or between the thumb and first finger.

– Cold-weather cycling gloves look like normal gloves but with padding on the palms, and some have extra insulation on the backs.

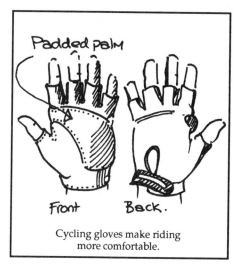

Padded palm

Front   Back.

Cycling gloves make riding
more comfortable.

BOTTOMS

Ordinary trousers are not great for
cycling. Jeans especially will soon
become uncomfortable on a longer ride
as they have a little bump of cloth
where four seams meet, right between
you and the saddle.

Lycra cycling-shorts offer three
benefits:

• They are tailored so that the seams
do not rub while you sit on the saddle.

• Cycling shorts have a chamois
leather or terry-towelling patch around
the crotch which reduces skin chafing
as your thighs go up and down. Like
the Scots and their kilts, racers wear
their cycling shorts without underwear.
If you are going to wear underwear
with your cycling shorts, make sure
you are not importing a bumpy seam.

• Cycling shorts cling aerodynamic-
ally to your body (as discussed in
Chapter 7).

Traditional cycling shorts have no
pockets, so if you don't like wearing
lycra and want pockets, it is possible to
get baggier 'touring' shorts which come
with a few pockets and the first two
features of cycling shorts.

For winter riding you can get
woollen or synthetic cycling longs that
combine the three features of cycling
shorts and look not unlike a sturdy pair
of long-johns. In really cold weather
you can add cycling leg-warmers over
the top. You could wear ordinary
long-johns underneath your cycling
longs but make sure the seams of the
long-johns won't rub. Ordinary long
trousers will get caught in your chain
unless you stop them flapping with
bicycle clips or straps. The
unembarrassable put their trousers in
their socks, some riders buy
ready-made clips or cloth bands, others
swear by loops of dressmaking elastic.

Long dresses and the like are not
much good for riding either as they can
easily get caught in the spokes,
although some bikes still have a mesh
dress-protector over the back wheel. A
handy bit of apparel for women riders
is a split skirt that looks like a skirt but
is actually a baggy pair of shorts.

TOPS

Ordinary shirts and jumpers are okay
for riding but the traditional cycling
jumper offers the advantages of pockets
on the back that won't get in the way
when you bend over, and a close, more
aerodynamic, fit.

Summer cycling tops are made with
short sleeves and of light materials but,
even so, they can be uncomfortable for
an ordinary rider, as they are
close-fitting. An ordinary, cotton
long-sleeved shirt with a collar can be
more comfortable and give better
ultraviolet protection.

Winter cycling tops are unbeatable as
they have extra-long sleeves that will
cover your wrists when you reach
forward to the handlebars and an extra-

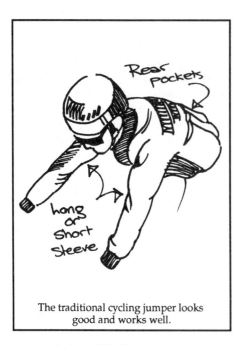

Rear pockets

long or short sleeve

The traditional cycling jumper looks
good and works well.

long back that will still overlap your
longs when you when you lean forward.
They are usually made of wool that will
go in the washing machine.

SUNGLASSES

An ordinary pair of sunglasses will
keep bugs, dirt, wind and ultraviolet
radiation out of your eyes. It is possible
to buy exotic cycling sunglasses that
cost ten times the price of a basic pair.

WET-WEATHER GEAR

Wet weather is a problem on a bike. It is
very difficult to ride a bike in the rain
and stay dry. Your feet, for example, are
always going to get wet. It is possible to
keep your top half out of the rain by
wearing a raincoat, but then you will
sweat. Some people prefer to get wet
from the rain than be drenched in sweat.

There is nothing wrong with this
plan as long as you don't get cold. The
speed of riding along makes a cold day
colder, especially if you are wet. So on a
cold, wet, long ride it is better to wear a
coat and sweat, while you might choose
to get wet if you are ten minutes from
home. Some people try to solve the
dilemma by buying a coat made from
materials like Goretex which claims to
allow your sweat to escape.

Traditionally, round-town cyclists
wore Dracula capes with a big hood,
but these capes make it hard to see
traffic and the air pressure makes it
harder to pedal. Capes are also likely to
get caught in the chain or spokes. An
ordinary raincoat such as you might
wear on a bushwalk is much better.

Better still are the special cycling
coats which are cut with long sleeves
and a long back like a cycling jumper,
often have venting panels under the
arm, can be tucked tight around your
wrists and come in highly visible
colours. Unfortunately these coats are
expensive.

Chapter 12

CYCLING FITNESS

Bike riding is an excellent way to improve your fitness and therefore your general health. In fact many people start riding bikes to get a bit of exercise.

Some of these people are easing themselves into exercise. You might be considering exercise as a way to support a new eating program or a decision to stop smoking. You might be recovering from illness, or trying to avoid it: cardiovascular disease is the number one killer disease in Australia and regular exercise will lower your chances of getting it. You might want to get into exercise just to feel better: psychologists always recommend exercise as part of a stress-relief program. Or you might just want to tone up a bit. Bike riding is a great way to get this sort of exercise. Unlike some other huff-and-puff activities, it offers an easy start: easier, in fact, than walking. If you can manage a brisk ten-minute walk, you are unlikely to have any problem getting out on the bike for an hour. A ride along the bike

path with some friends will not only be a good social occasion, it will also be doing you good.

Some people who already exercise regularly also ride. A bike ride provides a change in exercise routine. Runners and swimmers often find they have become triathletes. Joggers find it gives their bodies a rest from pounding the pavements. Nor does bike riding twist and bump you like tennis or basketball. If you are pregnant, you will be able to exercise for more of your pregnancy on a bike than you will, for example, on the aerobics floor. Steady cycling also puts less strain on the heart than the stop-and-sprint sports like football. In fact, cycling can be so gentle on the body that professional sports-people recovering from an injury often use a bike as part of their recuperation program.

You can also save time in a busy schedule by doubling up exercise with riding to work or down to the shops. If you are reasonably fit already, bike fitness offers you recreational possibilities, such as the annual organised bike rides, that will refresh your spirit and strengthen your heart.

If you are interested in the bicycle as a way to get ultimately fit, you have come to the right place. Champion cyclists are only one or two spots away from the top of the athletic fitness table.

But your bike is not just a mobile exercise machine and many riders, including me, get into cycling despite rather than because of the need for exercise. If you are in this category, this chapter will explain how your bicycle motor - that's you! - works, how you can help it to do its job and how you can help it to pedal for longer, or go further or faster, or travel the same distance for less effort.

TWO KEY POINTS ABOUT BICYCLE FITNESS

• **Bike riding is more about the rider than the machine.** It is not the bike that decides how fast you ride or how far you can go: it is your fitness. Even if you have the best bike that money can buy, a cycling champion could beat you on the bike my Mum uses to go up to the shops (as soon as we fix the puncture in the back tyre). In other words, you can make an ordinary bike go better by being fitter. Riders, especially competition cyclists, do get increased performance from improved bikes but the advantage might be only a quarter of a second at the end of a race.

• **Bike riding is more about lung power than muscle power**. There is trade-off in human performance between speed and strength against endurance; for example, a champion sprinter can run fast for 100 metres whereas a champion marathon runner

does not go nearly as fast but covers 40 km. Some sports emphasise one part of the trade-off over another. Weight-lifting for example, emphasises strength: cycling, on the other hand, emphasises endurance.

You can concentrate on muscle power on a bike, but you won't go very far. A champion short-distance sprint cyclist can pedal up a surge of energy of about 1300 watts for 10 seconds – about the maximum power you can generate on a bike. Sprinters who compete in events that last around five minutes generate only 400 watts. No-one who rides for more than ten minutes can maintain this energy output because the human body runs out of power.

On the other hand, if you ride without trying to generate maximum power, you can go a long way. A Tour-de-France cyclist generates around 300 watts, less than a third of the energy of a champion sprint cyclist. But Tour-de-France riders can travel 200 km at 40 kph, day after day for nearly a month.

There are two morals to this story. First, if you ride for more than ten minutes, you will have to start emphasising endurance rather than strength. Second, ordinary bike riding will not give you thunder thighs like a weightlifter.

ENDURANCE RATHER THAN STRENGTH

A bicycle is powered by your muscles which are contracted by chemical reactions. These reactions can be either aerobic (including oxygen) or anaerobic (without oxygen).

AEROBIC REACTIONS

An aerobic reaction takes place in this way. You take a deep breath, filling your lungs with oxygen and other gases. The surface of your lungs absorbs the oxygen and passes it into the blood. The oxygenated blood is pumped by the heart to the muscle cells. The muscle cells mix the oxygen with the large fuel tank of carbohydrates, fats, and proteins stored in your body, and this sets off a chemical reaction which contracts the muscle. (This reaction gives off heat which is why you get hot when you exercise.) As long as there are fats and oxygen to burn, the muscle cells will keeping banging away contracting the muscles. This is how the Tour-de-France rider keeps going.

ANAEROBIC REACTIONS

If muscles are called upon to work harder than the oxygen supply in the blood can match (as is the case in intense effort such as a sprint), an anaerobic reaction occurs. The cells fire the chemical reaction using a supply of ready-to-go energy called glycogen. But the anaerobic fuel tank is small and it burns up quickly. That is why all-out running, swimming or cycling sprints are over in a dozen seconds. It can then take a day or so of rest to replenish the store of glycogen in the muscles. The anaerobic reaction also leaves behind a waste product called lactic acid. The bloodstream can carry away a small amount of lactic acid but during an all-out sprint there is no time for the blood to remove the wastes and the sprinter quickly becomes fatigued.

Cycling can improve the body's ability to perform both types of chemical reaction but the main improvement that comes from cycling is in aerobic fitness.

GETTING FITTER

Your aerobic fitness is determined by how much oxygen you can get to your muscles. Some people's physiology can convert more of the oxygen delivered by the bloodstream than others'. Your age also makes a difference: at forty years your potential aerobic fitness begins to fall (at eighty it is half what it is at twenty). But most people are so below their fitness potential that it is possible to get fitter as you get older, even though your potential fitness is falling.

So how can you – at any age – increase the amount of oxygen delivered to your muscles? You already have more lung surface than you need and the proportion of oxygen deliverable is fixed by your physiology. What you can increase is the total amount of oxygen delivered to your muscles. The main way is to strengthen your heart so that it pumps more blood at each stroke.

The rate of delivery of oxygen to the muscle cells is known as an athlete's 'VO$_2$ max' (the volume (V) of millilitres of oxygen (O$_2$) consumed per kilogram each minute). A top athlete's VO$_2$ max might be 80 or even 90, while a non-athlete's might be only 30.

A higher VO$_2$ max indicates that you have:

- more blood in your system,
- more oxygen-carrying red blood cells,
- more capillaries sending blood to each muscle,
- your heart is pumping more blood at each stroke.

This increased fitness will not only be of benefit in the saddle but gives spin-off benefits such as more puff in other sports or lower risk of heart disease.

HOW TO GET FITTER

Your VO_2 max will improve if you make your heart run a bit harder than normal. It is important not to push your oxygen-delivery system so hard that you risk damaging it. On the other hand, if you don't push it hard enough, you won't improve its performance.

Fortunately, there is a formula that will help you work out how hard is hard enough, in heartbeats each minute. (It is a rough formula and, because our physiologies are all different, you must get a doctor's advice before starting any exercise program.) The maximum capability of your heart can be estimated by subtracting your age from the top rate of 220 beats a minute, because your fitness potential reduces as you get older. So the maximum number of pulse beats your heart is capable of each minute is 200 if you are twenty, while it is 180 for a forty-year-old.

But you don't exercise at this maximum. A very fit person might train at 85 per cent of the maximum: around 170 beats each minute for a twenty-year-old. But this is dangerously high for someone starting to exercise. Beginners are encouraged to go at about 60-65 per cent of top speed. A twenty-year-old getting back into exercise should not take her heart rate above 130 beats each minute. Chart A on p. 133 gives you an idea of the training rate for people who are getting back into exercise. Confirm this estimate with your doctor.

You can check that you are pumping at the right rate by taking your pulse half way through the ride and then again at the end. You can find your pulse in your wrist or neck. Counting heart beats is so fundamental to fitness that many competition cyclists ride with a pulse meter to make sure their hearts are running at a good rate all the time.

This pulse-based training rate is used in all aerobic sports, such as running and swimming. Aerobic capacity you develop while cycling can be used in another sport and vice versa. Triathletes, for example, will be improving their VO_2 max whether they are swimming or running or cycling.

The muscular development you achieve in other sports is not so easily exploitable for cycling. Sports science suggests that each sport and each action in a sport develops muscles in a unique way. So even when sports appear to use similar muscles, (cross-country skiing and cycling are often put together in this way), there is little shared muscular benefit. In other words you will build up your cycling muscles only by cycling.

AN EXERCISE PROGRAM

How much exercise do you need to stay fit? The National Heart Foundation says that there is no minimum amount of exercise that will produce cardiovascular protection, as the 'more activity that is performed, the better the protection'. They do, however, suggest that above a certain level of exercise the benefits start to reduce. The Foundation hopes to increase the number of people in the community doing this 'useful-maximum' amount of exercise – equivalent, in our case, to cycling 15 km five days a week. (V M Jelinek, *The medical benefits of regular exercise.* NHF 1990)

Although there is no healthy minimum of exercise, we know that there is a minimum that produces an aerobic benefit. As a rule of thumb, if

CHART A: TRAINING CHART

Maximum heartbeats each minute	Age in years	Maximum heartbeat minus age	Heartbeats multiplied by 0.65 for gentle training
220	20	200	130
	25	195	126
	30	190	123
	35	185	120
	40	180	117
	45	175	113
	50	170	110
	55	165	107
	60	160	104
	65	155	100

CHART B: BUILDING UP TO THREE HALF-HOUR SESSIONS PER WEEK

Week	Day 1	Day 3	Day 5
	Minutes		
1	10	10	10
2	10	15	15
3	15	15	20
4	20	20	25
5	25	30	30
6	30	30	30

you do some rhythmic activity, such as cycling, for at least half an hour three to five times a week for a couple of months, you will improve your aerobic fitness.

If you have not been doing much exercise, you should build up slowly to the three half-hour sessions. Let's start at the beginning and assume that you can ride for 10 minutes. (It is usually better to measure cycle training by time, not distance, as you could ride quite a distance with little fitness benefit because of downhills and tailwinds.) As Chart B shows, it could take you six weeks to get up to riding regularly for half-an-hour. Your program could be something like this.

PREPARING FOR A LONGER BIKE RIDE

If you are going on a longer ride you have organised yourself, you can train as you ride, starting with short easy days and slowly building up the time you spend in the saddle. But you can't use this system on an organised bicycle ride where the distances are set beforehand. You might be faced with around 70-80 km to ride, for example, which could take you seven hours in the saddle. If you have done no physical preparation, this could be a difficult and unhappy task.

A careful person might follow a training schedule over three months something like the one shown in Chart C. This program has a slow build-up based on the half-hour training time; it is regular – at least three sessions each week – and it incorporates rest. By the time the long ride comes around, all your muscles, including those in your back and neck, will be used to the hours in the saddle.

If you can't follow this program, you should still follow the basic principles: try to do a little on a few days rather than a lot on one. It is better to do three half-hour sessions than a single one-and-half-hour ride on the weekend. There is no harm in making any of the regular rides longer. You might even want to go out for a seven-hour ride just to reassure yourself that you can do it.

TRAINING PROGRAM FOR A LONGER BIKE RIDE

Week	Weekend ride	Weekday ride	Weekday ride
		Hours	
1	1	0.5	0.5
2	1	0.5	0.5
3	1	0.5	0.5
4	2	0.5	0.5
5	2	1.0	0.5
6	2	1.0	0.5
7	2	1.0	0.5
8	2	1.0	0.5
9	3	1.0	1.0
10	3	1.0	1.0
11	3	1.0	1.0
12	3	1.0	1.0

A SENSIBLE EXERCISE PROGRAM
I think the tomato would be a good get-fit symbol. People look after tomatoes: they let them grow a little every day, feed and water them well, support the branches as they grow and don't become impatient because it takes a couple of months to get fruit off the plant. Any sound exercise program - whether for top athletes or those beginning to exercise - should follow the same principles:

• **A gradual, regular approach** allows your muscles, especially the heart, time to adapt. It also allows your ligaments and cartilages time to adapt to new workloads.

• **Rest** allows the body to recuperate. Six training sessions a week is the maximum, even for top athletes.

• **Stretching** before exercise prepares your body, and helps protect it from injury. Stretching after exercise helps the body recover. (Massage is also a good idea but not immediately after exercise.) Cyclists obviously need to stretch leg muscles but shouldn't forget their arms, back and neck.

There is a bit of a knack to stretching muscles. When you start to stretch a muscle it will contract to protect itself. Start stretching by putting a gentle tension on the muscle and holding that position until the feeling of tension fades. This will take around half a minute. Then you can gently change the position to add a little bit more stretch and hold that for another thirty seconds. The second half of the stretch is what will prepare your muscles for action. Bouncing the taut muscle is wrong, pain is wrong and doing a tug-of-war with your body is wrong.

• **Gentle start, gentle finish**. A gentle start to your ride will help your muscles ease into their work. Don't jump on your bike and set off at top speed. Don't end with a sprint either. A few minutes gentle pedalling will help the bloodstream carry away the waste products generated by your exercise.

• **No strain**. It is unnecessary to strain your muscles like a weight-lifter or to make your chest heave when you are riding. Cyclists should follow the runners' rule of thumb: you should be able to talk to the person running, or in our case cycling, alongside you.

• **Good days and bad days**. Some days you will ride like the wind and others you will feel awful. If you are having a good day, enjoy it. If not, don't despair, the good days will return.

• **Don't compete when you are exercising**. Some people will ride faster than you or further; others will ride slower and stop sooner. Neither fact tells you about your own fitness: keep going at your pace.

• **Recovery.** If you do overdo your exercise and hurt your body, you will probably recover. The training principles of rest and gentle improvement apply to recovery as well. Look on your recuperation as a chance to practise the approach that will prevent more injuries in the future.

HOW TO FUEL YOUR FITNESS
I wish I could quote university tests that show that large quantities of beer or pastries are the most efficient fuel for cycling. Unfortunately they aren't. The best fuel for cycling is a balanced diet, which means eating the right amount of the right sort of food.

THE RIGHT AMOUNT OF FUEL
The daily amount of fuel humans need is pretty well worked out. Men need

more fuel than women, bigger people need more fuel than smaller people, younger people need more fuel than older people and active people need more fuel than sedentary people. On average each day a 60-kg woman under 35 years old needs around 8500 kilojoules (2050 calories). A 75-kg man under 35 needs 12 120 kJ each day. You need less fuel as you get older: those over 35 need from 500 to 1000 kJ less fuel each day.

Extra exercise such as cycling will increase the amount of fuel you need, but it doesn't increase it that much. A one-hour ride would increase your fuel requirements by 600 kJ, equivalent to a stubbie of beer. Even if you were a Tour-de-France cyclist riding hard in the saddle for seven hours a day you would still only eat around 33 000 kJ each day, or about three times your daily allowance. So you can see that ordinary cycling will not allow you to stuff your face and still stay thin. If you are keen to get to your optimum weight, or don't want to gain weight, then it is probably worth drawing up a food budget, getting to know the value of different foods with one of those little calorie-counter books and eating within your fuel budget.

THE RIGHT SORT OF FUEL

There are no special foods you need to eat for cycling. Lawrence of Arabia, when he was at university at the turn of the century, cycled through France studying fortresses. He says that each day he ate 'bread, two pints of milk and fruit to taste, especially peaches (three for a penny) and apricots (six for a penny)'; with a more solid meal in the evening. His diet is not far off the balanced diet recommended by nutritionists.

The Australian Nutrition Foundation (ANF) promotes a pyramid concept as a guide to achieving that balance. The idea is that you should eat more of the big bits at the base of the pyramid – fruit, vegetables and cereals (complex carbohydrates) – and less of the little bits at the apex – sugar and fats.

You can measure your diet-and-exercise balance by weighing yourself. If your weight is steady, then the fuel balance and quantity is probably right for the exercise you do.

Complex carbohydrates: most of your diet

Complex carbohydrates include bread, pasta, rice, potatoes, lentils, beans, broccoli, spinach, apples and bananas. The body digests these foods and turns them into glycogen. Around 50-80 per cent of your diet should come from this section of the pyramid.

If you eat a steady supply of fruit and vegetables, raw or lightly cooked, you will also get both the vitamins and minerals that you need. You always need a steady supply of the vitamin alphabet, especially since some of them, such as B and C, can't be stored. That might incline you to use vitamin pills, but then you might overload the supplies of those vitamins that the body can store, which is not a good idea. Too much of some vitamins can also reduce glycogen in the muscles.

Vegetables and fruit also supply important minerals such as salt, iron, potassium and magnesium. These days bananas are popular with racers who want to replace the potassium they have sweated out, but potatoes would work just as well.

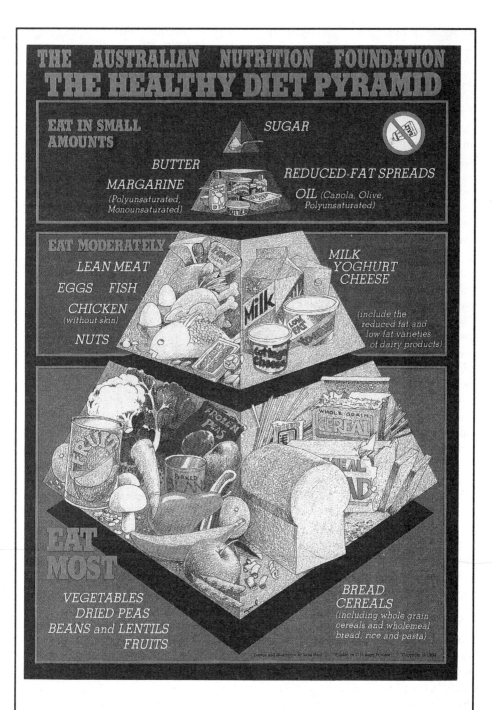

Protein: up to a fifth of your diet and dairy products: a third of your diet

The body also needs dairy products and proteins for body-building and energy generation. The foods in the middle section of the pyramid include milk, cheese and yoghurt, eggs and lean meat, including skinless chicken and fish. (Many dairy products now come in low-fat versions.) Nuts, olives and avocados are also included in this section. If there are not enough dairy products and carbohydrate in your fuel intake, the body will burn proteins instead of using them to build or repair tissue.

You don't need to eat large lumps of protein-filled steak to fuel your cycling. Normal adults only need 0.8 grams of protein per kilogram of body-weight each day. You will not get double the benefit if you eat twice as much protein as you need. If you are a keen athlete and a keen vegetarian, you will, however, have to do some research on how you can make sure enough proteins get through to the muscle cells. Lean red meat will also provide iron which will help women who lack iron.

Added sugars, fats and oils (small amounts)

At the top of the pyramid are the fats and the added sugars like honey, glucose, cane sugar and so on. The ANF says you should only eat small amounts of these foods.

You don't need extra sugar to fuel your cycling. You might think that eating straight sugar would help fill the muscle cells with glycogen. But if you do that, the body spots the glycogen surge and sends out insulin to calm everything down which will actually lower your blood sugar. So straight sugars will make you worse off. Steer clear of sugar-filled soft drinks. Sometimes towards the end of a long race professional racers might drink a fluid containing a little glucose but a can of soft drink, which contains about eight level teaspoons of sugar, would set off an insulin reaction. The electrolyte solutions that are used by sports people can also set off an insulin reaction as they often contain glucose. If you do use them, make sure they are well diluted. The ANF suggests that you steer clear of simple sugars in the hour before competition. Large quantities of sugars in the stomach or intestine pull fluid into the gut and can bring on nausea, stomach cramps and vomiting.

TIMING YOUR DIGESTION

It is not a good idea to try to cycle while digesting a heavy meal. Combining physical activity and digestion is hard work for the body, as digestion drags blood away from the muscles. One way to avoid this problem is not to eat things that are hard to digest, including fibre, processed meats, nuts and dried fruit. Another way of avoiding having to digest a big meal is to eat small amounts of food more frequently. It is even more important to keep up a steady intake of small amounts of food if you are out for a long ride. Eating before you are hungry will ensure you have a steady supply of energy.

An easy-to-digest breakfast could be breakfast cereal, low-fat milk and canned fruit, followed by toast with jam or Vegemite. Lunch could be a salad roll, fresh fruit with low fat yoghurt or a low-fat milk shake with a real banana. On the night before a strenuous ride, a cyclist is looking for a meal that matches the pyramid structure, composed mostly of fruit, vegetables and complex carbo-hydrates, with a small amount of protein, low in fat, sugar and salt. One example could be a spaghetti dish with a light sauce and a salad or vegetables on the side; dessert could be low-fat icecream with fruit. Alcohol, they say, should be avoided 48 hours before a strenuous ride as it dehydrates your body. You should drink plenty of water if you are drinking alcohol.

WATER

This is a case of saving the most important thing till last. Three-quarters of the human body is water. A lot of our body systems run on water: the system that carries oxygen and nutrients around the body is based on water and so is the waste-removal system. Just on an ordinary day we need to take in three litres of water to keep these systems going. Dehydrating drinks – like alcohol, coffee, cola and tea – further increase your need for water.

Exercise increases your need to drink. You could easily lose six litres a day on a longer ride. On a warm day you are likely to lose a litre an hour – more if you have a big build. If you don't replace the lost fluid, you won't cycle as well. A three-per-cent drop in your fluid level is enough to cause a loss of performance.

The trick is to keep up a steady intake of small amounts of water. Always take more water than you think you will need on a ride and keep drink-ing it often in small amounts. 'Drink before you are thirsty' is an old cycling maxim. But that is not the whole story:

• Start drinking the night before you go riding.

• Drink before you begin to ride; maybe around half a litre about a quarter of an hour before you start.

• Drink while you are riding; a couple of mouthfuls every 15 minutes is a good rule of thumb. On a long ride you should aim to finish a bottle each hour.

• Keep drinking when you have stopped riding.

The colour of your urine during the day will give you an indication if you are dehydrated: dark coloured urine is a signal that you need to take in more water. If you get behind on your drinking it can take a day for your fluid level to rise back to normal.

As cyclists have realised the importance of water, the drink bottles that fit on the bike frame have almost doubled in size from the old pint to the new litre bottles. This is a good thing. Get a big bottle, fit two bottle cages on your bike, carry another bottle in your luggage, ride behind a council water truck, but make sure you have enough water. To borrow a phrase from the Victorian road-safety people: 'If you don't drink and ride, you are a bloody idiot'.

PREPARING FOR COMPETITION

PREPARING YOUR BODY

To some extent, all these suggestions for an exercise program also apply to a training program for a competition cyclist. The only difference is that competition cyclists or their coaches will monitor everything more closely.

A beginner competitor is unlikely to have the knowledge of someone trained in the appropriate scientific disciplines or experience in the sport, let alone the tactical cunning of a coach. For those reasons many riders look to a club or individual coach for advice.

With or without a coach, you will need to work on three things: riding technique, diet and a training program.

• **Riding technique** includes things like learning a fast pedal-cadence, selecting the optimum gear (both discussed in Chapter 7), finding the best position on the bike (discussed in Chapter 9), and developing good breathing. It also includes the particular skills of your event (which we look at in Chapter 13): for example, BMX riders practise their starts, Madison riders practise the sling and road racers practise sharing the lead in the bunch.

• **Diet**. Keen competition cyclists will keep a diet diary of the food they eat and regularly weigh themselves to make sure they are not gaining or losing weight.

• **Training program**. You will need a training diary to record your progress, measuring equipment like scales and heartbeat counters and probably some form of rollers – a stand that allows you to pedal your bike in the garage or living room – that will allow you to train without leaving home.

Most importantly, you will need to develop a daily schedule that will take you through the phases of basic fitness, controlled improvement, and peaking. For example, competition cyclists start the first half of the year with a rest period of one to two months when they ride but don't train much. A road racer, for example, will then spend the balance of the first half-year in preparation. In the half year devoted to competition, a top athlete might spend 24 hours in the saddle each week.

Keen competitors are liable to make the mistake of overtraining, so the daily schedule will also ensure you get adequate rest. Peak performance, for example, does not follow the day after a massive training effort but occurs when the body has recovered from that extreme effort and has made precautionary preparations in case you do it again. Adequate rest also avoids overuse injury and ensures riders give their bodies time to adjust. Fitness does not improve steadily, like riding up an escalator, but goes up in steps: each new level of performance has to be consolidated before the body is ready to go up to the next step.

Quality not quantity is now the emphasis in cycle training so your daily schedule will give you a clear goal, such as to build strength, to extend endurance or to increase speed. That goal will be described by a time and pulse rate.

Your training will also strike a balance between aerobic and anaerobic improvement. Developing your aerobic capacity by riding at the maximum rate you can sustain is useful in all events, even sprints. Developing anaerobic capacity is a complex subject and it is worth hunting out a good coach or taking a lot of care in setting your own training program. Some coaches recommend 'intervals' such as pure, anaerobic, 40-second bursts, or a semi-sprint that is largely anaerobic for about four minutes. These interval sessions can build your speed and power but they have to be carefully matched to your current fitness level. Some coaches don't like intervals at all.

Weights and cross training
Your training program might include some weight-training or cross- training.

Generally cyclists don't rely heavily on weight-training, as riding is so much about aerobic fitness. There can be some benefit in weight-training for areas like the stomach and back muscles. You are likely to use light weights and fast repetitions.

Cyclists do not do a lot of cross-training specifically to improve their cycling, but any aerobic exercise will contribute to cycling performance and another form of exercise can be a refreshing change. The triathlete, of course, always cross-trains and always in sequence because the events are always in the same order: starting in the water and ending with the run. Usually triathletes train in pairs of events such as swim-cycle or cycle-run. There's not much point, when you think about it, in always running with fresh legs, as they won't be fresh on the day. The trick in triathlons, rather like aerobic training, is to tackle each event at a speed that won't spoil you for the next leg of the event but that will be fast enough to be competitive with your last time or those other people out in front.

The next chapter gives more information on competition cycling.

Chapter 13

COMPETITION CYCLING

THE EXCITEMENT OF COMPETITION

Bicycle racing is a great sport, whether you are in the saddle or on the sidelines. For the competitor there is a huge variety of events, like sprints and relays that emphasise athletic achievement to competitions that emphasise handling and daring. This variety means you can find a bicycle event to suit your interest or abilities.

There are many routes into cycle racing; it doesn't matter how old you are or how little bicycle experience you have. I think of one friend who used to do a bit of running and a bit of swimming and this got him interested in triathlons but he hadn't ridden a bike since he was a teenager. He bought himself a bike, set himself a serious training program and started to improve his technique. Within a year he had finished a race near the front and won his first points in competition – not bad for someone who wasn't a bike rider. Even if he has to give up running

as he gets older, he won't have to give up cycle racing. Cyclists keep riding and keep competing decades after other people have had to give up their sport.

Another route into cycle racing is through a school program. Some of the schools near my home, helped by the local cycling club, run afternoon programs down at the velodrome, which give kids the basics on track racing and an introduction to club members. It is not only track racing that benefits from this sort of program. Someone I know who started in one of these programs has left the smooth surface of the track and does most of his competition on a mountain bike, belting along dirt tracks.

For spectators, cycle racing has a lot to offer. Right from the early days there have been Australian champions and cycling heroes, from Frank White's transcontinental ride from Perth to Rockhampton and back in 1898, to Hubert Opperman's win in the 1931 Paris-Brest-Paris to Kathy Watt's gold medal at the 1992 Barcelona Olympics and Danny Clarke's worldwide domination of track racing. That tradition is carried on today and you have probably seen some of the modern breed during the Olympics. But cycling in Australia seems to have lost spectator involvement over the years. Bike racing used to be as popular as one-day cricket. Each city had a number of spectator velodromes and crowds filled big stadiums like the Melbourne Cricket Ground for the Austral Wheel Race. In the thirties a hospital in Melbourne tried hard to get rid of the velodrome across the road because the noise of the crowd was upsetting the patients. You don't hear many complaints about noisy cycling crowds these days. Yet in Europe people still crowd into the velodromes and line the roads for the big races. The excitement is still there for the spectator: don't miss out.

I hope that this chapter will either entice you down to your local cycling club to ride, to help out or just to watch. I have included, in Appendix 6, a list of contact addresses for each type of racing, which will allow you to participate or watch events. At the very least I hope you will turn on the television when the bikes are racing and support this proud sport with its heroes and villains, its brave achievements and funny stories.

CYCLING EVENTS

There are four factors common to every bicycle competition: sprinting, tests of handling skill, tests of climbing speed and tests of physical endurance. On this foundation, cycling builds an exciting array of competitions on all sorts of different bikes and on every sort of surface, from the polished wood of an indoor velodrome, through the asphalt or stone cobbles of a road to the mud and dust of an off-road course. The well-established cycling events are heading towards their second century, but, all the time, new events such as 'off-road enduros' and triathlons are being developed for the pleasure of participants and spectators. Broadly, there are three main groups of cycle events: road racing, track racing and off-road racing.

ROAD RACING

Stage races: a team on the road

To most people 'a bicycle race' means a long road race such as the Tour de France or the SunTour in Australia. These races go for a number of days, with each day's *stage* ending in a different town. A similar race that only lasts one day is usually called a *classic*. The oldest cycle race in the world is the Melbourne to Warrnambool classic over 260 km. If you do it in under six hours you are in with a chance of winning.

An ideal course for a road race will have enough flat riding to let the powerful riders do well, enough hills to give the good climbers a chance of winning, and a number of sprints throughout each day to encourage the sprinters. Riders usually compete in a team composed of climbers and sprinters and back-up riders, called *domestiques* in French, who are there not to win but to help put the stars in a good position. Individuals and teams then compete for the various prizes. At the end of each day there is the winner of the stage. At the end of the race there is a prize for the best sprinter, for the best climber and for the best team. Then there is the overall winner: the rider who has completed the course in the fastest time. Sometimes, after over 3 000 km of racing, the overall winner can squeak in by less than ten seconds.

The excitement in stage racing has as much to do with tactics as athletic performance and most tactics are based on air pressure (see Chapter 7). Most of the effort in cycling is in overcoming air pressure and if you can ride in the pressure shadow behind another rider, you can travel faster, or ride with less effort at the same speed. In a stage race the riders travel in groups or *bunches* and *draft* each other by pedalling behind a lead rider. The formation is called a *paceline* if the riders are in line astern or an *echelon* if there is a sidewind and the riders are almost side by side. After a short time out in front, the lead rider drops to the back of the bunch and another takes the lead. In this way a bunch can go faster than a solo rider, which explains why the average speed for the Tour de France is around 40 km an hour, a lot faster than individuals could maintain on their own.

Much of the tactical interest in a stage race is in the forming and reforming of these cooperative bunches. Sometimes a bunch will break away from the main group of riders or *peleton* and try to get to the finish line first. There will be struggles by the teams to get one of their riders into the escaping bunch, and battles in the bunch to cut out unwanted members. This sort of racing is not for the faint-hearted, as the tactical moves are sometimes enforced with a clash of bikes, elbows or fists. Often the peleton will catch the break-away riders, but sometimes even solo riders can sustain their lead to the end. Of course if Team A riders are in the breakaway, Team A riders in the peleton

won't be trying too hard to help the main bunch catch them. They could ride slowly at the front of the main bunch trying to hold back the pursuit or just coast along in the main bunch saving themselves to go out in front if their team-mates are caught. But if the race leader has broken away, all the teams will cooperate to haul him back.

Much of the athletic contest in the race is in climbing and sprinting. Usually the first few riders over each summit earn a time bonus or points towards the overall climber prize. The best climbers are light, wiry, little riders. If the climb is long enough, a good climber can sometimes get far enough in front of the peleton to win the stage. On the hill it helps to look tough. If the climber can look fresh while all around are in pain, and can keep up a steady pace, that can help discourage other riders and help open up a useful lead.

Sometimes the domestiques will spend their energy helping a senior team-mate up the hill. Team B might not have the best climber but their moderate climber could be a fearless downhill rider and, by taking the downhill side at high speeds, could catch the champion climber.

Throughout each stage there are markers that earn the first few riders who pass a time bonus or points towards an overall sprint prize. Each stage ends with the sprint for the line. Poor sprinters try to raise the pace of the bunch or peleton a long way before the line, hoping to make the faster short-distance sprinters burn up their energy too early. Other riders make their 'jump' a kilometre from the line and try to hold out the chasing bunch. Good sprinters might jump with 500 m to go. Still others will save a winning blast for the last few metres. To win a stage, riders have to know their individual abilities and the potential of the other riders around them.

The great riders in stage races are those who can ride strongly, climb hard, sprint fast and have a good team to back them up. Saying Joe Bloggs won the Tour de France is a bit like saying Don Bradman won the Ashes: the star has to do well, but you can be sure that he didn't do it alone.

Time trials, endurance rides and triathlons: individuals on the road

There are some team time-trial events but most time trials are tests for the individual. Stage races usually include a couple of individual time trials to bring the champions out from behind the team and see what they can do on their own. The time trial is a test of speed and endurance, usually over a 40-km course. The time trial does not involve race tactics so there are no sprints or surges. Rather, it is a measure of concentration and cycling technique. Each rider tries to maintain a steady effort over the whole course to keep the bike going as fast as possible, ideally crossing the line with no energy to spare. Drafting is not allowed, so the bike and rider are streamlined as much as possible under the rules. Some riders use custom time-trial bikes, which lower the front of the frame and run on disc wheels.

Some time trials emphasise speed over endurance. Popular examples include: the one-kilometre Olympic event in which Russell Mockridge won Olympic gold for Australia at Helsinki in 1952, where the record is just over a minute; the one-hour ride against the clock, where you would have to go

further than 50 km to get into the record books; and the 100-km event which takes just over two hours.

Other time trials emphasise endurance. A famous example is the Race Across America, the cycling equivalent of the Sydney-to-Melbourne running marathon. It takes the riders just over a week to ride from the west coast of the United States to the east and they don't get much sleep. A more sedate endurance time trial is the Paris-Brest-Paris which takes riders 1200 km out to the western coast of France and back. Those who are back in Paris in under four days get an official certificate of completion.

The most popular time trials are part of the increasingly popular triathlons. If you have a refreshing swim before riding your time trial, and then run home, you have completed a triathlon. The race began in Hawaii in the late seventies, as winners of the local endurance swim, bike race and marathon argued over who was doing the most work. The first triathlon put these three events together: a 6.4-km swim, a 180-km time trial and a full 42-km marathon. These days triathlons come in all sizes. The longest standard event is the same as the original but with a 3.8-km swim. Aussie Michellie Jones was World Champion in 1992. The prototype Olympic event is a 1.5-km swim, a 40-km time trial and a 10-km run. The sprint or short triathlon has grown in popularity as an entry-level event. These short courses are usually a 500-m swim, 20-km time trial and a 5-km run.

Criteriums: a track race on the road

The shortest road races are called *criteriums*. These sprinting and cornering races are held on city streets and often staged as part of a festival. About 50 laps of a 2-km circuit would be a long criterium; some are as short as 40 km. The last day of the Tour de France is traditionally a criterium around the streets of Paris. The winner of a criterium can be the first rider over the line or the person who collects the most points for lap wins on designated laps. If a rider – or better still a bunch of riders – can get out in front and help each other with drafting and go fast through uncongested corners, they can wrap up a criterium.

Criteriums are popular with spectators who can get close to the action as tightly bunched riders corner fast and sprint down the straights. Best of all you can see the riders lap a short course a number of times. Racers like these events because they are good money-earners. For example, anyone who wins a stage in the Tour de France will be paid to be the draw-card at criteriums all around Europe in the weeks after the Tour.

TRACK RACING

Perhaps only in Europe can you get an idea today of what track racing used to be like in Australia. In Europe the six-day races, with top cyclists whirling around the tight circuit close to the excited spectators, still draw big crowds.

Track bikes are quite distinctive: they have no brakes, only one gear (which the coach and rider pick before the race) and no freewheel, so the rider can't back-pedal. The frames are built with steep angles and sensitive steering. The fragile wheels have the minimum number of spokes and the lightest tyres with the highest pressure.

There are a number of popular track

events: the matched sprint, the time trial, the points race and the six-day event.

In the matched sprint two riders jockey for position over 800 m, and then race the clock and each other over the last 200 m. The best tactic is to start from behind, draft the other rider and then jump past, but some riders can hold out in front through sheer power. Many riders contest these paired competitions in heats that lead to a final between the top two. In Japan, cyclists and punters make a lot of money from keirin – matched sprints between ten riders – a sort of cycling Melbourne Cup.

Time trials are run on the track as well. Some time trials are as short as one kilometre: a one-minute sustained burst of power. Then there is the *pursuit*, a time trial where two riders start on opposite sides of the track. The riders race against the clock but can use the other rider like an electric rabbit in a greyhound race as motivation to go faster. Kathy Watt picked up her silver medal at Barcelona in 1992 in the 3 000-m pursuit. In a *team pursuit* it is the time of the third team member over the line that is counted. You might remember the Aussie 4000-m-pursuit team winning gold in Los Angeles in 1984 against the United States on their high-tech bikes.

When the criterium principle is applied to the track, it is called a *points race*. Designated laps score points and the rider with the most points at the end is the winner. Sometimes in a points race the last few riders are eliminated on designated laps which creates excitement at both at the front and the back of the pack.

If you stir all the track events in together, you get the *six-day race*. These are usually held in winter and road riders join in. Two riders form a team in six-day racing, one riding and the other resting. The rested rider then pedals up to their partner who grabs their hand and slingshots them back to racing speed. Over six days there are all sorts of competitions and each team competes with a dozen other teams for points, in sprints and surviving eliminations, to win the prize. A short race of this type in the United States is called a *Madison*. The Tasmanian, Danny Clark, has won over 50 six-day races in Europe.

OFF-ROAD RACING

Bicycle racing 'off-road' on rough courses or hilly tracks has boomed in the last ten years. Off-road riding requires all the fitness and technique of on-road riding but the rough surfaces put more emphasis on bike handling. There are more spills in off-road riding and some would say more thrills. There is a great range of competitions open to hobby riders, serious amateurs, professional racers and even children.

BMX and Freestyle

Bicycle Motor Cross or BMX was the first of the off-road cycle competitions to boom in Australia. The early high tide of popularity has receded leaving an established amateur and professional sport across the world. Our world champion in 1992 was Tanya Burrows. In a BMX race, riders (some as young as four years old) start in a long line behind a mechanical starting gate, like racehorses. When the gate drops, the riders surge around a banked and humped dirt track to the finish. The dirt circuits are sculpted into jumps, table tops, banked turns and camel humps

Freestyling is gymnastics on a bike.

and it takes a lot of skill to ride the track at top speed on your own, let alone in a crush of riders. The tangle of bikes all trying to get best position and the riders flying through the air make an exciting race for spectators. Like Grand Prix motor racing, gaining a front position just after the start is worth a lot in this race. The BMX bike is an off-road track bike. It has a single gear and straight front forks which give sensitive steering. It has a strengthened frame to cope with the jumps, and knobby tyres to grip the dirt.

A BMX club is a great place for your child to make friends and improve bicycle handling skills.

Riders who had developed the handling skills needed to fly off jumps and negotiate the other obstacles of a BMX track created another sport called *Freestyle*. Advanced Freestylers use a metal wave like a skateboard ramp to ride up and do somersaults, flips and other tricks. Down on the ground freestylers can do front and back wheelstands, all sorts of jumps and can 'surf' their bikes standing on the saddle and handlebars. These bicycle gymnasts can also climb all over a stationary bike rather like acrobats in the circus, handstanding for example, on the handlebars.

Mountain bikes
If BMX is comparable to track racing on dirt then mountain-bike racing is more like road racing on dirt. Early mountain bikes were old clunkers ridden by folk who liked flying down firebreaks in forests. As the bikes evolved, becoming lighter and more sophisticated, mountain biking became a craze that swept the world, and the social afternoons in the bush turned into formal competition. Now hundreds of people all across Australia compete in mountain-bike events. Even city riders find they enjoy the features of the mountain bike: the strong and stable frame with lower centre of gravity and wide, soft tyres.

There are many mountain-bike racing events. In the time-trial descent the rider dodges through poles like a skier. (Ben Munroe won the World Junior World Downhill title for Australia in 1989.) Another event is to ride up an unclimbable hill to see who gets furthest. Other competitions include time trials up a rideable hill and off-road criteriums with a massed start on a 10-to-25-lap up-and-downhill course. Mountain-bike championships often include *enduros* which, like their motorcycle namesake, set riders an obstacle course and a predetermined speed for the circuit. Then there are the

pure handling events or observed trials which test the rider's ability to clamber up and down over rocks and logs. Penalty points are added if you put your foot down during the circuit and the rider with the least points wins.

TRAINING FOR COMPETITION
To read about training to be fit enough for competition, see 'Preparing for competition' in the previous chapter, pp 139-141.

PREPARING AND IMPROVING YOUR BIKE
Proper preparation of your bike can gain or lose you a small but significant advantage in a race. Whatever the quality of your bike, it should be in peak condition before a race. The tyres should be pumped to the right pressure, the bearings running perfectly, the drive train clean and lubricated, the brakes in good nick, and so on. Anything that looks like it might not survive should be replaced. It is silly to drop out because your gear cable broke during the race.

Though the condition of the rider is far more important than the state of the bike, it is possible to improve the performance of the bike by, in order of priority:
- getting some system of locking your feet securely to the pedals;
- improving your aerodynamics, especially if you are time trialling;
- reducing the weight of your machine, especially if you are climbing.

One way to improve your bicycle overall is to buy a high-quality, second-hand racing bike. There is a good chance that a cycle shop that specialises in races will have some good used machines for sale from someone who has upgraded to an even better bike, or changed over to lawn bowls.

As you gradually improve your racing machine you might want to consider having two bikes – one for training and one for race day. This will make it easier to keep your best machine in tiptop condition for race day while the training mule soaks up the belting from your training. If you are training on the road, which most cyclists do whatever their event, then you can fit the training bike out with mudguards for comfort and lights and reflectors for safety. A halfway step to a training bike is to get a more durable set of wheels for your bike and keep the best pair for race day.

WHAT TO WEAR

Apart from the usual cycle clothing discussed in Chapter 11, such as helmets, gloves, glasses and chamois riding shorts, the racer has to consider aerodynamics. The slipperiest cycle clothing is a one-piece suit and a teardrop helmet, but this sort of gear is usually only worn for track events. Otherwise riders tend to wear traditional tight-fitting clothing which is practical as well as aerodynamic. The traditional racing jersey comes with three pockets at the back for food and drink, quite important if you are out on the road for a while. The jersey is usually worn with an undershirt to provide a sliding layer that will protect the skin if the rider falls. Racers often wear cycling shorts with braces or shorts made like bib overalls, with shoulder straps to stop the shorts sliding down. If you are riding a few times a week you will probably need a few sets of gear so you can wear a clean set while the others are in the wash. Riders who spend hours in the saddle are always prone to 'crotch rot' and clean gear is one good way to keep it at bay.

The next problem is staying comfortable in cold weather without rugging up and thus catching too much wind. If you are waiting for a start on a cold day, your riding jumper can be supplemented by a neck scarf or a sleeveless sweater made out of a plastic rubbish bag, both of which are removable when you warm up. Plastic bags as socks can help keep your feet warm in cold weather.

If you are competing in an event that emphasises handling skills and therefore are likely to take a fall, especially on dirt, then it is worth covering up. BMX riders add elbow and knee protection to their all-over suits and mountain-bike riders use knee and shin pads. Don't believe you're too skilful and tough to need protective gear.

Chapter 14

KEEPING YOUR BIKE IN GOOD NICK

Many people find bike maintenance boring. Fortunately a bicycle is such a simple and efficient machine that it will continue to serve you faithfully without a lot of mechanical attention. But a cared-for bike is easier to ride, less likely to let you down and safer. Looked at in that way, maintenance is an important contributor to the thrill of cycling.

This chapter starts with advice on how to avoid maintenance and then takes you through five levels of maintenance jobs, each requiring more mechanical skill, giving you an idea how to do them and whether it is worth attempting them yourself. You might find that maintenance is something you come to enjoy both for itself and for the satisfaction of riding a bike that's running sweetly.

AVOIDING MAINTENANCE
There are two ways to avoid bike maintenance: preventative maintenance and giving the job to your local shop.

PREVENTION
All the best maintenance programs, such as those of the reliable airlines, are based on pre-empting repairs and breakdowns. Here are five ways to practise prevention:
• **Start with a quality bike**. A quality bike will last longer, will be less likely to fail and, when something does go wrong, there is a good chance that it can be repaired easily. Cheap bikes and cheap bike bits break easily, go out of adjustment easily and are hard to repair.
• **Fit reliable parts**. Good-quality components will let your bike go longer between mechanical intervention:

– Thorn-proof inner-tubes, anti-puncture tape and kevlar-belted tyres all dramatically reduce the number of punctures you will get.

– Thick spokes and well-built wheels will resist distortion and breaking.

– Sealed bearings in the hubs, pedals, crank axle and derailleur tension or jockey wheels last longer between servicing and take longer to go out of adjustment.

– Three-speed hub gears will let your drive train last longer.

Your local shop will have other suggestions. You could buy a bike that has these features or fit them to your current bike when the old bit wears out.

• **Renew parts early**. If something penetrates the tyre, consider getting a new tyre rather than just a tube, as un-worn tyres will help prevent punctures. If one brake cable breaks, fit new cables on both brakes. Look on part failure as a chance to upgrade to a longer-lasting part.

• **Service the bike regularly**. Cables will break sooner and chains will wear more quickly if they are not lubricated. Bearings that are not regularly serviced are more likely to fail. A twice-yearly service would inoculate most bikes against going wrong. Once a year is enough for many bikes.

• **Clean your bike**. This gives you a chance to inspect it for little problems that are about to grow into big problems. There is a quick inspection list below for those who hate to clean.

Your reward for all this preparation, expense and attention is that you will reduce the number of repairs your bike will need and you shouldn't be faced with a repair at an inconvenient time, outside, in poor weather and with rudimentary tools.

GET SOMEONE ELSE TO DO IT
Another way to avoid maintenance is to take your bike regularly to a shop for a service. People who have found a reliable bike shop rarely do their own servicing and repairs because a good shop will have: the right tools, the right parts, a proper workstand, a skilled and experienced mechanic. It will also be good value for money. The shop makes a small profit on the bits they fit but if you bought the bits from them and did it yourself, you would pay what they charge you anyway. Your labour, at zero dollars an hour, is cheaper, but you have to include your investment in tools and learning time.

As there isn't a reliable bike shop within easy reach of every home, we need chapters on maintenance in bicycle books.

DOING IT YOURSELF
Poor service from a local shop also motivates people to do their own maintenance, but there are also some positive reasons for doing it yourself:

• It is not difficult. Unless you have four thumbs you will be able to do basic maintenance on your bike.

• It can be satisfying to learn a new skill and to feel the confidence that comes from having done a job yourself.

• You can't lose. If you need to take your bike to the shop, you might as well have a go yourself first. If you stuff it up or can't fix it, you are no worse off.

• You might get it done quicker at home. If there is a long queue at the shop, you might complete the job sooner even if you have to do it a couple of times to get it right.

• Once your skill level is up, you will, on many jobs, be able to do a more thorough job than the shop mechanic, as it is your pride and joy that you are working on.

• You can fix it next time. The knowledge and skills you gain as you learn to fix your bike will be with you wherever you go on the open road, often a long way from a bike shop.

Five levels of maintenance

This chapter looks at maintenance as a series of jobs requiring different levels of mechanical confidence and quantities of tools. Level 1 starts at the shallow end of maintenance, with recognising when something is wrong. Each subsequent level describes a task, lists the tools you need and gives you an idea of how to do the work. At each level the jobs become more difficult, require a larger investment in tools and are more likely to be left to the bike shop. Level 5 is down the deep end and describes things that only a determined few attempt. Unfortunately I can't guarantee that your bike will present you with a series of graded maintenance lessons, starting at 1 and working up; nor will the Level 2 problems be more frequent than those at Level 4. Whatever happens, have a crack at understanding the problem even if you aren't going to fix it yourself this time.

A few hints will help you at every level:

• **Use the right tool**. Using the right tool makes any job easier, but the wrong tool can make an easy job many times harder.

• **Use a systematic approach**. Bicycles are an ordered system. Each part has a right place to be. Don't be afraid to use pen and paper to keep track of what you are doing.

• **Work out the function and purpose of each part**. All the bits are

there for a reason. Often thinking about the purpose of a part will help you complete the repair.

• **Allow lots of time.** If you try to complete the job before friends arrive for tea, you put yourself under pressure and make it hard to be calm while you are trying-and-erring.

• **Treat the parts gently**. Although some effort is needed to deal with things that are tight, by and large maintenance is a gentle, careful activity.

• **Friends will help**. Working with someone else is probably the best way to learn. If you have no friends with cycling knowledge, find a formal course on bicycle maintenance. Contact your local bicycle group or adult education centre (See Appendix 5).

A TRAVELLING TOOL KIT

A number of factors influence how many tools to take on a longer ride:

• How much mechanical know-ledge do you have? Wherever you go, only take tools that you know how to use.

• How long is the ride? On a short ride you might only need puncture-repair tools. On a long ride the bike will have more time to think up something naughty to do.

• How near is a bike shop? If you are riding near bike shops, you might decide to let them solve any problems. If you are riding across the Sahara, you will need to carry quite a few tools and spares.

• How many people are on the ride? A group can share the weight of a comprehensive kit.

• Are you an improviser or an insurer? Some people are improvisers and are prepared to make do when a problem arise; others wear both belt and braces as insurance against their trousers falling down. In the end Murphy sets the rules: improvisers get stuck out in the mulga with an unrideable bike that could be fixed easily if only they had a so-and-so, while others carry a kitchen-sink tool kit that never gets called on.

Before you go
There is a good chance you will never need to use your tool kit if, before you go, you:
- service the bike
- check all spokes
- replace chain and freewheel
- fit new puncture-resistant tyres or thorn-proof tubes
- replace cables or carry spares cut to length
- fit new brake pads

Just enough tools for improvisers
A short general-purpose list might be:
- allen keys, (these sometimes come in a handy Swiss-army-style set with screwdrivers and spoke keys)
- electrical tape
- hand cleaning lotion, (a 35-mm film canister is usually enough)
- pump
- puncture kit (patches, glass paper, glue, pen)
- rag
- screwdriver (some Swiss army knives have screwdrivers as well as scissors and other useful things)
- small adjustable spanner (shifter)
- spare tube
- spoke tightener
- spray lubricant
- tyre levers

And for emergency botch-it repairs:
- pipe clamp (this can replace a

large expandable spanner and can pull cable like a pair of pliers, but they won't cut cable)
- pliers (will both pull cable and chomp through it, pliers can double up as a second spanner but not on big nuts)

A few more tools for insurers:
- chain breaker to shorten chain if the rear derailleur arm breaks
- copper wire (can be easily wound around a bracket that has broken or where a nut has disappeared)
- screwdriver, cross-head and flat blade
- spare bolts and washers, especially for securing your rack
- bearing grease
- crank tool
- chain lubricant
- degreaser
- toothbrush for cleaning

Tools for an expedition:
- correct-size spare spokes (strap them to the chainstays with some electrical tape)
- freewheel remover and spanner to get to spokes on rear wheel right-hand side – the most likely spokes to break
- spare brake pads
- spare tyre
- spare bearings
- hub spanners

LEVEL 1: KNOWING SOMETHING'S WRONG
Learn how to tell when something is wrong even if you aren't going to fix it yourself. If you only ride occasionally, inspect your bike each time you ride. Regular riders should run a quick check of their bike every week or so to make sure it is roadworthy. If you find a problem, get it fixed.

Quick tests

Tools for Level 1
The tools you need are your eyes, ears and fingers. Any crunching, squeaking, clattering or rattling sound indicates something needs attention. As you become more experienced, these tests will be running through your mind each time you get out your bike and as you ride.
  • **Brakes**
  – The pads should grip the wheel after the lever is squeezed only a short distance.
  – You shouldn't be able to squeeze the levers back to touch the bars.
  – The levers should move back and forth easily but be tightly secured to the bars.
  – The cables should move easily and not carry any rust.
  – The pads should have plenty of wear left in them.
  – The shoes should sit fully on the rim when you squeeze the brakes. They should never touch the tyre.
  – The pads shouldn't rub against the wheel when you aren't squeezing the brake levers.
  • **Gears**
  – The gears should work easily and accurately.
  – The bike should not slip out of gear.
  – The chain should not jump off the front or back sprockets.
  – The teeth on the front sprockets should not be worn or chipped.
  – The cables should move easily and not carry any rust.
  • **Tyres**
  – The tyres should be hard and hold their pressure when they are pumped up.

  – They should have no deep cuts.
  – They should have no sign of the fabric under the rubber.
  – The rubber surface should be smooth, not cracked, rough and brittle from age.
  – The valves should be sitting at right angles to the rim.
  • **Spokes**
  – Every spoke should ping like a guitar string when you pluck it.
  • **Wheels**
  – Wheels should spin freely and quietly, taking a long time to stop spinning.
  – They should not wiggle from side to side or hop up and down while they spin.
  – They should be held on tight by the nuts or quick-release lever.
  • **Cranks**
  – Cranks should be on tight. They should not wiggle if you try to lift or push down on them both together.
  – Cranks should turn smoothly without crunching or grinding.
  • **Pedals**
  – Pedals should spin with a flick of the finger.
  • **Headset**
  – When you put on the front brake hard and rock the bike back and forward there should be no movement between the forks and the head tube of the frame.
  – With the front wheel off the ground, the bars should swing easily from side to side.
  • **Chain**
  – It should be lightly lubricated; there should be no rust, or caked-on dirt and old lubricant.
  – You should not be able to lift the chain away from the teeth on the front of the front sprocket.

- **Check for loose components**
- Saddle, handlebars, brakes, mudguards, rack and other accessories should all be fixed tightly to the bike.

LEVEL 2: KEEPING YOUR BIKE GOING

Level 2 is designed to help you keep your bike on the road, or to get it going again if something minor goes wrong. You are likely to have some of the tools you need and the special equipment is not expensive. Nor are the jobs difficult. Most cyclists can have a go at Level 2.

Tools for Level 2
- **Necessary**
- set of spanners or a small shifting spanner
- all-purpose lubricant spray
- biro
- degreaser
- old cloth
- pump
- puncture kit
- screwdriver
- toothbrush
- tyre levers
- **Useful**
- chain bath
- chain lubricant
- tweezers
- work-stand

Pumping up the tyres
See Chapter 11, for more on different valves and pumps.

All cyclists have to pump up their tyres. Even without punctures, tubes slowly leak air, especially when they are old.
- Unscrew the dust cap.
- If you are using Presta valves, unscrew the knurled nut on top.
- Fit the pump connection to the

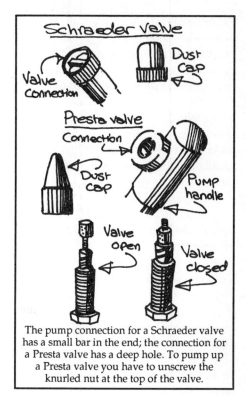

The pump connection for a Schraeder valve has a small bar in the end; the connection for a Presta valve has a deep hole. To pump up a Presta valve you have to unscrew the knurled nut at the top of the valve.

valve.
- The pump connection for Schraeder valves will have a small bar in the end to open the valve.
- The pump connection for Presta valves will look like a deep hole.
- If the pump has a locking lever, move it to the locked position.
- Pump the tyre until, when you pinch the tyre between your finger and thumb, sideways across the tyre or between rim and tread, you cannot squeeze it very much. You can be more accurate with a pressure gauge and match the tube pressure to the recommendation on the side of the tyre. Chapter 8 discusses tyre pressures in more detail.
- Reverse these instructions when the tyre is hard.

Taking a wheel off

It is likely that at some stage you will want to take a wheel off, to put the bike in the boot of a car, for example. The front wheel is the easiest to remove.

Front wheel

If the tyre is pumped up and your brakes are well adjusted, you will be unable to slide the wheel out between them.

- **Release the brakes**.
- Sidepull and centrepull. Look for a brake release lever on the brake lever or down by the brake calipers.
- Cantilever brakes. Unhook the V-shaped wire that runs to each brake pad.
- Cam-action brakes can be temporarily disabled by sliding out the cam that moves the brake arms.
- **Or let off the adjustment on the brakes**. Look for the barrel nut that adjusts the brake cable. Undo the lock nut and wind down the barrel nut until the brakes are far enough apart to let the tyre through. When you put the wheel back on again, make sure that you reset the brakes. (Quick adjustment of brakes is outlined later in this chapter.)

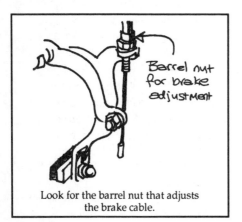

Look for the barrel nut that adjusts the brake cable.

- **Or let the air out of the tyre**.
- Schraeder valves: prod the valve pin in the centre of the valve with a match.
- Presta valves: unscrew the knurled nut and press the valve pin.
- **Release the wheel from the frame**.
- If the wheel is held on by nuts: loosen both nuts with a spanner.
- If the wheel is held on by a quick-release lever, this lever pivots through 180°, locking the axle in place, so undo the lever by swinging it open. If the wheel is still held in the forks, you might need to slack off the nut on the other side of the wheel. When you put the wheel back on, make sure the quick-release lever is on tight. It should begin to get stiff half way through its travel but not so stiff you can't push it right to the closed position. The quick-release lever should point to the rear when closed so something brushing past can't swing it open.

You should feel some resistance when you push the quick-release lever closed, but not so much that you can't push it right to the closed position.

Rear wheel

- **Derailleur bike:**
- Put the chain on the smallest rear sprocket.
- Release the brakes.
- Release the wheel from the frame.
- The derailleur has a pivot in it rather like a leg bent at the knee. Push the derailleur backwards, allowing it to

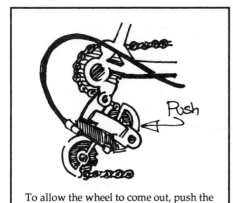

To allow the wheel to come out, push the derailleur backwards, so it bends at the knee.

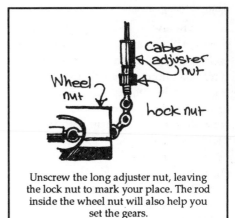

Unscrew the long adjuster nut, leaving the lock nut to mark your place. The rod inside the wheel nut will also help you set the gears.

bend at the knee and straighten.

– Slide the wheel down and forward if it hasn't already fallen out and dropped on your toe.

• **Hub-gear bike:**

– Put the bike into third gear, so the cable is taut but not tight.

– Release the wheel.

– Loosen the lock nut on the the cable adjuster and then screw it back lightly onto the long barrel adjuster.

– Unscrew the adjuster, leaving the lock nut to mark your place, until the cable is disconnected.

When you replace the wheel, screw the adjuster back up again until it reaches the lock nut, tighten the lock nut and your gears should be properly adjusted.

Alternatively you can use the mark inside the right-hand wheel nut to set the gears. See cable adjustment for hub gears later in this chapter.

Changing tyres and tubes

With the wheel off the bike, you can change the tyre and tube. If you are going to the trouble of taking off the tyre and tube it is probably worth fitting new tyres and tubes.

Parts

• New tyre if:

– you are regularly getting punctures.

– you can see the casing of the tyre through the tread.

– it has many cuts and holes in it.

– if the rubber feels rough, stubbly and perished rather than new and smooth.

• New tube if:

– it has many patches.

– it loses pressure easily.

• New rim tape. This tape protects the tube from the rough ends of the spokes.

• Make sure that you buy the correct size for your bike. Tyres and tubes come in an astonishing combination of diameters and circumferences, not to mention tread, colour and cost. Make a note of the numbers on the side of the tyre or take the old tyre into the bike shop to make sure you get the right-size replacement. Check:

– rim diameter,

– width,

– pressure,

– type of valve.

Tools

• **Tyre levers**. These are made of metal or plastic and have a rounded end for scooping up the edge of the tyre, and a hook at the other end to hook onto the spokes. Buy a set of two or three bike tyre levers. Don't use a screwdriver: it will cut up your tube and possibly the tyre.

Removing the tyre and tube

• Take wheel off.

• Let the air out of the tyre, unless it has already done that for you.

• Get the bead or wire hoop of the tyre up and over the rim of the wheel. This is hard as the bead is designed to prevent this in normal use.

– Dig around with the tyre lever until you have got the scoop end under the bead.

– Lever a small amount of bead over the rim.

– Hook the lever to a spoke to hold it in place.

• Use another lever and repeat the last step near the section you have just scooped out. Three of these scoops is usually enough to let you:

• Run your lever behind the bead that is outside the rim and peel the rest of the bead out of the rim.

• Complete the removal of tyre and tube by hand. Schraeder valves push out of the valve hole but Presta and Woods valves have a nut holding them to the rim.

• Remove the rim tape if you are replacing it. Sometimes this tape is cloth, sometimes rubber.

Refitting the tyre and tube

• Fit new rim tape so that the valve hole in the tape is over the valve hole in the rim.

• Prepare the new tube.

– Pump it up until it is tight. This gets the creases out of the tube and will make fitting easier.

– Let out most of the air until the tube can hold its shape but squashes easily.

• Sit one tyre bead inside the rim of the wheel.

• Push the bit of tube with the valve on inside the tyre and insert the valve in the hole in the rim. The valve should sit straight. A valve that's leaning over will be stressed and could fail and then you'll have to do all this again.

• Push the tube inside the tyre, starting from the valve. Make sure the valve stays upright and the tube does not twist. This is easier if there is some air in the tube.

• Seat the other bead of the tyre.

– Starting around the valve, encourage the other bead of the tyre inside the rim with your hands. You should be able to get three-quarters of the second bead on the rim, leaving only ten to twenty centimetres incomplete. The difficult bit will be opposite the valve.

– Push the valve up into the hole and hold it. Check that the bead has settled into place and is not pinching the tube, then let go the valve. Repeat this step to make sure. Again, it helps to have a bit of air in the tube.

– Go back to the section of bead still outside the rim. If you have strong thumbs, keep going and push the rest of the bead in. Award yourself the super-mechanic certificate. Otherwise hook a tyre lever in at one end of the difficult bit and encourage it to pop in centimetre by centimetre. You might need to hold another lever at the other end of the difficult bit to stop it

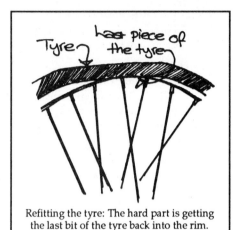

Refitting the tyre: The hard part is getting the last bit of the tyre back into the rim. Use your thumbs to roll it on.

popping out. Don't dig too deep with the levers or you will pinch and puncture the tube. Talcum powder will help the tyre bead slide on the rim. Keep going until the last bit of bead jumps into place.

• Make sure the tyre isn't pinching the tube.

– Put a bit more air into the tube but don't pump it up fully.

– Starting at the valve, push the wall of the tyre in with your thumbs and look into the gap between tyre and rim to see if the tube is caught under the bead. Turn the wheel and inspect another section. Keep going until you have been all the way round both sides. Push the valve in again to make sure it is not caught.

• Pump up the tyre.

Fixing punctures

Punctures nearly always happen on the road and usually at an inconvenient time. A quick way to get going again is to keep a new tube handy and fit it when you get a puncture. Then, at your leisure, you can fix the hole in the other tube.

Parts
– new tube
– glue
– patch

Tools
– glasspaper or scratcher in puncture-kit
– Biro
– a pair of tweezers

Finding the puncture in the tyre

• Take the wheel off the bike.

• Mark the tyre outer with the Biro to show where the valve comes through and the direction of rotation.

• Take the tyre off the rim but leave the tube on the rim.

• Check the tyre.

– Look around the outside of the tyre, squeezing and rolling it between your fingers as if you were rolling a cigarette. Pick out any bits of glass with tweezers.

– Look around the inside of the tyre. Be careful about running your finger around inside the tyre as whatever punctured the tyre could puncture you.

• Remove anything that might have punctured the tube.

• If you are fitting a new tube, you can now remove the tube and follow the steps above in 'Refitting the tyre and tube'.

Finding the puncture in the tube

• Remove the tube from the wheel.

• Locate the hole. There are five common ways to do this:

– If you have located the problem on the tyre, you can use the Biro marks on the tyre to find the corresponding place on the tube. (That's why you need the direction of rotation because a puncture at four o'clock on one side will be at eight o'clock on the other.).

– Roll the tube in your fingers like you did with the tyre.

– Pump up the tube, hold it underwater and look for bubbles. This is also a good way to check for a faulty valve.

– Pump up the tube and listen for escaping air.

– Pump up the tube and feel for escaping air with your fingers.

Whichever method you use, rubbing a bit of spit over the tube will confirm any possible holes.

• Mark the puncture. Whenever you find something that could have caused the puncture, draw a 20-cent-piece-size circle around the hole or an X with long arms that crosses over the hole.

• Check the valve by dunking it underwater or with a bit of spit on the valve. Check around the base of the valve, especially if it has been crooked. If the base of the valve is leaking you will probably have to buy a new tube.

Patching the tube
• Use the glasspaper or scratcher from your puncture kit to make a clean, rough area on the tube for the glue to grip. As soon as you start to scratch around the hole it will be hard to see exactly where the hole is. That is why you made the Biro mark. Make the scratched area bigger than the patch. A quick swab with methylated spirits will remove any grease, but this is not always necessary.

• Take the protective sheet off the patch and spread the glue thinly and evenly over both the patch and tube. Allow the glue to dry competely. This might take five minutes. Thick-and-wet might feel better but thin-even-and-dry works best.

• Place the patch over the hole. Make sure that the hole is in the middle of the patch. Thank heavens for that Biro mark.

• Put the patched tube on a smooth bit of ground, stand on the patch and count to 103. This pressure helps the glue to grip strongly.

• Refit tube and tyre (detailed above).

Hooking the chain back on
Sometimes the chain will come off the front or rear sprockets:

• Use your hands or a screwdriver to lift the chain out of any cracks or crevices it has got into.

• **Derailleur gears:**
– Grab the chain with a bit of cloth and pull the bottom half of the chain towards the front sprocket.

– Hook some links of the chain onto the front sprocket at about five o'clock and turn the pedals backwards. The chain should then drag itself on.

If the chain keeps coming off, you might have to adjust the screws that limit the movement of the derailleur arms (see 'Adjusting Things').

• **Hub gears:**
– Hook some links of the chain onto the front sprocket at about eleven and twelve o'clock and turn the pedals forwards. The chain should drag itself back on.

If the chain keeps coming off, the rear wheel might have slipped forward. In this case, release the axle nuts, pull the wheel back until it is straight and the chain is reasonably taut. Then tighten up the axle nuts again.

Lubrication and cleaning
The moving metal parts on bicycles need frequent applications of small

amounts of lubrication so that they move smoothly and without wearing each other away. Lubrication will also slow down the attack of rust if you are keeping a bike near the beach.

Once you have lubricated your bike, it will start to collect dirt from the road, and unless you clean it away, this dirt will act as sandpaper to grind away the metal parts. So each bicycle should go through a cycle of lubrication and cleaning, so that, as much as possible, the metal parts are sliding on clean lubricant.

Basic lubrication

Tools
- **Old bit of cloth**
- **Lubricant.** There are many bicycle lubricants. One that works well for most jobs is the all-purpose spray that also frees up rusted nuts and gets cars started on a wet day. The spray is adequate for chains and is certainly a lot better than household oil which does not have a lot of penetration, attracts dirt and washes off easily. A good bike shop will be able to recommend a purposed-designed cycle-chain lubricant.
- **Work-stand.** You will need some way of supporting the bike while you work on it. The better the work-stand you have, the easier any maintenance job will be. Get a good one if you plan to get serious about maintenance, or the family has a big fleet of bikes to work on. There are a number of possibilities:
  - **No stand.** The simplest way to work on the bike is to turn it upside down and stand it on its saddle and handlebars.
  - **Hanging stand.** Another simple solution is to hang the bike up, from the roof of the garage, for example. The

crank axle should be about the height of your waist when you are sitting or standing to work on it. Unfortunately this allows the bike to swing about.
  - **Homemade stand.** If you are handy with wood, you could build a cradle for the bike with cantilevered arms that go under the top tube, one near the head tube and one near the seat tube. Make sure that your design allows you to turn the pedals and change gear.
  - **L-rack stand.** If you have a L-rack for the towbar of your car (as we discussed in Chapter 4), you could build a concrete base that would turn the rack into a work-stand.
  - **Purpose-built stands.** Bike shops sell work-stands that stand on the floor or bolt to a workbench.

Chain
The chain is the part of the bike most in need of lubrication, especially if you have been riding in wet weather. You need some lubricant on the outside of the chain but most importantly you need it inside the links. Put a small amount of lubricant on the chain, let it penetrate the links and then run the chain through the cloth to wipe off the excess. Repeat this process a couple of times.

Cables
All cables need lubrication to help them slide back and forth inside their casings. Some modern cable-outers come with a teflon lining. If you don't have these outers you will need to convince some spray lubricant to creep down inside the cable outer. Pedants like to wipe exposed gear and brake cables with a rag dampened with lubricant.

Brake calipers and derailleur arm pivots

Every brake has a pivot which will work better if it is lubricated. Take care not to lubricate the brake pads or the rims as this will make the brakes ineffective. The front and rear derailleur arm pivots also need lubrication. Don't lubricate shift levers that rely on friction to hold the cable in the correct position.

Rear sprocket freewheel

The gear freewheel can be lubricated by spinning the wheel and spraying lubricant into the gap between the moving and the stationary part of the freewheel.

Hub gears

Hub gears need oil. On the body of the hub, between the spokes, there will be a little oil hole covered by a pivoting hat. Drop in a little sewing-machine oil.

Basic cleaning

Tools

- Some old cloth
- An old toothbrush
- A chain bath
- Kerosene or special degreasing fluids. Kerosene is a good cleaner, but look out for the effective new degreasers which claim to be less harmful to the environment. Degreaser can accelerate the decay of rubber parts so keep it away from tyres and brake pads. Don't use petrol: it is volatile and the lead and hydrocarbons will get through your skin and damage your body.

Chain

Some people like to remove the chain (described below) to bathe, scrub and rub it, but you can give the chain a pretty good clean while it is still on the bike.

- **Degrease the chain**
- **with a rag**. Dampen a rag with degreaser and, holding it on the chain, start turning the pedals, pulling the chain through the wet cloth. You'll need to swap the cloth around a lot until the chain is clean.
- **or with a toothbrush**. Dip an old toothbrush into degreaser and, holding a rag underneath to catch the drips, scrub the chain, link by link, inside and out. (Some degreasers will dissolve the toothbrush or make the bristles fall out.)

A combination of wiping and brushing will remove most of the dried lubricant and dirt.

- **or with a chain bath**. Chain baths are machines that combine the last two methods. These small plastic baths hold a small amount of degreaser. When you turn the pedals, the chain runs through the degreaser while being thrashed by brushes.
- **Remove the degreaser from the chain**. Get a clean rag and run the chain through it to dry off the degreaser. Once the chain is clean you can relubricate it so it is ready to get dirty again!

Brake calipers and derailleur arm

The pivots you so carefully lubricated will get covered in dirt.

- An old toothbrush and a strip of rag, dry or dampened with degreaser, will clean away all the dirt. Pull the rag to and fro like dental floss.
- Clean everything you can see, then relubricate. Don't get degreaser on the rim, tyre or brake pads.
- The two wheels on the rear derailleur will also gather old lubricant and dirt. Scrub them with a toothbrush dampened in degreaser and then wipe them dry with a cloth.

Rear sprockets

The front and rear sprockets and axles will also have a coating of dirt.

• Start by using a screwdriver or piece of wire to pick out large lumps of gunge from between the sprockets.

• Tear off a thin strip of rag and towel it to and fro between the rear sprockets and around the axle.

• There is no need to put lubricant on the sprockets.

Bearings

• Towel a thin strip of rag around the wheel axles, pedal axles, crank axle, headset and between the rear freewheel and the spokes.

• Don't spray or slosh degreaser directly onto the bearings as it will dissolve the grease inside the bearings.

• Don't put lubricant on the bearings as it will dissolve the grease.

Cosmetic cleaning

• A clean rag will do most of the other cosmetic cleaning on your bike.

• If you have coated the bike in mud, then a light spray with water first might speed the cleaning job up, but it will also speed up the need for a Level-4 service. A spray in clean water might be worthwhile if you have been riding on the beach, as bikes rust slower in fresh water than they do in salt water.

• If you are entering a concours d'elegance you can polish the paintwork with car wax (not the abrasive kind) and car-chrome polish. Use cutlery polish on aluminium parts.

LEVEL 3: TUNING YOUR BIKE

The maintenance jobs at this level will help you tune up your bike and make it run better. Level 3 requires a step up in skills and you will need more tools, so a

lot of people leave this sort of thing to a bike shop. But there is no harm in having a go, the shop will always be able to fix up any mistakes.

Nuts and bolts

Most of the tuning adjustments on your bike requires working with nuts and bolts.

Tools

For the nuts you will need:

• **Spanners**, which could be:

– ring spanners or

– sockets. These two types of spanner pull evenly on each of the flats of the nut.

– open-ended spanners. These are good but only pull on some of the flats.

– an adjustable spanner or shifter. These are never quite a perfect fit and they only pull on some flats. You are more likely to mash up a nut with an adjustable spanner.

For the bolt heads you will need:

• **Screwdrivers**:

– cross-bladed or Phillips screwdrivers and

– flat-bladed screwdrivers. Like spanners, screwdrivers come in different sizes. Your screwdriver should be thin enough to drop to the bottom of the slot and wide enough to reach to each end of the slot.

• **Allen keys**. Some bolt heads will have a recessed hexagonal hole. To turn one of these bolts you need an allen key or 'hex' key. This is usually an L-shaped, hexagonal piece of metal about half the length of a pencil. Like spanners and screwdrivers, allen keys come in different sizes. Most bikes will use metric allen bolts.

Hints for nuts and bolts

These are some of the tips worth

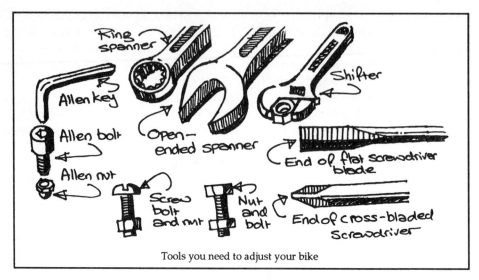

Tools you need to adjust your bike

remembering when you are working with nuts and bolts:

• **Tighter and looser**. Imagine a man in the pub getting tighter and tighter as he watches the clock go round. Nuts and bolts also get tighter as they turn clockwise and get looser as you turn them counter clockwise. Non-drinkers might prefer the memory aid: 'Turn it right to make it tight'.

• **Clean and lubricate threads**. Always clean threads with degreaser or spray lubricant and a cloth or toothbrush. Spray the threads with a little lubricant before you do them up.

• **Match the thread** in the nut with the thread in the bolt. There is only one correct path down a thread and if you do up a nut and bolt on the wrong path they will never work properly again. This mistake is called cross-threading.

– To avoid cross-threading, press the nut and bolt together gently and wind one part – the nut, for example, counter clockwise. Somewhere during the counter-clockwise turn you will feel a little click when the thread drops down a small step. This is the start of the correct path and you can begin to wind clockwise.

– To make sure you are on the right path, do the nut and bolt up by hand for a couple of turns. Your fingers won't be able to turn the nut if it is cross-threaded.

• **Too much force**. Most people think of metal as totally hard but metals actually come in different grades of softness. Many metals used on bikes are quite soft, either because they are light or because they are cheap. With a hefty swing of a spanner you will be able to strip threads off and break or distort nuts and bolts. Make sure you use the right-size tool and use it gently.

• **Too tight**. It is possible to do up a nut or bolt so tightly that it distorts or damages the thread. Experience will teach you what 'too tight', 'too loose' and 'just right' feel like. Bike shop mechanics use a 'torque' spanner which shows the pressure exerted on a dial.

• **Lock washers**. Use lock washers to attach any accessories like lights, mud-guards, toe clips or a rack. They keep the nuts and bolts from shaking loose.

There are a number of things that make life difficult with bicycle nuts and bolts:

• **Metric or non-metric**. Most bikes these days have metric nuts and bolts for which you need metric spanners and allen keys. But some bikes have non-metric fittings. These non-metric nuts and bolts will need different spanners and allen keys.

• **Thread variation**. It can be hard to get the right replacement nut or bolt if you don't have the old one with you. Nuts and bolts on your bike are all different sizes and different manufacturers use different sizes for the same job. It is always worth taking the bike or part to the bike shop to make sure you have the correct replacement.

• **Thread incompatibility**. Sometimes a bit from one bike will not fit on another and sometimes an apparently similar replacement nut or bolt will not match up properly. That is because there are more types of thread on bicycles than you can imagine. Even within the metric world of bicycles there are at least two standards. If you are having trouble getting two threads to mesh, you might have two incompatible pieces.

• **Left-hand threads**. Unfortunately one or two things on a bicycle have a left-hand thread which gets tighter when it is turned counter clockwise. The left-hand pedal often has a left-hand thread, as does the right-hand cup of the crank-axle bearing.

Adjusting things

If you learn to adjust things on your bike yourself, you can save yourself some trips to the bike shop. For example, you can adjust your bike to fit

better, you can keep the brakes working well, the gears shifting accurately and the bearings from premature failure. You might also need to 'adjust' your bike to take it with you on a plane or bus.

Tools
 – spanners
 – allen keys
 – hammer
 – large screwdriver
 – pliers
 – string or specialist brake tools called 'third-hand' or 'fourth-hand' tools, which grip brakes and cable.

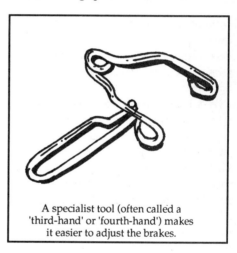

A specialist tool (often called a 'third-hand' or 'fourth-hand') makes it easier to adjust the brakes.

Saddle height

The calculations for saddle height are discussed in Chapter 9. To change the height of your saddle:

• Slack off the nut and bolt near where the seat tube, seat stays and top tube meet, and ease the seat post up or down. To release the seat post fully, you might need to lever the split in the frame apart with a screwdriver – gently.

• Move the saddle, then half tighten the nut and bolt and check the saddle height by measuring it, sitting on it, or

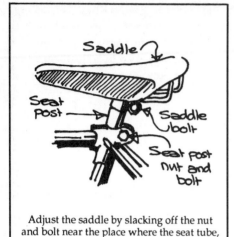

Adjust the saddle by slacking off the nut and bolt near the place where the seat tube, seat stays and top tube meet.

When you're adjusting saddle height, check that you can't see the maximum-height mark on the seat post.

both. You might need to repeat these two steps a number of times until you have the ideal height.

• Check that the saddle is pointing forward correctly.

• Check that you can't see the maximum-height mark on the seat post. This mark ensures that there is a couple of centimetres of post beneath the clamping bolt. If you can see the mark, you will need to buy a longer seat post or a larger bike frame.

• Snug the nut and bolt down tight.

Saddle tilt and position
Saddle tilt and the fore-and-aft position of the saddle are adjusted either by loosening a bolt on the top of the seat post or by loosening two nuts underneath the saddle. Follow the same procedure as for saddle-height adjustment.

Handlebar height
• Slack off the bolt on the stem. This bolt pulls up on a wedge-shaped nut that holds the stem into place.

• Protect the bolt head with a piece

of wood and tap the bolt head lightly with a hammer – hard enough to dislodge the wedge but not so hard that you damage the thread of the bolt. If the bolt does not move, you might have to spray some lubricant into the hole and tap it again. When the bolt drops down, you will be able to raise or lower the stem.

• Check that you can't see the maximum height mark on the handlebar stem. Like the saddle post, there should be a couple of centimetres of stem inside the frame. If you can see the mark you will need to buy a longer stem or a larger bike frame.

• Snug the bolt down tight when you are satisfied you have the ideal height and straightness.

Handlebar tilt
You can adjust the tilt of the handlebars by slackening the bolt at the front end of the stem.

Brake lever position
Brake levers can also be moved to a convenient position. The nut and bolt

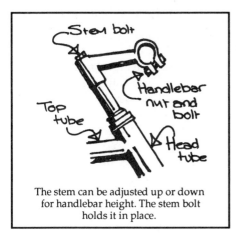

The stem can be adjusted up or down for handlebar height. The stem bolt holds it in place.

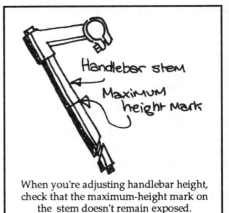

When you're adjusting handlebar height, check that the maximum-height mark on the stem doesn't remain exposed.

that holds the lever on flat bars is easy to find. The bolt that holds a racing-style brake lever is inside the hood at the top of the lever behind the cable. It is usually necessary to release the brakes to allow the cable to go slack, so you can get the tool in.

Brake adjustment

The brake pads on your bike should sit about a matchstick's width from the rim, and it should only take a small lever movement to bring them into action.

As you ride your bike two things will happen. The pads will wear down and the brake cables will stretch. Little by little it will take more and more lever movement to bring the pads onto the rims. If you allow this process to continue, eventually you will be able to pull the lever all the way back to the bars without engaging the brakes and they will be completely 'out of adjust-ment'. In other words they won't work.

Ideally, little by little you will adjust the brakes to compensate by turning a knurled adjuster bolt. This is a quick job.

• Find the adjuster bolt: it will be near the lever or near the brake caliper.

• Slack off the lock nut.

• Unscrew the hollow adjuster bolt with your fingers so that the cable is pulled tighter and the pads sit closer to the rim.

• Check that you have not gone too far. Squeeze the brakes on and off a few times, then lift the wheel off the ground and spin it. If it spins freely without hitting the pads, and if the levers don't have to move far to put the pads on the rims, the adjustment is good. If the pads rub the rim, you have moved the adjuster too far. Slack it off until it is in the best position.

• Tighten the lock nut so that the adjuster will stay where you have set it.

Re-clamping the brake cable

If you have no cable adjuster bolt, or the adjuster has already been moved to the limit, you will have to clamp the cable in a new position. This is a longer job.

• Strap the brake pads onto the rim. This can be done with a bit of string or a special tool called a 'third hand' which grips brakes and cable.

• Slack off the adjuster lock nut and wind the adjuster down to zero. This

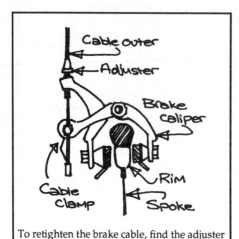

To retighten the brake cable, find the adjuster bolt near the brake lever or caliper.

few times, then lift the wheel off the ground and spin it. Ideally the pads will be a matchstick's width off the rim and you will have the adjuster at zero for future changes. If the pads are rubbing you have moved the clamp too far up the cable and you will have to start again.

will enable you to cope with further stretch and wear.

• Use two spanners to loosen the nut and bolt that clamp the cable. The cable clamp will be somewhere near the pads. Usually the cable will pass through a hole in the bolt and, as you tighten the nut, it will clamp the cable against the head of the bolt.

• Grab hold of the end of the cable with a pair of pliers or a 'fourth-hand' tool. (You will gather from the names of these special tools that this job is easier if you have extra hands.) Pull on the cable so that it is taut. Check that the cable end is still properly fixed in the brake lever by squeezing the lever.

• Keep the cable taut and slide the clamp a little bit above the spot it was in before. You can usually find the previous clamping spot by the kink in the cable.

• Tighten the clamp. The clamp needs to be pretty tight: it's vital it doesn't let go of the cable.

• Check your work by undoing whatever is holding the brake shoes to the rim, squeeze the brakes on and off a

Derailleur arm movement

Both front and rear derailleurs need adjusting occasionally to stop them swinging too far to the left or right and throwing off the chain. On each derailleur there are two adjuster bolts that limit the travel of the derailleur arm. They are often marked H and L for High and Low. To stop your derailleur swinging too far:

• Support the bike (see 'Workstand' above) so that the rear wheel is off the ground and you can turn the pedals and change gears.

• Check the swing to the outside. Turn the pedals and move the gear lever so that the chain moves to the middle of the rear freewheel (rear derailleur adjustment) or the left-hand front sprocket (front derailleur adjustment). Then, while turning the pedals, throw the gear lever swiftly to the downhill position. Do this a few times and watch what happens.

− If the chain is thrown off the sprockets to the right, tighten the H adjuster bolt.

− If the chain did not make it to the furthest right-hand sprocket, loosen the H adjuster bolt.

Repeat this process, adjusting the derailleur limit little by little, until the chain goes to the outside sprocket but no further.

• Test the swing to the inside on both derailleurs in the same way by

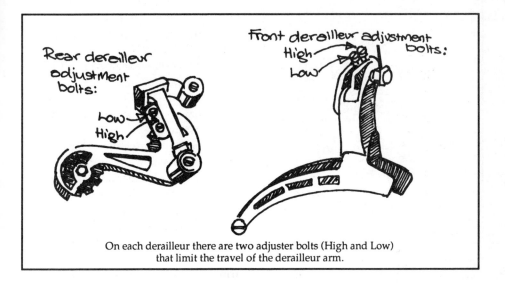

On each derailleur there are two adjuster bolts (High and Low)
that limit the travel of the derailleur arm.

throwing the gear lever swiftly to the
uphill position.

• Check your work by turning the
pedals and changing gear so that the
the chain swaps rapidly from inside
sprocket to outside sprocket and back.
On a friction system, when the H and L
bolts are in the correct position, the top
guide-wheel of the rear derailleur
should sit underneath the largest and
smallest sprocket at each limit of travel.

Friction cable adjustment
Derailleur gear cables should be taut
when the chain is on the smallest
sprocket. If the cable is too loose, there
might not be enough pull in the cable to
get the chain to move to the largest
sprockets.

• Support the bike.

• Move the gear lever until the
chain is sitting on the smallest sprocket.

• Use the adjusting bolt near the
derailleur arm to make the cable taut. If
the adjuster is already fully unscrewed
you will have to re-clamp the cable, as
described for brakes above. If you make

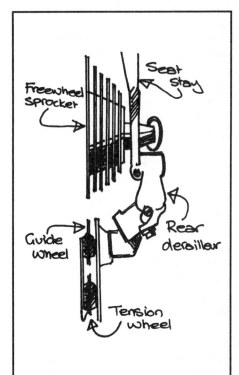

On a friction derailleur the guide-wheel
should sit underneath the largest and
smallest cog at each limit of travel. On a
click system the guide-wheel should sit
just inside the biggest and smallest cog.

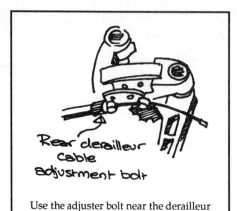

Rear derailleur
cable
adjustment bolt

Use the adjuster bolt near the derailleur
arm to make the cable taut.

the cable too tight, you might stop the
derailleur moving enough to put the
chain on the smallest sprocket.

• Check your work by running the
chain rapidly from inside sprocket to
outside sprocket and back.

Click system cable adjustment
Your click derailleur system will stop
working properly when the cable
stretches.
Quick fix:
Sometimes a problem with a click
system can be fixed by a half-turn on the
cable adjuster. Turn the adjuster clockwise to slacken the cable, if changing to
a higher gear (smaller rear sprockets) is
a problem; tighten the cable if the
system hesitates before changing down.
If the quick fix doesn't work you might
have to reset the system:
To reset the system:
• Support the bike.
• Change gear until the chain is on
the smallest rear sprocket and on the
largest outside sprocket.
• Turn the pedals and move the rear
derailleur one click:
– If the chain goes past the
second-smallest sprocket, the cable is

too tight.
– If the chain doesn't make a move,
the cable is too loose.
• Use the cable-adjusting bolt to
change the tension on the cable.
• Repeat the last three steps until
you are happy that the cable is just right
for the first jump.
• Then, with the chain on the
second-smallest sprocket, tighten the
cable with the adjuster until the jockey
wheel is underneath the second-
smallest sprocket.
• Turn the pedals and click to the
third-smallest sprocket.
• Check your work by putting the
chain back to the smallest sprocket.
Click to second smallest, click to the
next. If everything is okay, then you are
finished. If not, it is back to the
beginning again.
On a click system the top guide-
wheel of the rear derailleur should sit
just inside the biggest and smallest
sprocket at each limit of travel.

Hub gear cable adjustment
Cable adjustment is equally important
for hub gears. If the cable is too taut or
too loose you will lose your gears.
• Support the bike.
• Put the bike in the middle gear,
sometimes called normal.
• Slack off the small lock nut in
front of the cable adjuster.
• Look through the hole in the right-
hand wheel nut. Pull the chain that
comes out of the axle nut and move the
rod so that you can see through the
hole. The end of this rod must be
aligned with the end of the axle which
you can see through the hole. Sometimes there is a mark on the rod and on
the axle to show you the correct
position.

• Move the adjuster until the rod is in the correct position.

• Check your work by clicking between the gears and turning the pedals.

• Tighten the lock nut on the cable adjuster.

Front derailleur alignment

Sometimes the front derailleur will not lift the chain onto the outside front sprocket. Try adjusting the cable, but if that doesn't work it could be because the front derailleur is not aligned properly.

• Support the bike.

• Move the chain to the largest sprocket.

• Loosen the clamp that holds the derailleur on the seat tube.

• Align the derailleur so that the arms are parallel to the chain. When the cable is fully taut, the outside arm of the front derailleur should sit just above the teeth of the largest front sprocket.

• Tighten the derailleur arm in position.

• Check your work by moving the chain back and forth between the chainwheels.

Replacing consumables

The more you ride, the more things like brake pads and cables wear out.

Parts
  – new cables
  – new brake pads

Tools
  – spanners
  – file
  – a sharp blade
  – cable cutter or pliers.
There is one trick to replacing cables

and that is cutting them. A well-cut end will be easy to thread through holes and cable covers. A badly cut cable can be impossible to thread. Bicycle cable-cutters with V-shaped jaws always give you a well-cut end. The specialist cutter is not expensive and, because cables break regularly, it is worth having. Pliers will cut cables but usually make a mess of the end.

• A soldering iron or some five-minute glue could come in handy to seal the cut end of the cable and make it easier to thread.

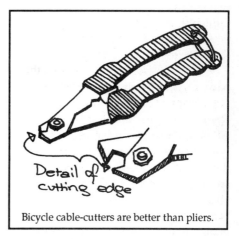

Bicycle cable-cutters are better than pliers.

Replacing brake pads

Replace the brake pads earlier rather than later and well before any metal in the pad-holder can make contact with the rim.

• Loosen the nut that holds the pad in place and remove the old pad.

• Insert the new pad. If you have been adjusting the brake cables as described above, you will probably have to back off the adjuster or re-clamp the cable to accommodate the extra thickness of the new pads.

• Adjust the pads. Make sure they are parallel to the rim, that all the pad lands on the rim and doesn't touch the

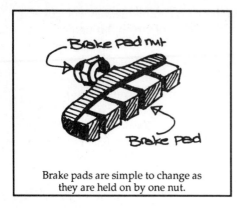

Brake pads are simple to change as
they are held on by one nut.

tyre. Squeeze the brake lever to hold the
pad in position against the rim and
tighten the nut gently.

• Check your work by squeezing
the brake levers a couple of times.

• Snug down the nut so that the
pads are held firmly in place.

Replacing cables and outers

All bicycle cables run through a cable
housing called an *outer*. The outer is a
flexible hollow tube, usually made of a
spiral of steel coated in plastic, which
allows the cable to be pulled around a
bend. Generally, where the cable is
being pulled in a straight line, it is not
put in an outer. Some outers are coated
inside with teflon to reduce friction
between the cable and housing.

Cables are a twist of small strands of
wire. Brake cables are thicker than gear
cables. You buy both types extra-long
with leaden nipples fused on each end.
One of the nipples will fit into the slot
on your brake or gear lever. The other
nipple is cut off and discarded. As we
have seen, the cut end of the cable is
gripped at the derailleur or brake by a
clamp.

It is worth knowing two emergency
repairs:

• If you break the front brake cable,

you can take the cable off the back and
fit it on the front, thereby keeping your
best brake.

• If you break your rear gear cable
the derailleur will dump you in your
most downhill gear. Use the H and L
travel-adjuster bolts to fix the bike in an
easier gear.

To replace a cable:

• Inspect the other cable and the
outer: if they are rusty or the outer is
kinked, replace them.

• Unclamp the end of the old cable
and pull it out of the cable outer.

• If necessary, replace the outer:

– Remove the old outer, noting
where it went on the frame and the
path it took. Ideally cable outers should
curve smoothly and not go round sharp
corners.

– Using the old outer as a guide for
length, cut through the plastic skin of
the new outer with a sharp blade. This
will reveal the spiral of metal that forms
the cable tunnel. Sit the blade of a pair
of pliers between the twists of the spiral
and snip through the metal spiral. The
spiral is quite tough and cutting will
take a bit of force. Try not to crush the
cable tunnel. You might need to run a
file over the cut end of the metal spiral
to smooth off any sharp edges.

– Thread the new outer back
through any guides that held it in place.

• Find the leaded cable nipple that
sat in your brake or gear lever and
compare it to the nipples on the new
cable or to the hole it will sit in. Cut off
the nipple that doesn't match yours.

• Melt some solder over the cut end
or dip it in five-minute glue.

• Thread the cable. Poke the cable
end through the brake or gear lever,
then through any eyes or guides and
through the outer. This is where your

cable cutters and five-minute glue will help you. A frayed cable or roughly cut cable is very hard to thread as the end can snag going through the outer and open out the spiral of small wires. If this happens, chop a bit more off the cable and try again.

- Run the cable through the clamp.
- Wind down any adjusters and clamp the cable lightly.
- Check that the nipple is sitting correctly in the lever and the outer and cable are correctly through the guides.
- Adjust the cable as described above so that the brakes or gears will work correctly.
- Cut the cable again so that no more than five centimetres sticks out beyond the clamp. You might want to solder or glue the end again.

LEVEL 4: HELPING YOUR BIKE LAST LONGER

Servicing the bearings and the drive train

Regular servicing of the bearings and drive train on a bike will do what a grease and oil change does for a car: make it run better and last longer.

As the bike is ridden, the races will shake apart, the lubricating grease will both wash away and draw in road dirt, which will begin to grind away the races. That is why it is necessary, every so often, to pull apart, clean, inspect and relubricate the bearings.

The drive train is even more exposed to rain and abrasive road dirt than the bearings. The cleaning and lubrication described above in Level 2 will keep the drive train going for a while, but every so often, like the bearings, the drive train will need to be pulled apart, cleaned, inspected and relubricated.

Service frequency

How often these things need attention depends on how often you ride and how much you ride in the rain. I suggest an annual service, when the rainy season's over. You could nominate a birthday for your bike and then each year, on its birthday, give it a service for a present. Or you could associate your bike service with a regular event like the local show or the Grand Final. Your bike may need two birthdays if you use it a lot. Bikes that are being ridden each day to school, for example, might need a service at the end of each term.

Servicing the bearings and drive train does not call for many more skills

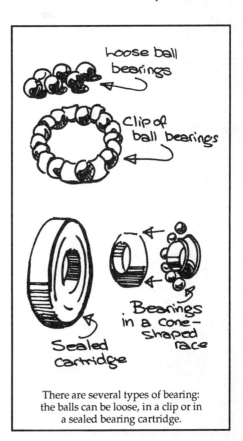

There are several types of bearing: the balls can be loose, in a clip or in a sealed bearing cartridge.

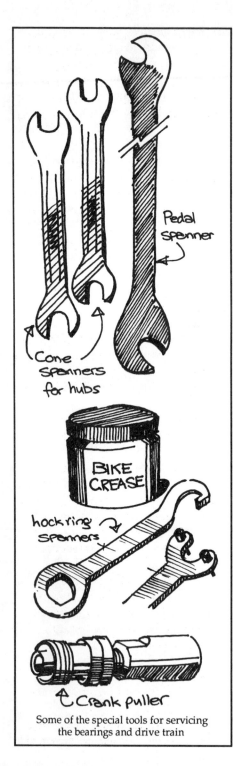

Some of the special tools for servicing
the bearings and drive train

than Level 3 but it does require more tools and and more time. For that reason most people leave this sort of work to the bike shop.

Bearings

Tools for bearings

To service bearings you will need some specialist tools:

- **Bearing spanners**. These tools differ:
  - from bearing to bearing. Sealed bearings need different tools from standard ball bearings. Pedal bearings can need a different spanner from wheel bearings. The more sophisticated and expensive the bearing, the more likely it is to need a special spanner.
  - from one component set to another. Sometimes the cheaper component set from one manufacturer will use a different set of bearing spanners to the top-of-the-range set from the same company.
  - from manufacturer to manufacturer.
- **Crank tool** to remove alloy cranks from the crank axle (see below).
- **Degreaser**.
- **Hub spanners**. These are special, thin spanners for the shallow bearing cups and lock nuts on standard wheel-hub bearings.
- **Pedal spanner**. These long spanners allow you to remove the pedal from the crank
- **Cloths**.
- **Wide-mouth spanner** for the extra-large lock nut on the headset bearing.
- **Standard spanners**.
- **Hammer** and a **punch**.
- **Cycle grease**. Make sure you lubricate your bearings with cycle

grease. There are many types of grease on the market that are wrong for bicycles. Motor-car wheel-bearing grease for example is made to be sticky when cold and only loosens up when it is hot. If you used this sort of grease in your bearings, it would never heat up enough to allow the bearings to run freely.

Testing bearings
Test your bearings to see if they need servicing. The bearing should move round smoothly. Sometimes you can feel when there is dirt or unhappiness inside the bearing by rotating it slowly and feeling for harshness or vibration. The following tests will tell you if you need to tune or service the bearing:

• Does the bearing spin easily or does the spinning come to a quick halt? A sticky bearing could mean:
– the grease is old and dried out or has gathered lots of dirt;
– the races are too close together.

• If you push and pull and wiggle the bearing, can you feel movement, apart from the spin that is supposed to be there? A loose bearing could mean:
– the grease has washed away from around the bearing;
– the races are too far apart.

You should take special care that the headset bearings are not loose. A bicycle with a loose headset can suddenly start to thrash the front wheel and handlebars from side to side. This frightening event (what motorcyclists call a 'tank slapper') is likely to throw you off the bike.

Servicing bearings
• Ignore some bearings:
– Freewheel bearings. There are bearings inside the freewheel which

allow you to pedal backwards and freewheel, but it is unusual to service them. Usually the body that holds the sprockets is replaced. By then the sprockets are usually worn as well and so the whole freewheel is replaced. (See 'Drive train' later in this chapter.)
– Don't attempt to service the bearings in a three-speed hub. If you have an old three-speed hub it is fun to pull it apart and marvel at the insides but reassembly is bicycle brain surgery.

• Remove the parts that stand between you and the bearing that you are after.
– Crank-axle bearings: remove cranks. (See 'Drive train' later in this chapter.)
– Wheel-axle bearings: release wheels from the frame, and remove the gear freewheel from the rear wheel. (See 'Drive train' later in this chapter.)
– Headset: remove stem and release front wheel.
– Pedal bearings can be attacked directly through the dust cap on the outside.

• Slack off the bearing lock nut.
– Crank axle bearings have a special lock nut on the left-hand side. You will be able to get a spanner that fits this lock nut. In an emergency you can tap the lock nut off with a hammer and punch.
– Wheel axle bearings have a special extra-thin lock nut. You can probably take the lock nut off with a standard spanner but you will need a hub spanner to put it back on.
– Headset bearings have a large lock nut which needs a large spanner.
– Pedal lock nuts are straight-forward.

• Unscrew the race. If the bearing has loose balls, they will all make a bid

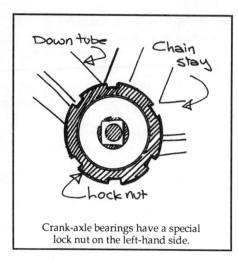

Crank-axle bearings have a special
lock nut on the left-hand side.

for freedom. Clips and sealed bearings
will just lift out. Use a craft-blade to
lever off the side panel of a sealed
bearing cartridge.

• Once you have unscrewed one
side of the bearing, the other side
should come out as well.

• Clean the dirt and old grease off
the races and balls with degreaser.

• Inspect the races for damage and
wear. The balls could have made
potholes in the race or have worn a
trench in the race. You will have to
replace worn races. Take the bits to the
shop to make sure you get the
correct-size replacement balls and races.
Ask for advice if you are unsure
whether you should replace them. Nine
times out of ten you will need to replace
the balls.

• Regrease the race or the sealed
unit, sit the balls or clip in the grease
and reassemble the bearing by lightly
screwing up the top or outside race.

• The next step takes a bit of trial
and error. You have to tighten the
bearing until it is loose enough to spin
but tight enough not to rattle.

• When you are satisfied, tighten

the lock nut without further tightening
the bearing. This is usually done with
two spanners, one on the race, the other
on the lock nut.

Drive train

Your main job when servicing the drive
train is to check for wear. Chain and
sprocket wear will be negligible on a
bike with hub gears but on a derailleur
the chain and sprockets wear quite
rapidly. This sort of wear shows up in a
number of ways:

• Gear changing becomes less
precise and less predictable. For
example, it can become hard to move
the chain to the larger sprockets. When
a chain is new, it has to be flexible so
that it can be guided from sprocket to
sprocket. But when it becomes too
flexible, though the derailleur arm
pushes it across, it can just bend and
stay on the smaller sprocket.

• The chain jumps out of gear when
you pedal hard. There are at least two
possible reasons for this.

– When the teeth wear, the chain
can slide off the top of the teeth when
pulled hard.

As the chain wears it also stretches
along its length which can mean that
the holes in the chain miss the teeth of
the sprockets.

As a general rule, a set of sprockets
will have two or three times the life of a
chain. But derailleur chains and sprockets
wear into each other. So if you replace the
chain and not the sprockets the new chain
can skip and jump over the partly worn
sprockets. Some people run two or three
chains with each set of sprockets, swapping the chain every so often so that the
sprockets and chains wear together. By
the time the set of chains has worn out,
the sprockets will need replacing as well.

Tools for the drive train

• Chain breaker. This tool pushes a pin in one of the chain links, allowing you to break or rejoin a derailleur chain.

• Freewheel remover. This is a small socket that fits the inside of the freewheel. Your bike shop will sell you the freewheel remover you need for your brand of freewheel.

• Chain whip to remove the sprockets from the freewheel body

• Crank tool. This controlled pushing tool behaves in a similar way to the chain breaker to remove push-fit cranks.

• Hammer and a punch
• Cloths
• Degreaser
• Long-handled spanner
• Vice

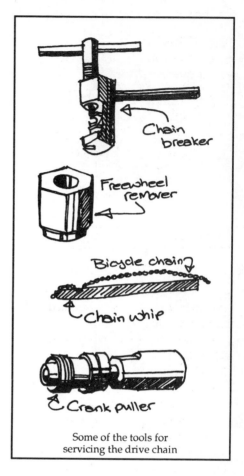

Some of the tools for
servicing the drive chain

Testing the chain

There are two ways to check if the chain needs replacing:

• Grab the chain at three o'clock on the front of the front sprocket and pull it forward. If you can lift the chain further than the top of one of the front sprocket teeth, then your chain is badly worn. A new chain will be hard to lift away from the front sprocket.

• Take the chain off (see below), stretch it out on its side and see how many pins there are in 30 cm, the length of a standard ruler. If you count fewer than 25 pins, then the chain is worn and should be replaced. If twelve links, from pin to pin, measure more than 30 cm, then the chain is worn.

Removing the chain

To remove the chain from the derailleur:

• Sit a chain link in the chain-breaker. The pusher rod should line up with one of the pins holding the

chain together.

• Gently screw the pushing rod of the tool forward so that it pushes the chain pin out of the inside link of the chain.

• Stop pushing the pin when the chain pin is held only by the outside plate of the chain link. Use the old mechanical principle of: Do a little bit and have a look.

• Lift the inner link of the chain out from between the outer links.

• Unthread the chain. It is likely that your chain will have to be removed through two holes, one through the rear derailleur and one through the front derailleur.

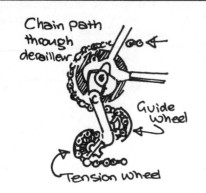

A derailleur chain runs in front of the guide-wheel and behind the tension wheel.

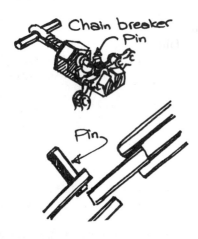

When removing the chain, turn the chain breaker a little bit and have a look to make sure you don't go too far.

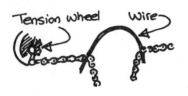

A U-shaped piece of wire will hold the chain against the derailleur spring while you use the chain breaker to rejoin the two ends.

Now you can clean the chain, test it for wear, swap it or replace it.

Reinstalling the chain

• Ensure the pin you pushed out is facing you and at the right-hand end of the chain. Lay the left-hand end of the chain over the top of the rear sprockets.

• Run the left-hand end in front of the guide wheel and behind the tension wheel of the rear derailleur.

• Cut a wire coathanger and bend it into a 'U' shape. Thread one arm through the left-hand end of the chain half-a-dozen links from the break.

• Take the right-hand end and lay it over the smallest chainwheel and bring it back towards the break. Insert the other arm of the wire 'U' a few links to the right of the pin.

Now you can sit the link to be joined in the chain-breaker and push the pin back into place.

Testing the sprockets

Check the rear sprockets for wear by:

• Comparing the shape of teeth on frequently used rear sprockets with teeth on sprockets you use less often.

• Seeing if the teeth on the front sprockets are symmetrical. On well-used sprockets the front edge will have worn away.

Removing the sprockets

Front sprockets can usually be removed by undoing the nuts and bolts that hold the chain ring onto the crank. Sometimes the sprocket and crank is made in one piece, in which case you have to undo the crank-axle bearings.

To remove the rear freewheel:

• Release the rear wheel.

• Unscrew the axle nuts or quick-release levers.

• Fit the freewheel remover inside the smallest sprocket on the freewheel.

• Fit a long-handled spanner to the remover and give it a big heave. It gets hooked on quite tightly with you pedalling all the time.

• As soon as the freewheel breaks free, put down the spanner and continue unscrewing it by hand. It is easy for the hard threads on the freewheel to damage the soft threads on the wheel hub.

• Now you can clean the freewheel thoroughly or replace it. Don't bathe a freewheel in kero as that will dissolve the grease in the bearings. Removing the freewheel will also allow you to repair a broken right-hand-side spoke (see below).

To separate the sprockets from the bearing body, you have to unscrew at least the top sprocket.

• Grip the larger sprockets in a vice.

• Fit the chain whip onto the smallest sprocket and unscrew it.

Sometimes all sprockets screw off the freewheel body. On some freewheels the smallest sprocket screws on but the rest slide onto a splined or toothed shaft.

Now you can disassemble and service the bearings on the freewheel body. Even bike shops rarely do this. You can also swap worn sprockets or swap the size of your sprockets.

Testing cranks
Cranks must be on tight. They will either be held on with a wedge-shaped pin called a cotter pin, or be pushed onto the crank axle.

Cotter-pin cranks
Many bikes have a steel crank secured to the crank axle with a wedge-shaped pin held on by a nut. When this soft

cotter pin distorts under heavy use, the cranks become wobbly. To tighten these cranks you will have to replace the cotter pin.

To replace a cotter pin:

• Support the crank on a brick or a piece of wood.

• Undo the nut securing the pin.

• Tap the threaded end of the pin.

– If you think the pin is okay and want to put it back, you will have to tap it out gently. Put a piece of wood over the threaded end to protect it and tap it with your hammer.

– If you intend to replace the pin, you can belt it straight out with the hammer and punch. But don't be too enthusiastic, as the hammer blows are also falling on your crank bearing.

• Take your old pin to the shop to make sure the new one is the correct size.

• Make sure the cranks are sitting opposite each other and are in line.

• Slide the new pin into the hole in the crank with the flat side facing the flat spot on the crank axle.

• Tap the pin gently to seat it.

• Tighten the nut on top of the pin.

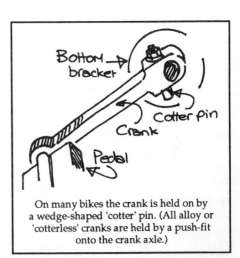

On many bikes the crank is held on by a wedge-shaped 'cotter' pin. (All alloy or 'cotterless' cranks are held by a push-fit onto the crank axle.)

Push-fit cranks

Some steel cranks and all alloy cranks go onto the crank axle with a push fit. They have no cotter pins and so are sometimes called *cotterless* cranks. To tighten or remove these cranks you will need the appropriate crank tool for your make of crank.

- Remove the dust cap at the axle end of the crank. This cap screws into the threads that the crank tool will use. Some dust caps have an allen key socket, some take a screwdriver.
- Undo the bolt in the crank head with a socket spanner. This is usually built into one end of the crank tool.
- Hold the threads on the outside of the crank tool and unscrew the pusher until it is fully backed up.
- Screw the outside threads of the crank tool into the dust-cap threads on the crank.
- Tighten the pushing rod so that it eases the crank away from the axle.
- Inspect the square hole in the crank head for distortion. Because the crank is soft and the axle hard, any problems will show up in the crank.
- If the hole in the crank head is undistorted, fit the crank back on the axle.
- Do up the bolt in the crank head.
- Tighten the bolt with the socket spanner.
- Replace the dust cap.

Removing pedals

If you want to take the pedals off the cranks, remember the left-hand pedal is atypical and undoes clockwise. To remove the pedals you will need a spanner with a long handle for leverage and a narrow head to fit the two faces on the pedal axle. Sometimes an ordinary adustable spanner will do the job. If you are preparing your bike for travel by bus or plane, and you have a crank puller, consider removing the cranks instead. It is much easier than taking off the pedals. The only time you really need to remove pedals from the cranks is to install new ones.

LEVEL 5: FRAME AND WHEEL REPAIR

In Chapter 10 we looked at some tests to see if the frame or forks on a bike are bent. If they are damaged the shop will often recommend replacement rather than repair. For example, frame damage might be impossible to fix if the frame is made of aluminium, carbon fibre or titanium.

Minor fork damage can be repaired by fitting the forks into a jig and bending them back into shape with a lever. A bent steel frame can be repaired by pulling it apart and fitting new tubes. This is quite expensive as the bike has to be stripped of parts, the tubes cut out and replaced. Then the frame will need repainting and the parts reinstalled. It is often cheaper to get a new frame.

You are unlikely to be able to do this sort of work at home to the same standard. But if you like cutting and welding, let me encourage you to experiment. There are plenty of homemade tandems around and, in Canberra, I met the owner of a homemade bicycle-and-sidecar which the family use for kids and goods.

Wheel repair and construction is something that requires skill and experience to get a good result. It is also much easier with expensive purpose-built tools which are only worth having if you are going to repeat the job. But when you are out on a longer ride it is worth knowing how to fix broken spokes and, personally, I got a lot of satisfaction from building my own wheels. It took me a long time and the ones I built will never be used as a World Standard of Roundness, but they are quite adequate and the spokes have never broken, which was the problem I was trying to solve.

Why spokes break

When each spoke in a wheel is under the same tension and therefore shouldering an equal amount of work, the wheel will last a long time and resist breakage. You can test the relative tension of your spokes by plucking them. If they are the same tension they will sing the same note. The well-built wheel is also both round, without up or down bumps, and true, with no left- or right-side warps. You can test for round and true by spinning the wheel and watching as the rim goes past a fixed point, the brakes for example. The rounder and truer a wheel is, again the more it will resist breakage. Unfortunately some wheels don't meet these three criteria and so the spokes break.

Probably the most common spoke breakage is on the right-hand side of the rear wheel on a derailleur bike. That is because there is a designed-in weakness. On the right-hand side the spokes are at a steeper angle and therefore at a higher tension to make room for the gear sprockets. These tauter spokes have both to transmit the force of the pedals and to take most of the weight of the rider. Their job is even harder if you put a heavy rider or heavily laden rear panniers on the bike and go riding down rough roads.

There are two ways to reduce recurring spoke failure:

- Get your wheel built by a skilled wheel-builder.
- Use heavy-gauge spokes.

Racers especially rely on wheel builders, as they have their wheels built from light-gauge spokes.

Wheel repair

If a few spokes have broken or if there is a small distortion, this can usually be corrected. But if the wheel has developed a large distortion or spokes are breaking regularly, the wheel may have lost its integrity and have to be scrapped.

Tools for wheels

To repair a wheel or to build a new one you will need:

- A spoke key, or spanner that fits the nuts on the threaded end of the spokes.
- A jig, which will help you measure for round and true. It is possible to use the frame of the bicycle as a jig but professional wheel-builders use a purpose-built jig.
- A tension gauge, which clips onto a spoke and indicates the tension. Old hands and home repairers use their fingers.
- File.

Replacing a spoke

Replacing a spoke is easy, as a spoke is only a long-handled hook with a nut, or nipple, on one end.

- **Release the wheel** and take off the tyre, tube and rim tape. If the broken spoke is on the right side of the rear wheel, you will need to remove the gear freewheel.
- **Remove the bits** of the old spoke.
- **Check that your new spoke** is the

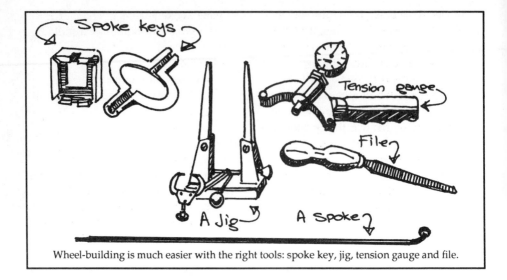

Wheel-building is much easier with the right tools: spoke key, jig, tension gauge and file.

correct length and gauge.

• **Poke the spoke through** the hole in the hub left vacant by the broken spoke. Make sure the spoke follows the pattern of the remaining spokes. Four spokes further round the rim is another spoke that is doing the same thing that your new spoke will do. Guide the new spoke over and under the other spokes according to the pattern and feed the threaded end through the hole in the rim.

• **Screw the nipple** onto the end of the spoke

• **Tighten the spoke** until it is the same tension as the others. This can be done on the outside of the rim with a screwdriver on the head of the nipple or with a spoke key on the shaft of the nipple inside the rim. Check it by twanging the spokes like guitar strings till the new one sounds the same as the old.

• **File down** any part of the threaded end of the spoke that is sticking out past the head of the nipple.

Now comes the difficult part of the operation: restoring the wheel to round and true.

Restoring true

A wheel can go out of true, or develop a warp with all the spokes intact, but it is more common in a wheel where one or more spokes are broken. A reasonable aim in this case is to make the bike rideable again. It will take quite a bit of skill to make the wheel perfect or to restore it from serious damage.

• **Reinstall the wheel** in the frame without the tyre, tube and rim tape.

• **Mark the warp**. Hold a pencil against the brakes with its point nearly touching the wheel rim. Spin the wheel and let the pencil mark the bulge as it comes round.

• **Adjust the spokes**. Slack off the group of tight spokes that are pulling the wheel into the warp and tighten the loose spokes that aren't pulling hard enough in the other direction. This should be done by a series of small adjustments, say a quarter of a turn, to a group of half-a-dozen spokes.

In the worst case you might find that some of the spoke nipples are frozen in place or that you mash the face of the nipples so you can't tighten them any further. Or both. If the nipple is mashed, you will have to cut out the recalcitrant spoke and replace it. If things are going really badly, it makes sense to start again with a new wheel.

• **Spring the wheel**. After a small turn on each of the twelve spokes, release the wheel and lean gently on the rim at every opposite hour of the clock with the axle on the ground. Lean on three and nine o'clock and then let go. Lean on four and ten o'clock and so on. Do both sides of the wheel. You will hear the spokes grumbling as they sort themselves out.

• **Reinstall the wheel** and spin it with the marking pencil ready. If you have fixed it in one go you are a genius. Everyone else will repeat the sequence of adjust and spring until the warp is under control.

• When you are finished, **file down** any part of the threaded end of the spokes that might puncture the tube and reinstall the tape, tube and tyre.

Restoring round

This is just like removing a warp except the distortion is happening from top to bottom and not side to side. Hold the pencil on the brakes with the point at the top of the rim to find the bump. This time, instead of loosening the spokes on one side and tightening those on the other, you will be tightening spokes on both sides at one point of the clock and loosening the spokes on the opposite side of the clock face. If the bump is at twelve o'clock, tighten the twelve-o'clock spokes and loosen the six-o'clock spokes.

Assembling a wheel

Parts
- new hub,
- new rim,
- spokes, of the right gauge and length.

Method

Copy a completed wheel. When you take a close look at a wheel you will see that it has four basic characteristics:

- There are two sets of holes in the rim, one set for each side. The spokes from the left side go to the left holes in the rim while the right-side rim holes are for spokes from the right side of the hub.

- Half the spokes on one side are angled one way. The other spokes sit between them and splay in the opposite direction. These are sometimes called pushing and pulling spokes.

- The cross pattern varies from wheel to wheel. Your wheel will probably be *three cross* – that is, each spoke crosses three others on its way to the rim.

- Finally, on a well-built wheel, two spokes from the same side should run parallel on either side of the valve hole to make it easy to get a pump to the valve.

• Copy the four features of the spoke pattern, lacing one side first and then the other. Lacing the second side requires some careful weaving of the spokes to get them around the spokes you have already put in.

• Once you have assembled the wheel, sit it in a jig or stand. An upside-down bicycle makes an adequate jig. With nuts and bolts you can set up fixed points to test for warp or bump.

• Tighten the spokes little by little, each by the same amount, testing continually that the wheel is true and round.

• After a circuit of tightening and testing, take the wheel out and spring it as described above.

• Reinstall the wheel in the jig the other way round to check for symmetry. This is especially important for the rear wheel which needs the rim to be centred between the axles even though the hub is not in the centre.

• Repeat this process until the spokes are as tight as you can reasonably get them or they make a similar ping to the spokes on the completed wheel.

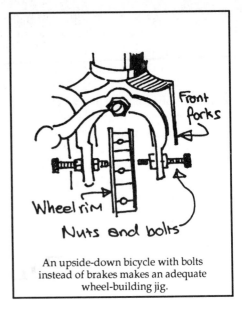

An upside-down bicycle with bolts instead of brakes makes an adequate wheel-building jig.

Chapter 15

BEFRIENDING BICYCLES

We have had so many new transport toys to play with over the last hundred years that many people have lost sight of the bicycle and what it has to offer, categorising it as a child's toy or an anachronism like detachable collars. But around the world there are communities that are still getting the same thrill out of the bicycle that we did a hundred years ago.

China sticks to the bike because it is a cheap way to get around: in Chinese cities such as Tianjin 80 per cent of the traffic is bicycles. Densely populated countries like the Netherlands have put a lot of money into bicycle travel and in cities like Groningen more than half the travel is by bike (with higher than average bicycle use in wealthy suburbs!). However much they spend on bikes – and a new one-third-more bicycles plan is underway – it will cost the Netherlands a lot less than importing oil or finding the space for more roads. Environmentally conscious countries like Germany are emphasising bicycle use, working to lift the proportion of bicycle travel in towns like Erlangen up from its one-third share. In Basel, Switzerland, bicycles do 20 per cent of the transport job despite the snow and hills, while Odense in Denmark manages to achieve 25 per cent despite the rain.

Australia's chance

I hope that you are reading this book because you too have found or rediscovered the thrill of cycling. If that is so, then you are not alone. Australians are on the way back to a more sensible approach to mobility and one that has a big role for the bicycle.

Unfortunately, we have a lot of ground to make up. Over the years, a lot of money and effort has gone into making it easy for people to drive cars in our cities and towns while cycling has been ignored and even discouraged:

• Suburbs have been designed without short-cuts for walking and cycling.

- It is hard for cyclists or walkers to cross the rivers of car traffic.
- Traffic lanes are often made too narrow to share with a car.
- There are few schools served by a safe cycle route.
- Planning regulations require car parking in new developments but there is no requirement to provide secure, undercover bicycle parking.
- Even recreational paths are badly designed with narrow, dangerous surfaces and impossible corners. Often the paths are poorly maintained and rarely upgraded.

As a result it can be hard to ride to work, to train for a triathlon, to enjoy a ride on the weekend, or to ride to school. The statisticians tell us that in Australia between 1 per cent (Sydney) and 6 per cent (Perth) of our trips are made by bike.

We have paid a price for this neglect of the bicycle. We have world-standard pollution in our cities: lead that destroys children's brains, particles that aggravate asthma and make the hay-fever season twelve months long; gases that provoke cancers and accelerate global warming. But even if our cars cleaned the air, they would still be a bad bet for city transport compared to bicycles:

- The space each car takes up has made us spread ourselves thinly across the land and moved us further from friends, work, school or the sports club and even cut communties in half with rivers of traffic.
- We have spent millions of dollars on freeways which, clogged with private cars carrying only the driver, become car parks during rush hour. In terms of increasing mobility, this money could have been spent to more effect on other transport projects, including

encouraging bicycles, not to mention other uses such as investment in education or industry. In this way we have subsidised car travel to a far greater extent than any money put into public transport. In Germany, one estimate put their road subsidy at 80 per cent – that is, car drivers pay only 20 per cent of actual road transport costs.

- More than half the surface area of a modern city is asphalt and concrete when what everyone wants is bigger gardens or more city parks.
- This emphasis on the car in Australia, especially since the Second Word War, has meant that we have wasted our investment in public transport by, among other things, failing to continue to attract large numbers of people to connect to public transport by bike. The station carparks we build, big as they are, rarely provide enough passengers to fill one train.

And really, after all this emphasis on the car, we aren't any better off. The speed of peak-hour travel in Melbourne is 20 kph whereas the bike riders on the bike path next to the Yarra River travel at an average of 30 kph. We have found that these bike riders are well-paid professionals with a good car at home who are not only travelling faster by bike but are saving time they would have to spend after work on exercise.

The way back
The encouraging thing is that we can easily change our cities into cycle-friendly ones like Amsterdam and Odense. We don't have to change the places we go to: many of our car trips are so short they could be replaced with a bike ride. We don't have to change geography or climate: those cycle-

friendly places are hillier, rainier and colder than anywhere in Australia. We don't have to have huge promotional campaigns to educate people about the benefits of cycling: people are ready to ride when the conditions are right. Nor do we have to spend heaps of money and land creating a complete off-road system for cyclists as the British did in new towns like Stevenage (only 4 per cent of the cycle network in the Netherlands is on off-road paths).

We just need to do what the cycle-friendly cities have done, and that is to make it easier for cyclists to get about on the roads. Successful on-the-road initiatives include:

• Making the road surface smooth so it is easy to cycle.

• Making the lanes on the road wide enough for a car and a bike to share.

• Marking a special bicycle lane on the road, sometimes with a white line, sometimes sealing the lane in a different colour.

• Creating special lanes for bikes and buses.

• Building safety islands to help cyclists cross other roads.

• Allowing cyclists to go the 'wrong' way down a one-way street or to use a pedestrian street.

• Installing bicycle traffic-lights to get riders through difficult situations either by going green early or by stopping a flow of cross-traffic.

• Painting stop lines for bikes ahead of those for cars.

• Lowering the speed of the cars on roads that cyclists use.

• Encouraging bikes to park at rail stations and allowing bikes to be taken on buses and trams.

• Requiring offices to provide bike parking and showers.

These changes to legislation, engineering and traffic management are already underway and are creating an environment that encourages cycling. Little by little, the bikes are coming out of the garage and onto the road.

As you have probably realised in reading this list, it is not a matter of giving bicycles special treatment: these improvements are exactly what we have been doing for cars over the past twenty years. Making the roads better for cars has encouraged a boom in car ownership and use: doing the same thing for bicycles will have a similar effect.

Bicycle changes often bring with them other changes. Our cycle-friendly cities will also favour fast, convenient and reliable public transport and give priority to pedestrians in built-up areas. We will be able to cut our travel time as planning laws and incentives encourage people to live near their friends, work and recreation. We will enjoy these cycle-friendly places with reduced air pollution, reduced noise, cheaper and quicker travel and an improvement in general health and won't feel the need to 'escape' where we live. Paradoxically, increased cycling will reduce unnecessary car trips and so make it easier to get about by car.

JOIN THE MOVEMENT FOR CHANGE

This transformation of Australian towns and cities into cycle-friendly places cannot be done by hoping. It will require hard work, determination and, above all, your support.

Membership

The first thing you can do is join your State bicycle group. You will find addresses in Appendix 5. Even if you only send in your membership fee and do nothing else, you will be helping the process of change. Your money will help the campaigns and your name will swell the size of the group. This will help the advocates when they speak to business people, bureaucrats and elected officials.

Don't forget the other groups you belong to like schools, community-service groups and work-based social clubs. They too can help cycling along by going for a ride or making sure that there is a safe cycle route to the school or local swimming pool and that there is bike parking at work.

Letter writing

Your membership of a bicycle group will mean that you receive the group's newsletter and news of the changes that the group thinks are the most important at the time. There is a good chance that one of those changes will be one that you also think is important. It is here that you can make your biggest contribution to change: write to the elected officials responsible for the current situation and ask them to support the change. Write to your:

• Local councillor or alderman if it is a local government matter. You might have two or three in your ward.

• State or territory representative if it is a State matter. You might have two in your electorate: one in the upper house and one in the lower.

• Federal member and your senators, if it is a Commonwealth matter.

'Why would anyone take any notice of my letter?' you might ask. The answer, and the strongest reason for writing, is that even one letter can make an enormous difference. Politicians usually make a mental calculation when they receive a letter and multiply it by the number of people that haven't written. Your letter may mean there are a hundred people who think like you. That is a powerful influence on someone who wants to stay elected.

Even politicians who support the change you want might be distracted by a dozen other debates. Your letter will help remind them of the importance of the issue: it is the squeaky wheel that gets the grease.

Finally, letter-writing shouldn't always be negative. If something happens that you support, write and say well done.

Other support

There will also be other opportunities to support your State bicycle group, through donations and fundraisers, in parades and celebrations. If you support the change they are aimed at, stand up and be counted.

Finally, your State group might be able to put you in touch with neighbours who are working to make the roads more cycle-friendly. A local group can be surprisingly effective at changing things: often it is local government that controls the things that cyclists need to have changed. It takes patience and determination to see through any change but the satisfaction of riding a path or using a bike lane that you helped create is considerable.

I hope, in some way or other, you will join us. If you do, our towns and cities will become cycle-friendly that much more quickly.

Appendix 1

FRAME HEIGHT CONVERSION CHART

Frame height			
Metric standard (cm)	Imperial equivalent (ins)	Imperial standard (cm)	Metric equivalent (ins)
40	16.0	16.0	40.0
41	16.4	16.5	41.25
42	16.8	17.0	42.5
43	17.2	17.5	43.75
44	17.6	18.0	45.0
45	18.0	18.5	46.25
46	18.4	19.0	47.5
47	18.8	19.5	48.75
48	19.2	20.0	50.0
49	19.6	20.5	51.25
50	20.0	21.0	52.5
51	20.4	21.5	53.75
52	20.8	22.0	55.0
53	21.2	22.5	56.25
54	21.6	23.0	57.5
55	22.0	23.5	58.75
56	22.4	24.0	60.0
57	22.8	24.5	61.25
58	23.2	25.0	62.5
59	23.6	25.5	63.75
60	24.0	26.0	65.0
61	24.4	26.5	66.25
62	24.8	27.0	67.5
63	25.2	27.5	68.75
64	25.6	28.0	70.0
65	26.0	28.5	71.25
66	26.4	29.0	72.5
67	26.8		
68	27.2		
69	27.6		
70	28.0		

Appendix 2

GEAR RATIOS CHART

The chart on the next page tells you how far a bike will travel in one turn of the pedals for any given sprocket combination. It is worked out on the formula: *70 cm (wheel diameter) x 3.14 (Pi) x the ratio of the front to the rear sprocket*. For example, a 40-tooth front sprocket and 22-tooth back sprocket means you go 4 metres for one turn of the pedals. The answer would be slightly different for a 65-cm wheel (3.7 metres from a 40-22 combination), but 65-cm-wheel owners can still use the chart to evaluate the relationship between their sprocket combinations because the relative proportions remain the same.

Front sprockets (number of teeth)

Rear sprockets (number of teeth)

Front \ Rear	30	29	28	27	26	25	24	23	22	21	20	19	18	17	16	15	14	13	12
58	4.25	4.40	4.55	4.72	4.90	5.10	5.31	5.54	5.79	6.07	6.37	6.71	7.08	7.50	7.97	8.50	9.11	9.81	10.62
57	4.18	4.32	4.47	4.64	4.82	5.01	5.22	5.45	5.69	5.97	6.26	6.59	6.96	7.37	7.83	8.35	8.95	9.64	10.44
56	4.10	4.24	4.40	4.56	4.73	4.92	5.13	5.35	5.59	5.86	6.15	6.48	6.84	7.24	7.69	8.21	8.79	9.47	10.26
55	4.03	4.17	4.32	4.48	4.65	4.84	5.04	5.26	5.50	5.76	6.04	6.36	6.72	7.11	7.56	8.06	8.64	9.30	10.07
54	3.96	4.09	4.24	4.40	4.57	4.75	4.95	5.16	5.40	5.65	5.93	6.25	6.59	6.98	7.42	7.91	8.48	9.13	9.89
53	3.88	4.02	4.16	4.31	4.48	4.66	4.85	5.06	5.30	5.55	5.82	6.13	6.47	6.85	7.28	7.77	8.32	8.96	9.71
52	3.81	3.94	4.08	4.23	4.40	4.57	4.76	4.97	5.20	5.44	5.71	6.02	6.35	6.72	7.14	7.62	8.16	8.79	9.52
51	3.74	3.87	4.00	4.15	4.31	4.48	4.67	4.87	5.10	5.34	5.60	5.90	6.23	6.59	7.01	7.47	8.01	8.62	9.34
50	3.66	3.79	3.93	4.07	4.23	4.40	4.58	4.78	5.00	5.23	5.50	5.78	6.11	6.46	6.87	7.33	7.85	8.45	9.16
49	3.59	3.71	3.85	3.99	4.14	4.31	4.49	4.68	4.90	5.13	5.39	5.67	5.98	6.34	6.73	7.18	7.69	8.28	8.98
48	3.52	3.64	3.77	3.91	4.06	4.22	4.40	4.59	4.80	5.02	5.28	5.55	5.86	6.21	6.59	7.03	7.54	8.12	8.79
47	3.44	3.56	3.69	3.83	3.97	4.13	4.30	4.49	4.70	4.92	5.17	5.44	5.74	6.08	6.46	6.89	7.38	7.95	8.61
46	3.37	3.49	3.61	3.74	3.89	4.04	4.21	4.40	4.60	4.81	5.06	5.32	5.62	5.95	6.32	6.74	7.22	7.78	8.43
45	3.30	3.41	3.53	3.66	3.80	3.96	4.12	4.30	4.50	4.71	4.95	5.21	5.50	5.82	6.18	6.59	7.07	7.61	8.24
44	3.22	3.33	3.45	3.58	3.72	3.87	4.03	4.20	4.40	4.61	4.84	5.09	5.37	5.69	6.04	6.45	6.91	7.44	8.06
43	3.15	3.26	3.38	3.50	3.64	3.78	3.94	4.11	4.30	4.50	4.73	4.97	5.25	5.56	5.91	6.30	6.75	7.27	7.88
42	3.08	3.18	3.30	3.42	3.55	3.69	3.85	4.01	4.20	4.40	4.62	4.86	5.13	5.43	5.77	6.15	6.59	7.10	7.69
41	3.00	3.11	3.22	3.34	3.47	3.60	3.75	3.92	4.10	4.29	4.51	4.74	5.01	5.30	5.63	6.01	6.44	6.93	7.51
40	2.93	3.03	3.14	3.26	3.38	3.52	3.66	3.82	4.00	4.19	4.40	4.63	4.88	5.17	5.50	5.86	6.28	6.76	7.33
39	2.86	2.96	3.06	3.17	3.30	3.43	3.57	3.73	3.90	4.08	4.29	4.51	4.76	5.04	5.36	5.71	6.12	6.59	7.14
38	2.78	2.88	2.98	3.09	3.21	3.34	3.48	3.63	3.80	3.98	4.18	4.40	4.64	4.91	5.22	5.57	5.97	6.42	6.96
37	2.71	2.80	2.90	3.01	3.13	3.25	3.39	3.54	3.70	3.87	4.07	4.28	4.52	4.78	5.08	5.42	5.81	6.26	6.78
36	2.64	2.73	2.83	2.93	3.04	3.17	3.30	3.44	3.60	3.77	3.96	4.16	4.40	4.65	4.95	5.28	5.65	6.09	6.59
35	2.56	2.65	2.75	2.85	2.96	3.08	3.21	3.34	3.50	3.66	3.85	4.05	4.27	4.53	4.81	5.13	5.50	5.92	6.41
34	2.49	2.58	2.67	2.77	2.87	2.99	3.11	3.25	3.40	3.56	3.74	3.93	4.15	4.40	4.67	4.98	5.34	5.75	6.23
33	2.42	2.50	2.59	2.69	2.79	2.90	3.02	3.15	3.30	3.45	3.63	3.82	4.03	4.27	4.53	4.84	5.18	5.58	6.04
32	2.34	2.43	2.51	2.61	2.71	2.81	2.93	3.06	3.20	3.35	3.52	3.70	3.91	4.14	4.40	4.69	5.02	5.41	5.86
31	2.27	2.35	2.43	2.52	2.62	2.73	2.84	2.96	3.10	3.24	3.41	3.59	3.79	4.01	4.26	4.54	4.87	5.24	5.68
30	2.20	2.27	2.36	2.44	2.54	2.64	2.75	2.87	3.00	3.14	3.30	3.47	3.66	3.88	4.12	4.40	4.71	5.07	5.50
29	2.12	2.20	2.28	2.36	2.45	2.55	2.66	2.77	2.90	3.04	3.19	3.35	3.54	3.75	3.98	4.25	4.55	4.90	5.31
28	2.05	2.12	2.20	2.28	2.37	2.46	2.56	2.68	2.80	2.93	3.08	3.24	3.42	3.62	3.85	4.10	4.40	4.73	5.13

Appendix 3

SHIMANO PRODUCT HISTORY

Like all component manufacturers, Shimano sells a number of 'groups' of components. Each group includes pretty much everything needed for a bike, barring the wheel rims and frame. The 22 groups improve in quality and increase in cost from left to right. Each group was sold in the year indicated until superseded by the next name in the same column. (Talk to your specialist bike shop for the latest information.)

ROAD BIKE GROUP

Year	Exage 300EX	Exage 400EX	Exage 500EX	RX100	105 SC	600 Ultegra	Dura-Ace
1982					Golden Arrow A105	600 EX	DA EX
1983							
1984							6-speed
1985					New 105 1050	SIS	SIS
1986							7-speed
1987		Action	Sports			7-speed	UG
1988	Motion A250	A350	A 450	Sports LX A452	D/Blue 1051		8-speed UG
1989	A300	A 400	A 500	A550	1055	HG	HG
1990							HG STI
1991						8-speed STI	
1992							

OFF-ROAD BIKE GROUP

Year	Exage 300LX	Exage 400LX	Exage 500LX	Deore LX	Deore DX	Deore XT	XTR
1982						M 700	
1983							
1984							
1985							
1986					New Deore MT60	New Deore XT SPD SIS M730	
1987		Trail M350	Mountain M 450				
1988	Country M250			Mountain LX M 450	Deore 11 7-speed HG	7-speed HG	
1989	M300	M 400	M 500	Deore LX	Deore DX	7-speed STI	
1990						ST M092 BR M732	
1991						ST M905	M090
1992							

BUDGET BIKE GROUP

Year	200CX	500CX	TY10	TY20	R552	70GS	100GS	200GS
1986								
1987			TY10					
1988					R552			
1989				TY20				200GS
1990							100GS	
1991	200CX	500CX				70GS		
1992								

Appendix 4

READING MORE ABOUT BIKES

Magazines

You will find quite a selection of glossy Australian, British and North American cycling magazines in the newsagents. They are a good way to extend the general knowledge you have built up through reading this book, as well as to find out about new bikes and the latest and brightest components and accessories. The large-circulation magazines will carry stories on all sorts of riding, but if you have a special interest – in triathlons or BMX competition, for example – you can find magazines that specialise in that topic.

Books

There are many good books on cycling. Here is an introduction to the basic categories of bicycle books, with some recommendations. You can get a catalogue which includes all up-to-date State-oriented material, such as guides to bike paths and trails, from the:
Bicycle Institute of New South Wales
    Mail Order Bookshop
GPO 272, Sydney NSW 2001,
Tel (02) 212 5628, Fax (02) 211 1867.
(*Check this address in an up-to-date directory before writing or calling.*)

General books on cycling
- *Richard's New Bicycle Book* – Richard Ballantine
- *The Mountain Bike Book* – Rob Van der Plas
- *The Complete Book of Bicycling* – Eugene Sloane

These three authors have written many books on cycling and each has its strength. They are overseas writers though, and their books do not always cater for Australian conditions.

Beautifully presented books on cycling
- *The Ultimate Bicycle Book* – Richard Ballantine
- *The Complete Book of Performance Cycling* – Phil Ligget (Phil covers the Tour de France for SBS TV.)

A bike-shop book on maintenance
- *Sutherland's Handbook for Bicycle Mechanics* – Howard Sutherland

Another view on cycling in traffic
- *Effective Cycling* – John Forester
John is the most widely known and controversial bicycle educator in the USA.

Guides to off-road touring
- *Cycling the Bush* – Sven Klinge
Sven's guides cover a number of States and, confusingly, all have the same title.

Guides to on-road touring
- *Bicycle Tours of Southeastern Australia* – Julia Thorn
This is only one of Julia's books; her typewriter keys have gone up and down as much as her pedals.

Armchair bicycle tours
- *Full Tilt* – Dervla Murphy
Dervla, now a famous travel writer, wrote her first book about the fulfilment of a childhood dream of riding her bike from Ireland to India. A great story, with the moral that anyone can do it.

Appendix 5

STATE BICYCLE GROUPS

Australian Capital Territory
Pedal Power ACT
GPO Box 581
Canberra, ACT 2601
(06) 248 7995

Newcastle
Newcastle Cycleways Movement
PO Box 58
New Lambton, NSW 2305
(049) 45 9350 (AH)

NSW
Bicycle Institute of NSW
GPO Box 272
Sydney, NSW 2001
(02) 212 5628

Queensland
Bicycle Institute of Queensland
PO Box 5753
West End, Qld 4101
(07) 899 2988

South Australia
Bicycle Institute of South Australia
GPO Box 792
Adelaide, SA 5001
(08) 271 5824

Tasmania
Bicycle Tasmania
Environment Centre
102 Bathurst Street
Hobart, Tas 7000
(002) 34 5566

Victoria
Bicycle Victoria
GPO Box 1961R
Melbourne, Victoria 3001
(03) 328 3000

Western Australia
Bicycle Transportation Alliance
35 Geddes Street
Victoria Park, WA 6100
(09) 470 4007

(These addresses and especially phone numbers do change, though they were correct when going to press in 1994. Be sure to check them in the directory before calling or writing.)

ACCESS TO CLUBS
There are hundreds of small cycling clubs in Australia that can give you a ready- made set of cycling-minded friends. There is bound to be one to suit you. There are clubs that teach kids road- safety skills, commuter groups, touring clubs and gung-ho racing clubs for triathlons, off-road riding, as well as track and road racing.

Sometimes the clubs are quite formal, with membership fees, international affiliations and so on. Others are quite informal. In one town, for example, there is an understanding that the race back into town starts each Sunday morning at a certain time by the old tree at the turn off. Whoever turns up is in the race and in the club.

There is usually no obligation to join a club on your first outing. You can see if you like the people and see if you like the cycling they do.

Your State bicycle group will be able to put you in touch with local recreational clubs. If you are interested in racing, contact the competition associations (see Appendix 6).

Appendix 6

COMPETITION ASSOCIATIONS

To contact your local road and track racing association, both amateur and professional, write to the addresses below. Please enclose a second, blank stamped envelope so your letter can be forwarded to your local association and a stamped, self-addressed envelope if you want material sent to you.

(These address and especially phone numbers do change, though they were correct when going to press in 1994. Be sure to check them in the directory before writing or calling.)

For road and track racing associations, contact:
Australian Cycling Federation
68 Broadway
Sydney, NSW 2007
(02) 281 8688

For BMX associations, contact:
National Secretary
BMX Australia
39 Jamieson Crescent
Kambah, ACT 2902

For mountain bike racing associations, contact:
Martin Whiteley
Australian Mountain Bike Association
c/o Australian Cycling Federation
68 Broadway
Sydney, NSW 2007
(02) 281 8688

DEAR READER,

I'd be pleased to receive your
constructive suggestions on this
book, to ensure that a second
edition is as comprehensively
useful as I hope it to be.

Please write to:
Harry Barber
The Better Bicycling Book
c/o Bicycle Victoria
GPO Box 1961 R
Melbourne, Victoria 3001

INDEX